REMARKABLE
AMERICANS

Washburn triumphs spanned a full range of world settings, from the
remote woods of the Telos Canal in northern Maine to the glittering halls
of the Tuilleries Palace in Paris (shown here burnt out after the
Commune of 1871).

REMARKABLE AMERICANS

The Washburn Family

Kerck Kelsey

TILBURY HOUSE PUBLISHERS
GARDINER, MAINE

TILBURY HOUSE ⌂ PUBLISHERS
2 Mechanic Street • Gardiner, Maine 043345
800–582–1899 • www.tilburyhouse.com

First hardcover edition: February 2008
10 9 8 7 6 5 4 3 2 1

Library of Congress Cataloging-in-Publication Data
Kelsey, Kerck.
  Remarkable Americans : the Washburn family / Kerck Kelsey.--1st ed.
     p. cm.
  Includes bibliographical references and index.
  ISBN 978-0-88448-299-4 (hardcover : alk. paper)
  1. Washburn family. 2. Brothers--United States--Biography.
  3. Legislators--United States--Biography. 4. Businessmen--United
States--Biography. 5. Livermore (Me.)--Biography. I. Title.
  CT274.W373K45 2007
  974.1'820440922--dc22
  [B]
                                    2007027266

Jacket photograph of The Norlands by Brian Vanden Brink
Copyediting by Genie Dailey, Fine Points Editorial Services, Jefferson, Maine
Photo scanning by Noah Krell, Pure Photographic Goodness, and Just Black and White, Portland, Maine; jacket silhouettes by Integrated Composition Systems, Spokane, Washington
Printed and bound by Maple Vail, Kirkwood, New York
Jackets printed by the John P. Pow Company, South Boston

To Billie Gammon

———•••———

the best friend the Washburns ever had

Contents

The Washburn family [has] towered above all others
in adding not only to the fame of Livermore
but to the State and country as well."

Hannibal Hamlin,
at the dedication of the Washburn Library,
August 5, 1885

I cannot in these lines begin to tell you all that house, those
steadfast hills represent. I shall not try, but if ever you are
in trouble, go up there and walk in the woods and fields,
sit in the little church alone — go back to that house
so full of dear ghosts — they will ALL help you.

From a letter by Rosalind Wright,
granddaughter of William Drew Washburn,
to her cousin, Elbert Baldwin, shortly before he left
for duty with the OSS in Italy in 1944

Introduction

———•———

The Washburns of Livermore

TELOS LAKE LIES JUST NORTH OF KATAHDIN in the northern wilderness of Maine. In the spring of 1846, it lies seventy-five miles of rutted wagon track from the nearest town. The weather on this particular spring day is cold and windy—the ice hasn't been gone for long, and the snow is still deep in the silent woods. A crew of lumberjacks, well toughened by months of winter work, are winching a large raft of logs across the lake toward a sluiceway at its eastern end. As they approach the head of the sluice, a crowd of between fifty and sixty hard-looking men—imported from Bangor for the purpose—appear along the shore, barring the way. Butcher knives are seen, and other armament is presumed. The boss of the rafters is informed that the new owner of the sluice will allow no passage of logs without the payment of a steep toll on each log floated through. The gang on the shore looks eager to enforce collection with whatever force is necessary.

The resulting standoff, although bloodless, was called the Telos War. Because the right to use the waterways was crucial to the entire lumber industry, this confrontation in the woods had major implications. It was resolved several months later by the brilliant arguments of a diminutive and bespectacled frontier lawyer from Orono named Israel Washburn, Jr. He was the self-taught son of a failed storekeeper from Liver-

more, Maine, and his victory helped earn him a seat in the
United States Congress.

Twenty-five years after that confrontation, and half a world
away, a much more elegant meeting took place in one of the
grandest buildings in France. In a glittering ballroom at the
Tuilleries Palace in Paris, the emperor of France, Louis
Napoleon, gave a state dinner to honor the new American
minister. The emperor, in the wake of his disastrous adventure
with the puppet Maximilian in Mexico and his sympathy for
the lately defeated Confederacy, was working hard to regain
the favor of the Americans. Nothing was spared in the elaborate ceremony. The guest of honor that evening was the
American minister plenipotentiary to France, Elihu B. Washburne, a younger brother of the peacemaker of the Telos War.

These brothers were just two of a brood of ten remarkable
children who grew up on a simple farm in remote Livermore,
Maine. Their advantages were few, but together they left a
record of achievement in politics, in business, in diplomacy, in
the military, in their church, and among their own children
that will probably never be equaled again by a single generation of any American family.

They lived in tumultuous times. The decade of the 1850s
was critical for the future of America, although few people
besides the Washburns saw it that way. The influence and
power of southern states in every branch of the national government, especially in the two political parties that competed
for control of that government, had never been more pro-
nounced. At the same time, floods of ordinary people were
moving from eastern to western states, and forcing a change in
the balance of power. There would be a revolution in
American politics in the 1850s and a civil war in the 1860s.

Driving this revolution were the furious efforts of five different Washburn brothers from Maine to California. Four were

elected and reelected to the U.S. Congress from four different states. Two of the four would later be separately considered for Republican nomination for president and vice president of the country. Their accomplishments while in public office were as impressive as the phenomenon of their being elected.

The Washburns were not self-promoters. They made little effort to publicize their roles in creating the Republican party, in bringing it to power, and in leading the North to triumph in the civil war that resulted. They sincerely felt that what they did was so morally right that it would have happened inevitably, with or without them.

Later, after their great cause had triumphed, their stubborn resistance to being controlled by machine politics, and their loyalty to old friends, ended their greatest days in the public spotlight. In the self-serving world that followed the Civil War, their public records, unstained by any hint of self-enrichment, slowly faded from view. Although they left behind a unified country, respected both at home and abroad, their part in the drama received little acknowledgment amid the cloud of self-promotional histories and autobiographies that emerged from the war.

Their political accomplishments were impressive enough, but this remarkable group of siblings did more than that. They left memorable records in the courtroom, made substantial contributions to the Northern victory in the war, built great corporations, and endured great hardship in their country's interest overseas. They changed the shape of the land itself, from the prairies of Montana to the wilderness of Upper Michigan, and from the Yazoo swamps of Mississippi to the Falls of St. Anthony in Minnesota. Without them, there might never have been a city of Minneapolis. Their adventures included a duel in California, cleaning up after a shootout in Iowa, a tussle on the floor of the House of Representatives, and an enormous mill explosion in Minnesota. Through it all, they maintained their Yankee rectitude and left a fierce record of Yankee integrity.

Even the lesser lights of the group were impressive in the variety of enterprises they undertook: a ship's captain who became a lumberman; a newspaper editor who wrote novels and invented an early version of the typewriter; a storekeeper who became a banker; and three sisters who overcame plain appearances and lack of polish to find husbands, establish new lives in new worlds, and raise respectable families. Washburn siblings also produced children who made memorable contributions of their own.

The Washburns were liked and admired by politicians and princes, lumberjacks and theologians, prairie farmers and judges. They served before the mast and before the bar. They harnessed waterfalls, redirected rivers, cut down forests, built railroads, milled wheat, dug coal, and even led a national religious movement. They were either bitter enemies or trusted allies of at least eight different American presidents. They wrote and spoke eloquently and often—from political inspiration to historical scholarship that is significant to this day.

In the end, they had towns, counties, orphanages, schools—even a railroad locomotive—named after them in at least six states. At one point, the two largest flour companies in the country, the Washburn Crosby Company and the Pillsbury Washburn Company, each carried the name—for the two different brothers who had created them. Both these companies are now one organization, united under the name General Mills.

The ten Washburn siblings grew up in the most humble of circumstances—in a simple farmhouse far removed from any advantages. By their own efforts, they lived the American dream: self-taught, weaned in a crucible of poverty and disgrace, but governed by the highest ideals, driven by furious energy and great visions of what they could do, and what they could help their country to do.

They deserve our attention because of their competence, the wide variety of their enterprises, and the genetic phenomenon that they all happened to be brothers and sisters. They are also worth our attention for the uncompromising moral compass by which they lived their lives. They were more admired by their contemporaries for this than for any other thing. For this reason, we too should take inspiration from this extraordinary group.

To modern eyes, images of the nineteenth century are defined by the necessities of early photography. Forced to hold still for long exposure times, the faces look grim, dark, and uncomfortable. On top of this, the clothing and the houses are also dark and heavy and uncomfortable—even dangerous, with all the open fireplaces that had to be tended.

But the heaviness and grimness are deceptive. These people could laugh and dance and sing as well as we can. However, their times also called on them to do great things. In America, the nineteenth century was a time of national crisis, of high moral principle and meanest venality, and of courage and cowardice. The Washburns embodied the best of nineteenth-century America. Their story is instructive of their time, and a model for ours.

This is the story of ten individual people. They happened to grow up together, but then dispersed in ten different directions. In trying to explain the phenomenon of their achievements, we should look at them first in their early years. Not only is this where their stories all begin, but it is these common experiences that supply the best answers to the nagging question as to just how all this talent could have come from a single group of brothers and sisters.

ONE

Was It the Water?

THE NUMBER OF WASHBURN SIBLINGS who went from their simple farm in Livermore, Maine, to positions of national leadership has never been equaled by any American family. Four of the sons served a total of twenty-one terms as congressmen from four different states. Three of them served at the same time—and actually roomed together. Two were later governors of their states, two were ambassadors, and one even served briefly as secretary of state. A fourth brother, almost a generation later, from still another state, served three terms in the House and then went on to win a seat in the U.S. Senate. Yet another brother (a fifth) was prominent in the politics of a yet another state, before being named an ambassador by Abraham Lincoln.

Their leadership was not just pro forma. They didn't just fill their seats. Their actions were instrumental in bringing about the political revolution that led to the nation's greatest crisis—and to a resolution of differences between sections of the country that even the founding fathers had not dared to address. In their various roles, these Washburns made huge contributions in the crucible of a great civil war, contributions that confirmed once and for all America's identity as a single nation rather than a loose collection of individual states.

Of course, they weren't all giants. Some led fairly ordinary lives, and all were of modest physical stature. But as a group, they left behind them great works: a new political party solidly in control of a centralized federal government, a nation newly respected abroad, and three commercial enterprises that have endured to this day.

The only thing they had in common was their family and their early years on the farm. Something unusual had to have been going on with this family. The span and scale of their accomplishments draws us back to that earlier time and place, and to the question of what could have happened to produce this particular group of siblings.

It was more than just the water. The remarkable confluence of talent, energy, courage, and leadership nurtured in this family was a product of many factors. These children were not cast in the same mold, but they were all shaped by the same place, the same family, the same faith, and the same events.

The place to start studying what made this amazing generation tick is the place that is easiest to see, namely the physical place where they all grew up. The Washburn property in Livermore, and the neighborhood around it, sounds and feels and smells today just as it did in their day. It has changed very little.

The first task for the curious visitor is to find the place. It is now, as it was when the Washburns grew up here, far from the beaten path. No airport or interstate highway is nearby. The visitor must find his or her way twenty-five miles north of Lewiston, or about the same distance west of Augusta, into the hills beyond the Androscoggin River. The roads to follow go from interstate highway to secondary highway to country lane. There is no direct route. Approaching from the south, the persistent traveler climbs the final rise and at last comes in view of the church and, shortly thereafter, the mansion now called The Norlands.

One's first impression is surprise. The whole place stands out markedly from its surroundings. The church jumps up from the land around it. Its white spire contrasts vividly with the fields and woods that gradually fall away on all sides. There is no village around this church, no tidy green. It is solitary and spectacular. Then the mansion behind the church comes into view, with farmhouse and barn attached to it, forming one very long building, also unlike anything in the neighborhood. Its Victorian chimneys and jutting eaves are unique.

Another surprise lies beyond the mansion. It is the library—a small edifice of stone and slate amid lawn and pasture—a heavy presence among the white-planked fences and livestock that browse around it. Within its solid confines, over its collections of family papers and musty volumes, serious oil portraits gaze down on the visitor.

There is history here. There are things worth remembering of great works and strong people. They, like the buildings they left behind, stand out distinctly from the surroundings that produced them all. The whole place is a monument.

The mansion, built by the brothers for their father in 1868, is an impressive structure, but it is hardly indicative of what the place was like thirty years earlier than that, when the ten Washburns were all growing up here. On a beautiful summer day, the scenery is glorious. But in the gray half-light of a winter afternoon, the wind howling over that frozen ridge can be savage. It was not by chance that the whole family heartily endorsed the lines from Tennyson that brother Charles used to name the place one winter day:

> The long dun wolds are ribbed with snow,
> and loud the Norland whirlwinds blow[1]

The property is still known as The Norlands. The Washburn brothers built the mansion here, on the site of the farmhouse where they all grew up, which had burned. The brothers then enhanced the project by making stately improvements to the church next door. The Gothic-styled library was the final thing they built here.

Over the years, all of the siblings undertook difficult trips to revisit the place for summertime holidays and mini-reunions. But despite the impressive enhancements they made to it, none chose to live here long, and only a few chose to be buried here. Mirroring the habit of millions of farm émigrés all over America, they preferred to visit their birthplace, to honor their memories here, but then to return to the lives they had made elsewhere. They did not wish to relive their early experiences here.

The main thing they did not wish to repeat was the isolation of the place. In 1809, when Israel Washburn, Sr., originally bought it, the farm was off what beaten paths there were, even then. The nearest town of any consequence was Hallowell, at the head of navigation on the Kennebec River. Hallowell, with its neighbor Gardiner, was about twenty-five hard miles to the southeast. It was a full day's ride to get there from the Washburn farm, although with the right conditions in the winter, you could do it faster. Most of the time, though, it was a bumpy road with steep hills all the way, and the trip also included a substantial river crossing, over the Androscoggin.

Hallowell was the home of the nearest newspaper and the access point for ships to Portland and Boston. It was the town from which was carved the municipality of Augusta. Afterwards, in order to resolve a tug-of-war between Portland and Bangor, Augusta was made the capital of the state. The legislature occupied a new capitol building there in 1832, and after that, the buzz of politics drew the Washburn boys in that direction like bees to a hive. Three of the four oldest started their careers in Hallowell.

There were more neighbors near the Washburns 150 years

ago than there are now, but the tiny community at the cross-roads was still small. Perhaps a dozen neighbors were within a fifteen-minute walk. All of them had more money than the Washburns.

Governmental services were virtually nonexistent, with the exception of the nearby one-room schoolhouse. This was only open for twelve or fourteen weeks during the winter months, depending on the state of the neighborhood's finances. If they wanted access to each other and to the outside world, the Washburns and their neighbors had to clear and maintain the roads themselves. They had to pay a toll to get across the Androscoggin River to their east. To get a church, they built one themselves, and, even then, they could only have religious services whenever a traveling preacher happened to stop by.

Isolation developed three important characteristics for everyone in Livermore. First, their isolation bred self-sufficiency. When something had to be done around the place or in the neighborhood, people used whatever was at hand to do it themselves. Whether mending a wall or mending a road, neighbors had a quiet confidence that they could take care of themselves. No one else was going to do it for them. Except for the village poorhouse, there were no handouts.

Second, their isolation bred independent thinking. People didn't go along with the crowd, because there wasn't much of a crowd to go along with. This is not to say that there were no outside influences. Indeed, the people were all subject to an occasional fire-breathing sermon on a Sunday morning, or a provocative editorial in the weekly newspaper, and always there was flowery rhetoric to be heard from the stump at election time. Dr. Bradford, the neighbor who delivered all the Washburn children, kept a library in his home. But people made up their own minds.

Third, especially for the Washburns, isolation was a factor to resist. All their lives, this family was furiously involved in the world outside its neighborhood. They were hungry for news of current events, and devoured every word of the great debates of their time as they were reprinted verbatim in the various journals to which they subscribed. No abridgements, no interpretations, no summaries would do for them. On the contrary, for many of their neighbors, the Washburns were the interpreters.

From his perch behind the counter of the family store, Israel Jr., the oldest son, became familiar with a wide range of issues of the day. He heard about the outrage of Maine's statehood in 1820, when the southerners in Congress forced the admission of Missouri as a slave state in order for Maine to come in as a free state. He rejoiced with his father over the election of soon-to-be Whig John Quincy Adams as president in 1825. He anguished as his beloved Uncle Reuel Washburn, who introduced him and his brothers to the world of books and the law, missed getting elected to the U.S. Congress by a miscounting of just five votes in 1829.

This exposure to public service at close range also provided the Washburn children with a sense of the public good, and of the importance of fairness and honesty in their dealings. In later life they were responsible for untold millions of public and private dollars from their clients, shareholders, taxpayers, partners, creditors, and friends, to say nothing of the cash they exchanged between themselves. Not one left any hint of malfeasance or mishandling of any of the monies entrusted to them.

Particularly during and after the Civil War, when venality and self-interest and a habit of cutting corners characterized many of the brothers' contemporaries, the Washburn record remained remarkable in its spotlessness. They were not always politic in their utterances, but they were absolutely honest in their actions. They left no doubt where they stood, and it was always on the side of integrity. They were stubborn about this. For them, politics was a high calling, and the welfare of their constituents and their country stood far above their own interests. They were governed by high ideals rather than political opportunism. When the great crises of the century loomed, their constituents realized this about them, and followed the Washburn lead.

There were other effects this property had on the extraordinary people who grew up here. To appreciate them, the visitor has to do more than experience the remoteness of the place, for most of Maine—and New England, too—was isolated in the early nineteenth century. It was a fact of life for most of the population in the young country. So beyond their isolation, what else helped shape the Washburns? As one looks around The Norlands with the perspective of 150 years, there are other formative influences to see and to imagine.

A major influence, recreated by the Washburn-Norlands Living History Center today, was the nature of life on a nineteenth-century farm. The sights and sounds and smells of the Washburn farm here have not changed in the past century and a half. The chores are the same, too. The animals still have to be fed, the stalls mucked out, the wood chopped, and the garden tended. Fences still have to be mended, roofs patched, water pumped, and meals prepared on a woodstove. All of these activities continue around Norlands to this day, mostly without the help of modern conveniences.

Thanks to many devoted volunteers, the nineteenth century is alive and well at Norlands for thousands of twenty-first-century visitors. Overnight guests sleep on horsehair mattresses under goosedown quilts, use an unheated privy, pump their own water, split their own wood, make their own biscuits on the woodstove, tend to the animals, swat the flies, or hitch up the sleigh—depending on the season. Special events include everything from maple sugaring to sleigh rides through the woods or ice-cutting on the pond, to a Sunday service in the church or a day with slate and birch rod and goose-quill pen learning lessons—and manners—in the one-room school. After doing these things, it is easier for the visitor to get a feel for the Washburn experience growing up here—and to appreciate their journey that started here. The living history experience at Norlands is authentic and rigorous. It serves as an appropriate environment in which to meet the Washburn family.

The work on the Washburn farm was unending, from dawn till dark, and no one was exempt. Drainage ditches had to be dug out each year. Rocks thrust up in the fields by the frost had to be lifted onto the walls that were needed to keep the animals from wandering. Plowing and planting could only be done when the fields were dry enough in May, and there were always fences to be repaired, apple trees and vegetable gardens to be tended, animals to be corralled. Only crops like hay, oats, and potatoes could be raised in the short growing season. Cows had to be fed and milked, pigs slopped, horses shod. Wagons, buggies, sleighs, and sledges had to be constantly repaired, along with bridles and harnesses. For the winter, roads had to be cleared and patched, snow rolled, and wood chopped. The women made the clothes, cooked or put up the food, and had and cared for the babies. Everybody sewed.

Here on this farm, two things happened that had a lasting impact on every Washburn child. First, they learned to work hard; the only work was *hard* work. Whatever it took to get a job done, they would do—and maybe more. There were no shortcuts. There was no quitting time. They quit when the job was done, and not before. Whatever had to be done, they did, usually in a hurry. That energy may have been something they were born with, but they learned how important it was as they labored on this farm.

As adults, the Washburns were all later admired for their formidable energy. Israel Jr.'s energy was so impressive that it had the effect of obscuring his message. During his first speech in Maine to announce the movement to establish the Republican party, an opposition newspaper reporter was in the audience. It was the most important political speech ever heard in Maine, yet the reporter never heard the message because he was so amazed by the messenger. He likened Israel to a galvanized bullfrog. "He is all gutta-percha, and bounds and rebounds at the utterance of every period," the reporter wrote.[2]

Israel's younger brother Cadwallader, who led enormous commercial enterprises across several midwestern states, was also always on the move, and was constantly on the lookout for young men of the same stamp. At a low point during his career in the army, he begged his congressman brother Elihu to get the War Department to approve a certain Samuel Rundle to replace his current quartermaster. "I feel very anxious," he wrote, "to get a man appointed who has some *snap* to him."[3]

He got his man, and many others, before he was through. Brother Charles, who preferred a furious pen as his instrument, produced over a thousand newspaper editorials in California in the run-up to the upset victory of the Republican party there in 1860. Behind him, the youngest son, William, early nicknamed "Young Rapid" by his older brothers because he was always in a hurry, was the force behind an amazing array of enterprises during his lifetime—dams, sawmills, railroads, flour mills, and even coal mines.

The second thing the siblings learned on the farm was equally deep-felt. Despite the sweet bucolic memories here, it

*Israel Washburn, Sr., and his wife Martha Benjamin Washburn,
known as Patty. He was a failed storekeeper...*

must be admitted: they all wanted out. In later years they glo-
rified the place, made huge improvements in it, and came back
for frequent visits. But their memories of growing up here were
not pleasant. It was difficult, dirty, and sometimes painful, and
worst of all, it didn't seem to go anywhere. They would work as
hard as they could for as long as they could, and at the end they
seemed still to be about where they were when they started.
Every Washburn sibling wanted more than this. To achieve
their dreams, they had to get off the farm. Here, on this farm,

...and she a barely educated country woman, but they raised what may have been the greatest single generation of any American family.
(COURTESY WASHBURN LIBRARY)

was born their fiery ambition to make something of themselves. They thirsted to get away and, in the end, every one of them succeeded.

The key to success in the outside world was self-improvement. Both the children and their parents were aware of the need to supplement the offerings of their local school. The children couldn't speak well or write well, their clothes were homemade and handed down, and their simple origin was obvious to everyone they met. All of the Washburn siblings were

aware of their shortcomings, once they reached the more polished world outside the farm. There wasn't a Washburn who
didn't spend years in fashioning himself or herself with skills
and manners to achieve the desired passport to a different life.

There were two other enormous influences that acted on
these children on this farm. The visitor can't see either one, but
they can be imagined. The first was the model that was provided for them by their family—both the parents close at hand
and the uncles and aunts who were sprinkled all over the neighborhood. The second model that influenced them was provided
by their church, both by what they learned there during the
services they attended, and by what they learned from discussions with visiting clergymen around the family dinner table.

On both sides of the Washburn family, there was no shortage of role models and inspiration. Despite their difficult circumstances, both Martha and Israel Washburn, Sr., came from
strong family traditions of service and integrity. Originating in
England, the elder Israel's first Washburn ancestor in America
was a secretary of the original Plymouth colony. John
Washburn owned a farm in Duxbury, Massachusetts, and his
descendants settled Bridgewater and then modern-day
Raynham. Israel Washburn, Sr., was the seventh generation of
Washburns in America since 1631, and the fourth consecutive
to be named Israel. Just prior to Maine's achieving statehood,
Israel Sr. was elected four times to represent his district in the
Massachusetts General Court. Both Israel Sr. and his brother
Reuel served Livermore long and faithfully in a variety of pub-
lic offices. Israel Sr. served as a town selectman, and for years
he settled grievances in the community as justice of the peace.
His children's regard for him was summed up by his son Elihu
on the occasion of his father's eighty-sixth birthday. Trapped in
Paris by the siege during the Franco-Prussian War, Elihu wrote,
"All hail to the glorious, great-headed, great-hearted, noble old

man; in truth the noblest Roman of them all. How intelligent, how kind, how genial, how hospitable, how true. Yet when in the course of nature, a kind Providence shall call him hence, I would have the hand of filial affection only trace this simple inscription on his monument: 'He was a kind father and an honest man.'"[4] Those words grace Israel Sr.'s stone at Waters Hill Cemetery in Livermore today.

Martha Benjamin Washburn, whom Israel Sr. married in 1812, was the daughter of one of the town's leading citizens, Samuel Benjamin, who had served as an officer in the Revolutionary army from Lexington all the way to Yorktown. "Patty" as she was called, had as much family history and pride as did her husband.

She, too, was a powerful influence on every one of her children. She was tough enough to survive the birth of eleven children in twenty years (one son, named William Drew as a subsequent brother would be, died at the age of thirteen months). One of nine children herself, Patty had brothers and sisters all over the Livermore area. They provided crowds of uncles, aunts, and cousins for her own growing brood. Her younger brother, whom the children knew as Uncle David, was as loved and respected by them as was Uncle Reuel, her husband's brother.

Patty was a fierce and loving figure for all her children, and they especially remembered her for her unflinching faith that they would all "raise themselves up" in the world. She died shortly after her oldest son Israel was elected governor of Maine, an event she had predicted when he was only ten. Although never blessed with much of a formal education, Patty Washburn made a lasting impression on the people who met her. After her death, no less a person than Hannibal Hamlin, former senator and vice president of the United States, gushed to an audience of her townspeople that "She was a remarkable woman, with whom the famed Spartan mothers and the matrons of Rome fail in comparison."5

Jeannette Washburn Kelsey, who with her sister was sent by Cadwallader Washburn to Livermore to live with her grandparents when their mother was hospitalized, remembered both of her grandparents' influence. She wrote that Patty "was a woman of strong character and indomitable will power, very ambitious for her children, determined that they should get on in the world and take a high place. She worked early and late, and while her husband gave his children the taste for literature which was one of their strong characteristics—most of the sons being omnivorous readers—...it was she who gave them their force of character. She was always encouraging them and urging them forward."6

The Washburns also inherited from their family an enormous interest in the world around them. The Washburn farm may have been remote, but it was a hotbed of thought and discussion about issues of the day. Israel Washburn, Sr., was a gregarious man, sprung from a family steeped in public service. He loved people, and his little store at the crossroads in Livermore—to say nothing of his dinner table at home—was a gathering place for neighbors, peddlers, preachers, and politicians. Every one of his children was exposed to every sort of discussion on the affairs of the community, such as it was, and on the world beyond. In addition, they had access to Uncle Reuel's library. In that library, over and above its legal tomes, there was available to every Washburn sibling a treasure trove of literature and letters.

It was from their family and their church that the Washburn children learned the steadfast moral code by which they were so well known in later years. It was from these models that they learned to be honest and fair in all their dealings, and to expect the same from their fellows. They learned to respect and honor all men as did their father, and from their father and his brother they learned that service to the public was a high calling, and that a debt incurred was a debt to be paid. They learned confidence because of their mother's confidence in them. From their uncle, they learned to respect and love learning. From their church, they learned to judge issues in terms of what was right, rather than what was expedient. And also from their church, they learned that every man had great potential, and that to keep men in bondage was a great sin. They learned some big ideas here about sin and redemption, and they learned the importance of these ideas. In this humble place, of all places, they learned about the potential of politics to give ideas voice and to provide the means of making ideas reality.

We don't hear much of the Universalist Church today. It originated in the late 1700s in reaction to the harsh and dictatorial overtones of Calvinism and its Puritan offshoots. Universalism expanded across New England like wildfire in the early nineteenth century. It professed the hopeful message that salvation was possible for *all* men—that the benefits of faith were universal. Universalism's tenets regarding fairness and equal opportunity also brought the church, and its Washburn faithful, into early opposition to slavery. Following the Civil War, much of Universalism's broad message was adopted by other faiths across the country. As a result, although we don't see many Universalist churches today, the Universalist message can be heard in almost every church in the land.

For the gregarious Washburns, Universalism's sunny optimism about the inherent worth of every man and the limitless prospects for the future through hard work was a perfect fit. In 1828 their father sold a piece of his own land so that there might be a church built right next door. Over a hundred people participated in the church raising.[7] When it was dedicated the next year, it was the first church in the town with a steeple. Israel Sr. provided room and board for many a traveling preacher who held services there. Details of faith were discussed at length over the Washburn dinner table. It was no accident that all the children were faithful churchgoers all their lives, and that both the oldest and youngest sons rose to national prominence in the Universalist organization.

The Washburn brood was not only shaped by their place, their family, and their faith. Certain events that happened on the farm were also hugely influential on the Washburns—especially the oldest children, who were the most affected.

Israel Washburn, Sr., had two hopes for the future. He could increase production through his own energy by clearing more land and increasing his herds, or through starting some enterprise on the side. In addition, he could hope for lots of children to increase his labor force in years to come. His wife did him proud with the latter, but the little store, his enterprise on the side, nearly put the whole family into the town's poorhouse.

During the nineteenth century Americans loved humble origins in their leaders. From "Old Hickory" Andrew Jackson to "Tippecanoe" William Henry Harrison and his "Log Cabin" campaign, to "Honest Abe" Lincoln, the rail splitter, political king-makers parlayed rural roots into successful presidential campaigns. Of course, most nineteenth-century American politicians were educated and polished political professionals—the products of middle-class, if not elite, backgrounds. But in the case of the Washburns of Livermore, Maine, the humble origins were real—painfully so.

For the Washburns in 1829, the high regard of their neighbors was tempered by financial disaster. That was the year that creditors from Boston suddenly showed up at Israel Sr.'s door with bills that were long overdue for payment. There was no money in the till to pay these obligations—probably because Israel Sr. had long been too liberal with credit, and too many of his customers couldn't pay their own bills. For example, an entry in the store's order book for one Samuel Park of Dixfield read simply, "three gallons of rum, one gallon of molasses, one pound of tea, and I will pay you in the spring."[8]

The Boston merchants called in the sheriff, and the family had to watch in shame as most of their worldly goods were sold off at public auction. Uncle Reuel stepped in to save the farm, but the following year the oldest children were shipped out to friends and neighbors to work off their father's debts. Elihu never forgot the brutal five months of dawn-to-dusk work he had to perform to pay off one $25 debt, plus another lonely year he had to spend with his elderly grandparents back in Massachusetts because there wasn't enough food at home for everyone. Years later, Cadwallader's ill-timed but candid admission that he had few pleasant memories of growing up on a farm led to his defeat by a farmer for reelection to the governorship of Wisconsin. As far as the Washburns were concerned, their humble origins were far from electioneering hyperbole. They were very real, and crushingly unpleasant.

The year 1831 brought some relief. That was the year that Israel Jr. reached the age of eighteen and left the farm to study law in Bangor. Thereafter, all the older boys also left soon after their eighteenth birthdays, so they too could earn wages and send money home, as well as lessen the number of mouths that had to be fed around the dinner table in Livermore.

Debt and poverty were not unusual in rural Maine. But their experience with it filled all the older Washburn siblings with a grim determination to make good, no matter how much effort it took. The hardships they endured as they grew up inspired them all with an enormous capacity for work, driven by an ambition to reach big goals.

At this point, we should note some differences between the
early Washburns and the later Washburns. The early Washburns bore the brunt of the family's hard times. The younger
Washburns, including Charles, Mary, Samuel, William, and
Caroline, had an easier time. Their early years were greatly
softened by the additional income being sent home by their
older siblings. Expectations were just as high for them as for
their predecessors, but there was much less uncertainty about
just how those expectations would be met. The younger Washburns, for example, were given far greater opportunities for
education and "polishing" outside of Livermore than their
older siblings ever received.

Of all the ingredients we consider vital for success in life
today, however, many were absent from the mixing bowl that
produced the older Washburns.

The first of these was formal education. Especially for the
oldest children, there was but a bare minimum of formal
schooling. Their one-room schoolhouse was only open for the
few months in the year that the children were not needed on
the farms. Teaching was by rote and the facilities were rudi-
mentary at best. Many of the young Washburns' first jobs were
at school teaching, and it was clear from their letters that physical control of the "scholars" was the most important talent
expected by the communities that employed them. The command of language, logic, literary referencing, humor, and eloquence expressed by the Washburn siblings as they grew older
were all self-taught. A world of letters was close by in Uncle
Reuel's library, but all of the siblings were on their own if they
wanted to take advantage of it.

Second, there were no important friends or relatives in
high places for the Washburns. Their relatives were well
regarded in the community, but unknown outside it. The siblings made their way outside of Livermore with little influence,

few letters of introduction, and no outside help. Any reputations they made, they had to make for themselves.

A third ingredient missing from the mixing bowl was financial support from the outside. For the Washburns, there was no financial legacy. No inheritance came their way, no unexpected windfalls, no gifts. Any advances they did receive came with obligations to repay—with interest. Indeed, brother Sidney, the first in the family to have any spare cash, in forty years went from loaning Israel twelve dollars to equip his first office, to providing his younger brothers Cadwallader and William with tens of thousands of dollars in revolving short-term notes. He was able to provide himself with a comfortable living back in Hallowell just from the interest on these notes.

It is an irony that the oldest Washburns—those who got the least in terms of material support—appear to have been morally tougher than some of their more advantaged younger siblings.

If you happened to meet one of the early Washburns, what you saw in front of you was what there was—homespun, rough-spoken, and eager. If you happened to meet the early siblings, you would also have seen their tight-knit family loyalty. As the first siblings grew older and began to experience success, their priority was to look out for their younger brothers and sisters. After Israel Jr. established himself in Orono in the late 1830s, he hosted for lengthy and repeated visits no less than five of his younger sisters and brothers: the former for introductions into society in their search for husbands, and the latter for private instruction in the field of law and for preparation for lives as professionals.

All together, somehow, for these ten children, what they got on the farm in Livermore was more than just the water. What they got was enough to light a fire of ambition for better things. They all took a chance and left the only world they knew as soon as they could legally do so, and with their parents' blessings. They went far and did much.

The story of their arrival in, and their departure from, the quiet world of Livermore, Maine, is a classic story of the birth of an American dream.

1. Alfred Lord Tennyson, *The Ballad of Oriana*, from an entry written by Charles Ames Washburn in the Washburn family journal for March 11, 1869 (Washburn Library).

2. *Eastern Argus*, June 13, 1854 (story dated June 6).

3. CCW to EBW, December 9, 1862 (Library of Congress, hereinafter LC).

4. Julia Chase Washburn, *Genealogical Notes of the Washburn Family*, privately printed, 1898 (Washburn Library), 42.

5. From *Dedicatory Exercises* pamphlet of the Washburn Memorial Library, remarks made August 5, 1885, (Washburn Library), 40.

6. From a journal of reminiscences of Jeanette Washburn Kelsey (Washburn Library), 7.

7. Ira Thompson Monroe, *History of the Town of Livermore and Its Pioneers* (Lewiston, 1928), 37.

8. From Washburn store records (Washburn Library), quoted in 1973 paper by Billie Gammon.

Two

Barefoot and Homespun

ISRAEL WASHBURN, SR., CAME TO THE DISTRICT of Maine from Raynham, Massachusetts. As several of his sons were to do later, his first employment, in 1806, was teaching school— first, for a two-month session in the Pownalborough section of Woolwich and the following year for three months at Damariscotta. There was plenty of time available for him to undertake other enterprises. In nearby White's Landing, now Richmond, Maine, twenty miles up the Kennebec River from its mouth, he and a partner named Barzillai White managed a store and also built a small schooner. They named the vessel *Portumnus*, sold it, and used the profits to build a second. Unfortunately, Jefferson's embargo of 1807, followed by the devastating British blockade along the coast of Maine during the War of 1812 removed all potential buyers from the scene, and the little vessel rotted on its stocks. Israel Sr. had often visited Livermore, where he had customers for his merchandise, where his brother Reuel had just hung out a lawyer's shingle, and where other friends from Raynham had settled. He liked the place, and in 1809 he purchased a small farm there from one Artemus Leonard, a man who would later be in business with three of Israel's sons in Hallowell. The farm consisted of a gambrel-roofed house and a small general store, plus about sixty-five acres of rocky land. It was located at a crossroads on a windblown ridge near the geographical center of the thinly populated township of Livermore. The house had originally been built by the settlement's first doctor, Cyrus Hamlin.[1]

The Hamlin and Washburn families would always be close, possibly because of their joint interest in politics. Hamlin's two sons, Elijah and Hannibal, would each become prominent politicians in Maine. Hannibal would be congressman, governor, U.S. senator, and Lincoln's vice president during the early years of the Civil War. Israel Washburn, Jr., would be instrumental in persuading Hannibal to give up his lifelong affiliation with the Democrats and become a Republican. They worked closely together to bring the party to victory, first in 1856 in Maine, and then in 1860 for the White House. It was a small world.

The spot where the farm was located was just a hilltop crossroads. Rocky fields alternated with patches of woods, as they do to this day. Just down the road there was a small tavern, and beyond it a blacksmith shop and a modest fulling mill. Beyond that was the farmer who doubled as a postmaster. There were three other crossroads settlements within a short ride: "The Corner," now North Livermore, was up over Waters Hill to the north, and Uncle Reuel and his family lived there. To the south and west, on Brettuns Pond about four miles away, was another settlement simply called "Brettuns." To the east was the settlement called Livermore Center, which had another dozen or so families, and beyond it was Hillman's Ferry, an alternate way of getting across the river to East Livermore, where the various Benjamin aunts and uncles and cousins lived. The Washburn family journals are full of visits back and forth, and the two families were always very close. There was a fourth settlement to the north, where the river boiled over a set of falls. Later there would be a bridge here, and then the railroad would come. Ultimately, Livermore's falls would attract the paper mills that are still there (and just upstream at Jay) today. But in 1809, when Israel Sr. bought the farm, all of this was decades into the future.

The Androscoggin River was a shallow, rock-filled waterway during most of the year. For the Washburns, it was the gateway to the outside world—not down it or up it, but across it. The Washburns usually crossed at a place called Strickland's Ferry. The ferry there was a heavy, flat-bottomed barge operated by the hand of a farmer of the same name. Mr. Strickland had to haul the barge across the river using a long cable attached to trees on each bank. If you approached the opposite bank at a moment when the ferryman happened to be busy doing something else, you might wait an hour for him to haul the barge over to you, and then haul you, your horse and buggy, passengers, or other load, in whichever direction you were going.

From the Washburn farm, the ferry was about five miles away—mostly downhill going to the ferry, and uphill coming back. Things changed a bit around 1851, when the railroad came to interior Maine. Sadly for the future of the Washburns' neighborhood, the first railroad line came up the east side of the river from the south and stopped at Strickland's Station. This was a mixed blessing for the Washburns, depending on the season. Using the train, they could get as far as Portland in a day, but the return trip could be perilous in the wintertime. During winter storms, thanks to delayed or broken-down trains, blinding snow, and drifts, to say nothing of the numbing cold and high winds, the job of meeting visitors and bringing them back to the farm in the middle of the night could be treacherous indeed. Israel Jr. recalled more than one trip in which he survived more by luck and a horse who knew the way, than by anything else.

Trips to the outside world were always a high point in the

lives of the young Washburns. Elihu remembered as a seven-year-old going on one of the twice-yearly buying trips for the store that his father took to Boston. The route for that trip was by schooner from Hallowell. Five years later he went again, this time overland with a drove of cattle—a trip that took nine days.

Also recorded was a famous trip south that Israel Jr. made in 1828. Unlike his younger brothers who had to work in the fields, the oldest son was allowed to clerk at his father's store and help with the business side of the farm. That year, fifteen-year-old Israel Jr. was in charge of a wagonload of goods to be sold in either Bath or Portland, wherever he could get the best prices. He went in convoy with two neighbors who were doing the same thing. When they came to the point where the road to Portland branched off, the neighbors went on to Bath, but young Israel decided to go to Portland. Perhaps he hoped for better prices in Portland. However, what he really wanted was to visit the state legislature, which was meeting there at the time. It turned out that the best prices were at Bath, and younger brother Elihu remembered his father ribbing Israel for many years afterwards. about this decision to go to Portland to see the "le-gis-la-ture."[2]

Although actual trips "away" were rare, the Washburn household was always interested in news from the world outside of Livermore—especially political news. This might come from traveling peddlers, but the main sources were the weekly newspapers. The family ultimately subscribed to several, from Augusta, Boston, and even New York. All were anxiously awaited—woe be unto the mailman who was late—and they were carefully perused by all who could read. The arrival of a fresh newspaper inevitably kicked off heated and lengthy discussions—in the store, over the dinner table, in the front parlor, perhaps out in the hay barn as well.

The Washburns were Whigs, the somewhat conservative party founded by Henry Clay in 1820 in response to Andrew Jackson's campaign against a national bank. Whig platforms were always sympathetic to business and found more support along Maine's commercial coast than in its agricultural interior; it was a minority party in interior Maine. Much of the region's infant economy was tied up in shipbuilding and the growing lumber trade, and the state had yet to have a single highway connecting its southwest and northeast boundaries. So the Whigs courted votes by supporting nationally funded internal improvements, a single national currency, and, above all, a strong national tariff on imports to protect Maine products, such as lumber, from being undercut by lower-priced competition from British Canada. The Washburn family heroes were John Quincy Adams and Henry Clay. Israel Jr. so much admired the Great Compromiser from Kentucky that in 1843 he named his own first son, Israel Henry Washburn, after him. This was in spite of the imbroglio over Maine's statehood that Clay's compromising had been meant to resolve.

Patty Washburn's impressive production of babies began in 1813 and continued for the next twenty years. None of her descendents ever approached her record at this (see Appendix A). For two eventful decades, the Washburn household was rarely without a new baby. The first four were boys, and in their choice of names for the four, the parents showed an imagination and love of history that was unusual for backcountry farmers.

The first child was Israel Jr., named after his father and grandfather. The following year Israel Jr. got the first of his brothers. The parents named this infant Algernon Sidney, after a Protestant political leader in London who was executed for treason in 1683. (Fortunately for the boy, he was always known as Sid.) In 1816 came the third brother, Elihu Benjamin, whose Old Testament first name probably came from an uncle. He would be the first of four different children to bear their mother's family name as a middle name. The fourth brother was born in 1818. They named him Cadwallader Colden, after a well-known physician, botanist, and loyalist leader in pre-revolutionary New York City. Finally, in 1820, the Washburns got their first girl. She was Martha Benjamin, named after her mother.

During these seven years, times were relatively good for the neighborhood around the Washburn store. By far the biggest issue on everyone's mind was being fought out in the U.S. Congress, well beyond their world of rocky fields and dusty roads. This issue was Maine's campaign for statehood.

Maine had long been a district in the Commonwealth of Massachusetts, but impatience with the Massachusetts government had been growing across the district. For her part, the Commonwealth was growing weary of the unceasing demands and dim prospects from her far-flung and poverty-stricken stepchild to the north. Israel Sr. was elected to represent Livermore in the Massachusetts General Court for four of the last six years that Maine was part of Massachusetts. He must have been right in the middle of the growing tensions.3

Finally, Massachusetts allowed an election to be held to settle the question. Elections conducted in Maine during 1819 returned landslide victories in favor of separation and, at year's end, in favor of a new "state" constitution. Now the issue went to Congress, where it immediately became part of another tug-of-war: the contest between northern and southern states over control of the central government. The rhetoric was about slavery, but the real concern was about maintaining a balance between slave states and free states in the U.S. Senate.

Eventually Henry Clay worked out the deal that has always borne the name of the other state involved in the struggle: The Missouri Compromise. In March of 1820 Maine was allowed to become a state without slavery, while Missouri was allowed to come in as a slave state—but with a clear line, north of which slavery was prohibited. That line, and its later removal, would provide the cause that propelled all of the Washburns into intense political activism.

Clay's compromise preserved the balance between north and south, but Mainers were outraged. Pulpits rang throughout the state: Maine statehood had been held hostage by the slaveholders, and only granted in return for the expansion of that evil institution. In fact, all seven of Maine's own representatives actually voted *against* the Senate version of the statehood measure.

Churchmen were not the only ones who were upset. From Monticello an aging Thomas Jefferson called the new Maine state constitution, with its generous bill of rights, "the knell of the union." Voters in Maine had no particular feeling about slavery one way or another, but the statehood battle marked the beginning of resentment across the new state about southern power in the central government. It was resentment that the Washburns would use thirty years later to help create a new political party and unite the northern and western states to fight in a war to preserve the country.

From their written reminiscences, one gets the impression of a particular togetherness among the first five Washburn offspring. There was a mutual experience of hardship and a mutual sympathy to high moral purpose. Although they scattered to places far apart from one another, their correspondence was copious—in the early days hand-delivered through friends to avoid the cost of postage stamps.

Israel Jr. was the most bookish of these five. Due to both his age and his intelligence, he was often excused from farm chores so he could help out in his father's store. In addition, he was often farmed out to Uncle Reuel when the larder got thin at home. This gave him access to Reuel's extensive library, which in turn resulted in his early love of literature and his ambition to become a lawyer. His voracious reading gave birth to an eloquence that served him well, both in courts of law and on the campaign trail. He passed the bar examination at twenty-one and was soon thereafter able to supply financial and other support to both his parents and his siblings.

Sid may have been the first to leave Livermore. Possibly as early as 1828 he was clerking in a retail store in Hallowell, a job that included room and board. Next he migrated to Boston to continue his mercantile career in a bigger venue. He was the first of the brothers to earn spare cash, which he unhesitatingly sent home or loaned out to whichever brother needed it. Israel, Elihu, and Cadwallader were all early recipients. All hated to be obligated, and all were able to repay promptly. All found themselves going back to Sid's well in the years to come, this time paying interest. Although Sid enjoyed the social life of a rising bachelor businessman in Boston, these loans would eventually evolve into a career as both a public and a private banker back in Maine.

Adding to the financial pressures on the family between 1820 and failure of the store in 1828, four more children were born on the Washburn farm: three boys and a girl. Charles Ames, possibly the weakest physically and certainly the dreamiest, arrived in 1822 and immediately became his mother's favorite. He was followed two years later by Samuel, who grew to be the most physically powerful and perhaps the least literary of the brood. A year after that arrived Mary, the second daughter and closest sibling to Sam.

Unfortunately, Mother Patty's string of eight flawless pregnancies now came to an end. About the same time that the family's most difficult financial times began, in 1827 a sixth son was born. They named him William Allen Drew, after one of their favorite Universalist ministers and the editor of one of the weekly newspapers they lived by. The child never achieved full health, and they lost him shortly after his first birthday in 1828. Thus, to the store's closing and Israel Sr.'s decision to try and make a living from the farm alone was added the sadness of a child's death.

The failure of the family store in 1828 was hardest on Elihu and Cadwallader and cemented a strong tie between them. Elihu, then only twelve years old, spent a hellish five months in 1830 laboring for a deaf old man named Lovewell up on Waters Hill to work off that $25 debt mentioned earlier. Cad, age ten, with all his bigger brothers gone, had to take their place laboring in the fields with his father to coax enough food out of their rock-filled acres to keep them all from starving. Even with the two oldest boys gone, there were still eleven mouths to feed, and sixty-five acres was a very small area in which to do it.

It is interesting to note here that Israel Sr. made no effort to start another store. He had no capital, of course, and he may have lost the store building as well. But neither he nor any of his neighbors ever moved to replace the little business. Everyone in the neighborhood knew of the generous "book" at the Washburn store, and most had probably benefited from it from time to time. But when it came time to pay the piper, no one except brother Reuel stepped forward.

The store's failure may have been a traumatic experience for others besides the Washburns in their little community, and the trauma lasted a long time. It was years—not long before Reuel's death, in fact—before the boys paid off their uncle for the mortgage he had taken in order to save the little farm.

Elihu thought that the four years after the store's demise were his mother's finest. Despite the hardship, the uncertainty, and the physical danger, she would deliver two more children.

Another son was born in 1831, and they named him William Drew after his departed brother. This was the same year that Israel Jr. celebrated his eighteenth birthday and departed for Bangor to study law on the frontier. The eleventh and final arrival came in 1833, the year before Israel Jr. hung out his law shingle in Orono. She was the third daughter—named Caroline—and she would become the most attractive and vivacious of the sisters. Thus there was a full generation's difference between the oldest and the youngest Washburn children. As things developed, this would work to the advantage of the youngest.

Somehow, Patty found time to attend to all of her children, get meals on the table, sew shirts and pants and dresses as needed, and impress everyone with her confidence in each child. Wood got chopped, cows got fed and milked, fences and walls maintained, and crops got planted, weeded, and harvested. At the same time, the children learned to read and write. Some of them even got additional tutoring in subjects such as Latin and Greek.

Also in 1833, at the age of seventeen, Elihu found a job as a printer's "devil" for a newspaper in Gardiner. His brother Sid was clerking at a store in nearby Hallowell, and they saw much of each other. Sid moved on the following year for greener pastures in Boston, but Elihu always remembered how kind Sid was to him during the year that the two boys spent their first time away from home. Patty still made Elihu's clothes, and he was able to send home nearly half of the clothing allowance he received from his employer. Unfortunately, the newspaper went broke, but Elihu, using hometown connections, managed to find a position teaching for a term in nearby Hartford, Maine. He boarded for a time with his Uncle Reuel to study Latin, and finally landed a job in Augusta as a printer's apprentice with the prestigious *Kennebec Journal*. This was one step up the ladder, and he learned much from a kind boss there named Luther Severance—later a political ally and friend to several of the brothers. Elihu was there, already hanging around the legislature, in 1836 when Cadwallader arrived in Hallowell to work in a store and part-time in the post office while studying to prepare himself to be a schoolteacher. All four oldest sons were now supporting themselves, and easing financial tensions at home through their remittances.

Home was still a very busy place. In 1835 fifteen-year-old Martha penned a letter to her brother Sid in Boston. In it she provided a glimpse into the dynamic state of the Washburn farmhouse: "The family is in their wonted uproar," she wrote. "Hurrah boys, slam bang the pigs are out, come Sam says Charles. The oxen are in the corn, why don't you drive them out. Such sounds are falling in the most admissible discord upon my ear as I sit in the kitchen upside the oven door penning this letter."[4]

Controlling "wonted uproar" was the main responsibility of the rural schoolteachers that Cadwallader, Elihu, Martha, and Mary would all, like their father before them, evntually become. In smoky one-room schoolhouses, amid the snowdrifts from Hermon to Hartford, East Livermore to Wiscasset in Maine, and later, all the way out in Davenport, Iowa, all of them would have to make unruly and energy-charged young people "toe the crack." When Elihu took his post in Hartford in 1834, the first thing he learned was that his rebellious "scholars" had "turned out" their teacher from the previous winter. Writing forty years later, he remembered subduing one young rowdy who was bigger and older than he was by shattering a large ruler "to atoms" over the young man's head. (The ferule was a standard piece of equipment for every teacher in those days.) The mutiny was quelled, and the term finished without incident, though Elihu remembered that "I disliked

All of the Washburn children were "scholars," and four of them were
teachers in country schools like this one painted by Winslow Homer.
Teachers were ill-prepared, school terms were short, and discipline was
the first requirement. Most school sessions took place during the winter,
but—from the childrens' bare feet shown here—this painting
must have been done during a rare summer term.
COURTESY ST. LOUIS ART MUSEUM

teaching more than anything I have ever done in my life." For
his three months in the teaching profession he was paid three
ten-dollar bills—most of which he used to pay for going back
to school himself.[5]

In about 1836, sixteen-year-old Martha was sent off to the
first of several terms she received at the Waterville Liberal
Institute. As the boys needed to be prepared to earn a living, so
the girls needed to be prepared to find a husband. For the
Washburns, these missions were of equal importance.

Fortunately for the girls, their oldest brother was getting
into a good position to help. Israel Jr.'s law practice in Orono
was a success, and he was gaining respect among a wide circle
of friends and clients. With help from his brother Sid, in 1840
Israel completed construction of a new house in Orono that
included a guest bedroom. The very next year, the young

lawyer married the daughter of one of the town's leading citizens, Mary Maud Webster. Over the next fifteen years, Israel and Maud were happy to host each of his three sisters for extensive and repeated visits. The sisters helped Maud with her babies, and were introduced to the lively society of the Orono-Bangor area, which at the time enjoyed the highest wealth per capita of any area in Maine. It was a successful effort. Two of the three girls met their future husbands while visiting Orono.

The older offspring were called on to help even more in 1843, when the house at the crossroads burned and had to be replaced. The new place was a white cottage with green shutters, French doors opening onto a piazza, and a space upstairs under the eaves where the younger boys slept. They named the new house Boyscroft.

Farm work was what the children did as they grew up. The boys helped with the animals and with the field crops at the same time that they undertook a regimen of outside studying to improve themselves. The girls helped in the kitchen and the house, and with the lighter outdoor chores like collecting eggs and fetching water. School provided them all with a different experience, but for no more than three months in the winter, between the time of last harvest and firewood cutting, and the time of first clearing and planting in the spring. With ten or fifteen other "scholars" of all ages in one room, they would learn their lessons—and their manners. Occasionally, if the neighborhood families felt flush, they would hire a teacher for a few more weeks in the summertime, before everyone was needed for the harvest.

The days were long, but not without entertainments. Israel remembered dances in the barn of a neighbor named Otis Pray, with his brother Cadwallader gliding gracefully around the floor under the low ceiling doing something called the "swing balance." All the older boys had fond memories of Livermore, but Israel's were the most detailed. Fifty years later he was able to fill thirty pages of the family journal with recollections of over 250 friends and neighbors he had known in the town. This was apart from the many more pages in his personal journal that he filled with memories and opinions about national political figures he had known in Congress and elsewhere. These pages are not only a tour de force of Israel's memory, but also a vivid record of the whole family's involvement with, and love for, the people around them.

The first challenge that had to be met by each of the oldest Washburn boys was simply to support himself. Each started his new position with only the clothes on his back, but all had a burning desire to better themselves. All realized that their best options were away from Livermore and that they needed a lot more of both social polish and vocational expertise than they had when they started out. All had dreams of achieving financial security far ahead of what the farm could provide, and of achieving respected positions in whatever society they found themselves. Despite their lack of finances, credentials, and references, they determined to go wherever they had to go in order to make good. Unlike most small town émigrés who aspire to the bright lights of the city, three of the four oldest Washburns came to a different conclusion. The frontier was where the action was.

One by one, each of these three found his way to a different community at the edge of the expanding country. That was where commercial activity was growing and opportunities would be best. Perhaps by design as well, each picked a spot well separated from his siblings. Although linked by constant correspondence and visits, each made sure that he had a field to himself.

* * *

The first thing needed by anyone who wanted to build anything on the frontier was lumber, and the earliest adventures of
the oldest brothers all began in or near the woods.

1. Information about Israel Sr.'s first years in Maine can be found in Julia Chase
Washburn's *Genealogical Notes of the Washburn Family* (privately printed, 1898,
and located at the Washburn Library).
2. From *Early Recollections*, private paper edited by Wayne M. Dimond, and written by Elihu in Archason, France, in March of 1873 (Washburn Library).
3. Monroe, 254.
4. MBW to ASW, Oct. 4, 1835 (Washburn Library).
5. From *Early Recollections*, 24–25.

THREE

—•—

Lawyers and Land Agents

AMERICA IN THE 1830S AND 1840S was expanding in all directions. Out on the edges of the country, floods of new people were arriving. For them, it was a once-in-a-lifetime chance to leave old lives behind and start new ones—where the soil had no rocks and the opportunities no limits. New states were being created, new resources were being exploited, and new investment money was flowing. For those who were young and in good health, great possibilities lay on the frontier. If you couldn't actually go yourself but you had a few dollars laid by, then it was a good place to risk your money.

In the East, the great forests of northeastern Maine made up the last frontier in New England. Most of it was drained by a single river—the Penobscot—and it presented a lucrative opportunity for speculators from Boston and New York. The land was cheap, and the great trees could easily be cut and dragged to a nearby stream bank. From there in the early spring, when the melting snow brought high water, they could be floated a hundred miles downstream. There the sawmills could turn them into lumber, and a vast fleet of schooners could take the lumber to booming markets as far south as Baltimore and Washington. Similarly, to the northwest, the government was opening up huge tracts of land across the new states of the upper Mississippi valley.[1] Natural resources such as lead, water power, and timber waited to be developed, as well as rich agricultural land. This was a hotbed of opportunity for settlers and for investors—investors who had no interest in what they were buying, other than what they could make by leasing it or selling it. As money was pouring into northern Maine, even more money was being plowed into investments in the upper Mississippi valley.

As the land was cleared, new towns appeared, and services—from surveying to schoolteaching to banking—were needed. Demand for land caused values to escalate and speculation to increase, so that prices went up further. In the rush to buy, little attention was paid to the details, and there was much competition and confusion. There were endless battles over land titles, boundaries, rights of way, and, above all, money: rent money, loan money, tax money, and wage money. Everything on the frontier was done on credit. Entrepreneurs struggled to find financing and pay their employees, distant vendors struggled to get paid, municipalities struggled to collect taxes, sellers struggled to find buyers, and buyers struggled to find sellers.

At the heart of all this activity stood the lawyers. As Israel, Elihu, and Cadwallader Washburn saw it, everyone on the frontier sooner or later would need a lawyer—and speculators sooner than anyone. Surveys had to be done, boundaries had to be drawn, titles had to be established and defended, taxes paid, rents collected, improvements made, and bills paid. A trusted lawyer could make a comfortable living acting as agent for a land company, a transportation company, or a bank. The Washburn boys had no problem with being trusted; formal training in the law was what they lacked.

In those days there were two ways of becoming a lawyer. Those who could afford it could be formally trained at one of the very few law schools in the country. Alternatively, if tuition money was not available, a candidate could apprentice with an established lawyer or judge, burn a lot of midnight oil studying on his own, and then be examined individually. Either way, it was possible to be admitted to the bar after two or three years of hard study. Israel Jr., helped by Uncle Reuel, passed the bar in Maine when he was just twenty-one. Later, Elihu and Cadwallader did it, in Massachusetts and Wisconsin respectively, when they were twenty-four.

Even the Washburn siblings who did not become lawyers took advantage of opportunities on the frontier. Although he never went farther than Boston, Sidney supplied goods to customers on the frontiers, including his brothers. From Sid's position in the city, he loaned them money to get started, and he shared in their investments in both Wisconsin and Minnesota. Younger brother Sam went to sea in the cotton trade that supplied the textile mills with what they needed to mass produce the goods that Sid sold. When Captain Sam later came ashore, it was to buy a stake in Cad's lumber camp in Wisconsin. Brother Charles, although he, too, received training in the law, found a métier with his pen at a newspaper in the gold fields of California. Youngest brother Bill was admitted to the bar in his turn—the fifth of the seven boys to train in the law—and then he, too, used Sidney's loans to leap into the land and lumber business on the frontier in Minnesota.

Even the three Washburn girls wound up on the frontier. Martha found a husband in Wisconsin, and later followed him to Illinois. Mary followed her husband first to Wisconsin and then to Iowa. Caroline stayed in Maine at first, but tragedy changed her world there, and she also went west, ultimately spending the rest of her life near her brother Bill in Minnesota. For all the Washburns, the frontier was where they wanted to be.

The first three Washburn brothers to become lawyers all achieved success, but followed very different paths.

From the huge forests to the north to the burgeoning cities to the south,
the whole economy of eastern Maine flowed down the
Penobscot River to the lumber schooners at Bangor.
COLLECTIONS OF THE BANGOR MUSEUM AND CENTER FOR MAINE HISTORY

Israel Jr. was the first to leave Livermore. Details are uncertain, but sometime around 1831, shortly after his eighteenth birthday, dressed in the clothes his mother had made for him, he bravely set his face to the northeast. He was bound for the booming town of Bangor, the head of navigation for the Penobscot River, where the sawmills screamed and the waterfront was filled with log rafts and lumber schooners, where more people were making more money than anywhere else in New England, and where the courts were busy with the clamor of competing interests large and small. No doubt carrying an introductory letter from Uncle Reuel, it was there, in the same court where he would plead cases for the next twenty years, that Israel found a sympathetic judge to supervise his self-instruction and, three years later, to examine and pass him as a member of the Maine bar. Back at Livermore, Uncle Reuel was so proud that he gave Israel a new suit—perhaps his first—to celebrate the occasion.

Israel Washburn, Jr., did not exude a commanding presence. He was shortest of the brothers—no more than five feet, six inches tall—and from an early age wore thick spectacles that made him look older than he was. However, he was smart, well-read (thanks to Uncle Reuel's library), and an excellent debater. Most important of all, he shared his family's integrity and work ethic. Years later he remembered the weeks of preparation he put into his first case before Judge Ether Shepley in Bangor.

The new lawyer knew exactly where he would start out. He had had three years to observe the area, and he had determined that the settlement of Orono, located eight miles upstream from Bangor, where the Stillwater River flowed into the Penobscot, was where he would hang out his shingle. Although the 1830 census listed only 1,473 people in Orono, there were far more than that when Israel first saw the place, and the volume of timber floating down from the north was steadily increasing. New dams were under construction to create holding areas for logs and to channel water to power the new sawmills. Local entrepreneurs jostled with Boston speculators in their eagerness to buy and develop the timberlands to the north. Although there were already three or four other lawyers in town, none were Whig—an important consideration, as young Washburn analyzed his prospects. Success in the practice of law required not only legal competence but also political sympathy, and a lot of the biggest potential clients in the area were Whigs.

The town of Orono didn't look very booming when Israel opened up shop there in December 1834. Winter was when the trees were cut, because of the relative ease of hauling them over snow and ice to the nearest riverbank. Hence, nearly all the men and many of the women in the town were working in the woods when Israel hung out his shingle. It was very quiet and very cold. Thanks to a loan of twelve dollars from his brother Sid, Israel furnished his new office with a table, two chairs, a candlestick, and some firewood. It was a long winter, and he had to borrow another six dollars from Sid to get enough firewood to make it through till spring. He found clients, or they found him, almost from the very beginning. Nineteen-year-old Elihu, the future minister to France, was then slaving away for pennies at a print shop in Gardiner. He reported with wonder to Sid in April of 1835, that Israel had made twenty dollars cash in a single week.

All kinds of improvements were coming to Orono. Within a year, the town had its first bank. It was joined by a second the next year, and there was regular stagecoach service through the town. Population topped 6,000, and there were more than twenty stores along the main street. In 1836 Samuel Veazie, one of the most spectacular of the Bangor timber barons, completed the state's first railroad—from Bangor to nearby Old Town. Orono citizens turned out to gawk as the little engine Lion and its two passenger cars, all imported from England, bumped and snorted up and down the line through the woods on the western edge of town.

As long as lumber prices stayed up, times were good. Israel remembered a land auction in Orono in 1836 where champagne was served in tubs, and there were signs of wealth that "rivaled the Arabian nights."[2] Bangor, where lumberjacks and schoonermen shared the muddy streets with gamblers and ladies of the night, boasted the highest per capita income in New England.

However, things could come down as fast as they went up. Overproduction brought a lumber glut in 1837, which worsened as the lumbermen cut more logs to make up for falling prices. Suddenly, the land boom became a bust. Stores closed, people left, and even food supplies got tight. Then, six years later, boom times returned, bigger than ever. The Penobscot was lined with more than 200 sawmills, and they cut hundreds of millions of feet of lumber every year. The scream of the saws and the smell of freshly cut wood was everywhere.

Volatility in lumber prices was one problem. Another problem was geopolitical. Far to the north and northeast, beyond the drainage basin of the Penobscot, the great pinery continued, but here the streams flowed north into the St. John River, and that, in turn, flowed to the sea through British Canada. Although the great trees were in Maine, the logs cut here had to be floated out via Canada, where duties had to be paid. The Canadians, mostly Loyalists who had been forced out of Boston and New York after the Revolution, were not well disposed toward their American neighbors. They controlled the sawmills and the waterfront at St. John's, the only place where finished lumber could be shipped out.

The problem was not just unfriendly sawmill operators. The actual location of the border between Maine and British Canada had been in dispute since 1817. Despite the wording of the 1783 treaty that had established the line, Canadians considered the entire St. John drainage basin part of Canada and were sending rival lumber crews up the river to cut trees there. These were trees that Mainers considered their own.

Confrontation escalated into violence in the winter of 1838. The Maine State Legislature, alarmed by Canadian "depredations"—the stealing of what they estimated was $100,000 worth of Maine trees that year—sent a 200-man "posse" north to stop the invaders. Impromptu trials of Canadian trespassers were held on frozen rivers, and horse teams were confiscated. Unfortunately, the land agent commanding the group, one Rufus McIntyre, somehow got himself captured by the Canadians and was thrown into jail at Fredericton for several weeks. Tensions built, and the next winter troops were raised on both sides of the border. The Maine legislature appropriated a million dollars to pay for theirs, and a considerable force marched north in the winter of 1839. Young lawyer Washburn watched them go by his front door. Eventually, American general Winfield Scott managed to arrange a truce between the two sides, and serious boundary negotiations began between the two countries. The so-called "Aroostook War" was avoided. Two years later, with the approval of the Webster-Ashburton Treaty, the border conflict was settled, albeit at great cost to Maine and great anger on the part of Lawyer Washburn of Orono.

Sometimes by accident and sometimes by design, the Washburn brothers seemed to attract historically significant events. The dedicated contingent of Maine militia marching past twenty-six-year-old Israel's front door, determined to take on the entire British Empire, was an early example. His being a member of the Maine legislature that was duped to decide the border question was another.

Washburn had risen steadily in stature and reputation in Orono. He was named moderator for the annual town meeting in 1839—the first of four times. In 1840 Orono and Old Town separated, and each became an independent town. Lawyer Washburn was elected to the Orono school committee. This was the year of the Whigs' high-water mark in both state and national politics, and Israel worked hard in both the state and national elections that fall. Afterwards, he was jubilant to report to brother Sid that the Whig vote in Orono had increased by 189 votes over the year before. The next year, Israel was elected to his first statewide office, becoming one of the new town's first representatives to the state legislature in Augusta.

Not much happened during the regular session, but fireworks took place during a special session called by Governor John Fairfield that summer. The British, led by Lord Ashburton, and the American secretary of state, Daniel Webster, had been talking in Washington about a comprehensive border settlement between the United States and what was to become Canada. Now they needed Maine to appoint representatives to approve what they had decided about the exact location of the boundary across northern and eastern Maine.

Both the governor and the legislature of Maine were opposed to any agreement that changed the terms agreed upon in the Treaty of Paris fifty years earlier. But the British now wanted the St. John Valley for a military road, expansionist American president John Tyler wanted concessions along the border in the west, Webster wanted to be president, and nobody cared much about who cut down whose trees in the wilderness of northern Maine.

To win approval of the new border line, Lord Ashburton by his own admission had to deal "somewhat irregularly" with the men of Maine that summer. His tactics included intimidation. The central government, pushed by representatives from New Hampshire, New York, Michigan, and Minnesota, wanted this deal. If Maine wouldn't take it, the next offer would be much worse, the legislators were warned. Falsified evidence was also used. A phony map of the 1783 agreement was presented by a Harvard professor named Sparks to prove the British claims. One of the world's first disinformation campaigns was mounted. A rumor was started that if the Maine men agreed to give up territory in the north, perhaps they might be given territory from southern New Brunswick in exchange. Finally Ashburton's "irregularity" included outright bribery. A leading Bangor newspaper editor was paid $14,000 to write editorials sympathetic to the treaty.

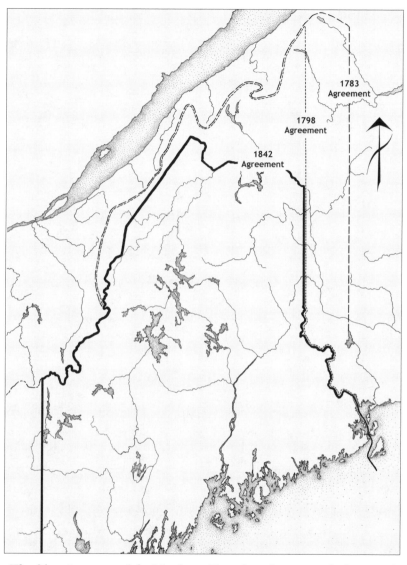

*The fifty-nine years of the Northeast Boundary dispute marked repeated
losses for the state of Maine. The line finally agreed to in the Webster-
Ashburton Treaty—only after a campaign of intimidation, bribery,
and misinformation—marks the present border of the state. For years
after this treaty was signed Israel Washburn, Jr., distrusted both the
British and his own government.* ORBIS MAPS © 2007

In the end, the legislature appointed the commissioners, and the commissioners went to Washington and were bullied into approving the deal. Israel Washburn, Jr., got his first lesson in power politics, and Maine became the only state in the union ever to give up territory to a foreign power. The total of land lost, compared with the agreement that both sides had lived by since 1783, was hundreds of square miles. The ratification of the Webster-Ashburton Treaty was a humiliation that Israel Washburn, Jr. never forgot.

For the rest of his life, Washburn was supersensitive to the fact that Maine was surrounded on three sides by a foreign power, and that the southern-dominated central government had little knowledge of, or sympathy for, the problems of its northernmost citizens. In his twenty-five years of public life, one of Israel's greatest accomplishments was to increase the national government's awareness of Maine's vulnerability in this regard.

Israel Washburn, Jr., was far more than a spectator in the Northeast Boundary Dispute. He would be involved with it for the next forty years. His clients would be hurt by it, his own pride in his state would be hurt by it, and his faith in the central government would be severely tried by it. After the Webster-Ashburton agreement was signed, he never again trusted either the British or Daniel Webster. In addition, he may have felt more than a little guilt over the way things turned out. He himself had been a member of the special session of the Maine legislature without whose approval the agreement never could have been signed. In the end, three years before he died, Israel's preoccupation with the Northeast Boundary Dispute would result in his most impressive work of historical scholarship.

Lawyer Washburn made a major improvement to his standing in Orono in 1841 by wooing and winning Mary Maud

Webster, the daughter of Colonel Ebenezer Webster, one the town's most influential citizens. Webster had earned his title in command of an Orono militia unit at the disastrous fight against the British at Hamden back in 1814. He was a major player in north woods lands and owned one of the new sawmills on the Stillwater River. Over the next forty years, Israel grew exceedingly close to the Webster family.

To house his new bride, and with the help of another loan from his brother Sid, Israel built a home on a fine lot that faced Orono's main street and backed up to the Penobscot River. It contained enough room for plenty of children, for nannies or visiting relatives, and for his office. To this day, it is still one of the handsomest homes in the town.

Washburn's reputation continued to grow. He was picked to deliver an oration at the Fourth of July celebration in Bangor in 1843, the year his first son was born. With his father-in-law, Israel helped establish the first Universalist society in Orono. They opened their first meetinghouse in 1844, just down the street from Israel's own new house. Both the Washburns and the Websters purchased pews.

In 1846 Israel got one of his most important cases. The biggest landowner in northern Maine was David Pingree, a successful businessman from Salem, Massachusetts, who became interested in the forest lands along the far reaches of the Penobscot drainage basin.

The height of land that separated the south-flowing waters of the Penobscot River from the north-flowing waters of the Allagash River was hardly a height at all. It was more a series of marshes and small lakes. Thanks to his brilliant agent, a man named E. S. Coe, David Pingree learned that by placing a dam across the Allagash River where it flowed out of Chamberlain Lake, he could raise the water level across the entire upstream drainage basin. If he raised it just eleven feet, he could reverse its flow. As a result, about thirty-five miles of the Allagash River headwaters, including Telos Lake and Telos Stream, could be made to flow south rather than north. This meant that logs cut across thirty-five miles of forest could be floated out to the south, through Bangor, rather than north, through Canada, where duties would have to be paid. As a result of this discovery, Pingree purchased five townships around Chamberlain Lake—one hundred square miles of timberland containing an estimated two hundred million board feet of prime lumber. Coe built the dam, Pingree started leasing the land out for cutting, and several important Bangor lumbermen signed up and began operations.

The key point where the flow of the water could be reversed was between Telos Lake and its neighbor, Webster Lake. In 1843 a ditch was dug between the two. This ditch was eventually widened and named the Telos Canal, and another dam, the Telos Dam, was built at the head of it to hold back the high water and extend the southward log-driving season. Despite protests from Canadians up on the St. John, the first logs began to flow south through the canal in 1843 and 1844.

In 1845 a sixth township came on the market. It was the township that contained the canal, but for some reason Pingree declined to purchase it. Instead, a freewheeling Bangor entrepreneur named Rufus Dwinel pounced on the property. Within months, Dwinel had an improved dam with locks constructed across the top of the canal, and announced that there would be a toll of two shillings (thirty-four cents) per thousand board feet to float logs through it. He backed his demand up with a gang of roughnecks imported from Bangor. Furthermore, he announced, the toll would go up to fifty cents the following year. If the lumbermen didn't like it, they could let their logs rot in the lake. Put up or shut up.

The lumbermen were stymied. The longer their logs stayed

floating in Telos Lake, the more the water level would go down and the greater the likelihood that they wouldn't be able to get them out at all that year. So, at last, they put up, but they didn't shut up. Pingree retained the services of Lawyer Washburn of Orono, late of the Maine State Legislature, and all the parties made a beeline for the legislature's Committee on Inland Waters in Augusta. The loggers complained that the waters were public property, open to all, and that Dwinel's tolls amounted to an undue burden on the public interest. With a brilliant argument, Washburn defended the classic right of eminent domain: public good over private rights.3

In 1846, over Dwinel's protests, the legislature responded to the Telos crisis with two acts. One act established an acceptable toll of twenty cents per thousand board feet, and the other act eliminated tolls altogether, if Dwinel didn't comply with the first act. It was a huge victory for the lumbermen. Dwinel would get some compensation for his investment, but Pingree and his lumbermen would be able to harvest trees around Chamberlain Lake and float them out to the south without undue economic hardship.

Washburn's victory reverberated all over the north country. In the days before railroads and tote roads penetrated the Maine woods, every lumberman in the state needed the streams to get their logs out. Now their right to use those streams was confirmed, and so was the reputation of the diminutive lawyer from Orono.

* * *

Israel's progress to reputation and respectability was duplicated by his younger brother Elihu, in a context similar to Maine's, but far removed from it.

The year before Israel passed his examination for the bar in Bangor, seventeen-year-old Elihu (in pantaloons held up by one suspender, he recalled) arrived at the tiny office of the *Christian Intellegencer* in Gardiner, Maine, to interview for the position of printer's "devil," the entry level of the printer's trade. He got the position, and found the work of sweeping out and lugging water and wood much easier than pulling rocks and hoeing potatoes back on the farm. He learned to set type and occasionally got to help out on the press itself. In his spare time he embarked on an intense program to improve himself. He read and studied furiously, resolved never to smoke or drink or play cards, and changed the spelling of his name to Washburne, the way his ancestors in England had spelled it. He was impressed by the "men of prominence" who lived in Gardiner, especially the lawyers and politicians.[4]

Unfortunately, the *Christian Intellegencer* failed in 1834, and Elihu was thrown on his "beam ends." He determined to get through the winter by teaching school in the Livermore area while continuing to seek an opportunity to pursue the printer's trade. He briefly thought about Hallowell for the latter, but Sidney advised him against it. Either there was something the matter with printers in Hallowell, or his brother thought they would each do better if they were in different towns. Evidence of the latter was strengthened in 1836, when young Cadwallader arrived in Hallowell and Sid left it for Boston. Throughout their careers, though fiercely supporting, partnering with, and defending one another, no Washburn brother was ever to settle permanently in the same town as any other.

Elihu retreated to the farm in the summer of 1834 and passed the time attending a private school in East Livermore, and working for an aunt to earn room and board. For a while his Uncle Reuel took him into his law office for some instruction in Latin. For three months in the winter of 1835, as Israel was enduring the frozen mud in Orono, eighteen-year-old Elihu was in charge of that previously mentioned schoolhouse full of rebellious "scholars" in the town of Hartford, Maine. Schoolmaster Washburne, now a solid five feet, ten and a half inches tall, having met the inevitable challenge to his authority with a preemptive strike, passed the rest of the term peacefully.

Although Elihu appreciated the respect with which he was treated by the people he boarded with in Hartford, and although he later wrote that he learned much through the experience, he hated teaching. Fortunately, he never had to do it again.

He took his earnings from Hartford—thirty dollars—to enroll at Maine Wesleyan Seminary in nearby Kents Hill, at the same time writing to newspapers all over the area for a position. In April, 1835 he got a job in a small print shop in Belfast, and then in May got an offer from Luther Severance of the *Kennebec Journal*. This was the man and the paper he had long yearned to work for, and the position proved every bit as good as he had hoped. Not only was he now a legitimate printer's apprentice with an important Whig publication, but he boarded with the Severances and got to meet many of the legislators who would later achieve national prominence. Jonathan Cilley, John Holmes, and Hannibal Hamlin were among these. Elihu continued to read and study in his spare time, and attended church every Sunday. Unfortunately, he began to feel the effects of a hernia, which ultimately prevented him from continuing as a printer. In April 1836, he sadly had to leave Augusta, but he had a new purpose. Like the politicians he admired, he, too, had determined to become a lawyer.

Elihu managed to go back to Kents Hill for a few months, but was again out of funds when a cousin put him in touch with Dr. Amos Nourse, the postmaster in Hallowell. Dr. Nourse kindly took him in. Again working for his board, he spent all his spare hours during the winter of 1836–37 studying French and Latin, reading extensively, and meeting the leading men in the town. He also kept an eye on his younger brother Cadwallader, who had just come to town, and he corresponded regularly with Sidney in Boston regarding opportunities there. The economic slump in 1837 brought a resurgence of Whig sentiment to the state and helped elect Edward Kent to the governorship, and Elihu shared the excitement of the campaign in Hallowell, which was a predominantly Whig town. At last, near the end of the year, he was invited to join the Hallowell law office of John Otis as a student. Otis also gave him room and board and later loaned him money to help with law school. Washburne spent the winter of 1838 in Otis's office, which he described as "a sort of rendezvous for the Whigs." He even tried for an appointment in the state legislature as assistant clerk to the house, but was "knocked sohigh and so quick that it made my head swim." He long remembered the cold, lonely walk afterwards, back to Hallowell in the snow.

Although Elihu Washburne had a long and effective career, he was frequently plagued with health problems. There were many intervals when he was in great pain or incapacitated altogether. One such event happened in the summer of 1838, during a visit to relatives in Massachusetts. He was suddenly overtaken by an excruciating pain in his hip that rendered him nearly unable to stand or walk. When he got back to Maine, Dr. Nourse relieved the pain by inserting a drain, which Elihu later repeated on his own, but the infection lasted several years.

The next winter, having over a year's experience with Lawyer Otis, Elihu decided to continue his apprenticeship at a larger law office in Boston, and to attend the law school in Cambridge, which would later be absorbed by Harvard. His friends in Hallowell loaned him money, and Mr. Otis helped him find a place with the firm of Derby and Andrews. This position gave Elihu experience with office practice and enabled him to visit the courts in Boston and to hear the great lawyers and judges of the day. In March the next term at the law school opened, and Elihu went out to Cambridge to enter it. He was there for over a year, studying hard and continuing at Derby and Andrews at the same time. Eventually the weight of his debts, and his unwillingness to incur any more of them, made him determined to get privately examined for admission to the bar in Massachusetts. Armed with letters of recommendation from two of his professors, including former U.S. Supreme Court justice Joseph Story, he had to try two different judges, but at last, on December 9, 1839, he made it.

His brother Cadwallader had gone west earlier in the year, and Elihu now resolved to follow him. With his brand-new license to practice law in Massachusetts—which would be accepted in any state in the union—and the blessings and good wishes of his relatives in Raynham and his brother Sid in Boston, in March of 1840 Elihu headed west. On the way, he visited Washington. He was fascinated by the debates in Congress and regretted that he could not be in both the House and the Senate at the same time. Hallowell representative George Evans, a good friend of all the Washburns, even took him to the White House to meet President Van Buren. Worried again about his budget, Washburne reluctantly left the capital after a week, and by rail, stage, and steamboat made his way west. He picked up letters of introduction as he proceeded, and even met the future Whig president, William Henry Harrison, outside of Cincinnati. He passed through Cairo, Illinois, which he observed was "infested with river thieves, gamblers, and cut throats." Little did he realize that significant events would take him back there twenty-one years later. St. Louis, Keokuk, and Burlington passed, and then at last, there was brother Cadwallader waiting for him on the dock at Stephenson (now Rock Island), Illinois.

Cadwallader had been through a kaleidoscope of adventures since 1837. He had clerked in a store in Hallowell and had also helped out at the post office there. Reading hard at night, he had prepared himself to be a teacher and had, for a term, tended a schoolhouse in Wiscasset. Then, also financed by Sid and determined to make his fortune in the most promising part of the country, he had made his way west, not stopping until he got to the Mississippi. He roamed down the river from Galena to Stephenson, in Illinois, and then across the river to Davenport, Iowa. He taught school, learned surveying, and carried out several federally funded surveys. He clerked in a store and considered other schemes, from publishing to farming. Frustrated by lack of funds, and driven by an ambition that was even fiercer than his brothers', Cad, too, started to read for a career in the law. He would become the third frontier lawyer in the family.

The brothers Elihu and Cadwallader huddled in Stephenson—two young men with the whole world before them. Although Elihu had been heading for Iowa, Cadwallader urged him to consider Galena, Illinois, located to the north on the Fever River just a couple of miles in from the Mississippi, and about halfway between St. Louis and Fort Snelling, up in Minnesota. There was considerable lead-mining activity around Galena, it was a major steamboating hub, land values were heating up, and there weren't many lawyers there. Elihu decided to take his younger brother's advice. Early in the morning of April 1, 1840, an unknown and solitary Elihu Washburne stepped off a gangplank and struggled up the muddy riverbank at Galena. The place was a bustle of lead miners, blast furnaces, and teams hauling "pigs" of lead to market. After a chat with the local Whig newspaper editor, a friendly man named Houghton, he decided to stay. He hung up his shingle on a log building on Main Street, across the street from

Galena, Illinois, thanks to lead mining, land speculation, and steamboat traffic, was the busiest commercial center west of Chicago in 1852. Elihu Washburne first hung out his shingle among the barrooms and bawdy houses on the riverfront, but was soon elevated to Bench Street, the more respectable area up the hill from the river — indicated here by the church steeples.

COURTESY ALFRED MUELLER COLLECTION, GALENA HISTORICAL SOCIETY

a livery stable across the street. He was the town's first Whig lawyer. All that summer, in a room next to his office, he shared a straw bed with Houghton, both of them kept awake by the bawling of cattle at the stable. Although he didn't know a soul in town, Elihu was determined to achieve success and respectability in as little time as possible. From the beginning he impressed people as having "an air about him that indicated energy and pluck."[5]

Elihu's progress provided some interesting similarities and differences when compared with that of his brother Israel at the other end of the country. Galena and Orono were both unruly frontier towns, busy with river-based commerce, and both were about the same size. They were raw towns, built on the exploitation of the resources of the country around them. In both places, from the lumberjacks to the lead miners, from the land speculators to the smelter owners, from the immigrant farmers to the steamboat captains, law and order were just beginning to be felt.

The lawyers were at the forefront of the process, which was an adventurous place to be. One of Elihu's first cases was the defense of a horse thief in Belleview, across the river in Iowa Territory. This was just days after a desperate gun battle that had killed or wounded ten people there, including several of the defendant's colleagues. The town was full of "angry people, loud talk, and bad whiskey." Elihu later recalled sharing a bed with the judge in the case, who slept with a Bowie knife under his pillow that Elihu estimated was at least four feet long. (The judge later assured him it was only two feet long.) Washburne was there about a week, got licensed to practice in the territory, defended his man, and returned to Galena with seventeen dollars above and beyond his expenses.

This adventure pointed to one major difference between Israel's and Elihu's early practices: Elihu did a lot more traveling than his older brother. The courts along the Mississippi frontier moved around a circuit, so the lawyers and judges were constantly on the move with them, pleading cases during the day and socializing together in small hotels and boardinghouses in the evenings. Elihu's early years of practice ranged from fifty miles north into Wisconsin, across the river westward into Iowa Territory to Belleview and Dubuque, and as far south as Rock Island and beyond in Illinois. Twice a year he endured three days of bone-jarring torture in an unheated coach to plead cases before the supreme court down at the state capital in Springfield. It was on one of these trips in 1844 that he first met Abraham Lincoln. The two rawboned country lawyers, both enthusiastic Whigs, liked each other immediately.

Almost everybody liked Elihu Washburne immediately. The town of Galena was built up a hillside that rose steeply from the waterfront, and one's respectability in the town increased with one's altitude on that hillside. Elihu's first office was among the saloons and gamblers on the waterfront, but within four months he had been invited to join the office of Charles Hempstead, the town's leading attorney, whose office was on Bench Street, halfway up the hill. Mr. Hempstead, due to ill health, needed a right-hand man, and Elihu was happy for the literal elevation. Shortly afterwards, Galena was incorporated, and Hempstead was elected its first mayor. Elihu attended church with the Galena establishment—first Episcopal, then Presbyterian. He became the first subscriber to the *New York Daily Tribune* in Galena. He established friendships with other young "comers" in the town, including the merchant Russell Jones and the bankers Nathan and Henry Corwith—all of whom would play a part in his later career.

In 1843 he met Charles Hempstead's niece, sixteen-year-old Adele Gratiot. She was a daughter of one of the area's first settlers, whose Huguenot family had been one of the first to settle St. Louis. Elihu bided his time for two years, and he built a house in the best part of town. He was soon followed by the Joneses and the Corwiths, and later by his sister Martha and her husband, Charles Stephenson. Then, in a ceremony that was postponed until brother Cadwallader could get there, he married Adele. She would bear him eight children, and despite his frequent absences, they would be devoted to each other for the rest of their very eventful lives.

Elihu did well enough financially to manage visits back to Maine almost every year. In 1843 these trips back east began to include Washington, D.C., for either political or Supreme Court business. He was also promoting his debt collection services to merchants in far-distant places, from Cincinnati to St.

Louis to Boston (via his brother Sid). His reputation was beginning to spread beyond the confines of Galena. In 1845 Illinois governor Thomas Ford appointed Elihu as the prosecuting attorney for Jo Daviess County, of which Galena was county seat.

* * *

In 1842 brother Cadwallader completed his self-directed legal studies in Galena under a judge named Joseph B. Wells. He was admitted to practice law in the Wisconsin Territory on March 29. He was well acquainted with southwestern Wisconsin, thanks to previous experience as a surveyor there. Cad elected to hang out his shingle in the lead-mining town of Mineral Point. Like Galena, it was a rough place. The year young Cadwallader got there, the big event was a public hanging, which brought some four thousand people into the town. Land prices were rising, and so was speculation by absentee investors. Cornish lead miners in Mineral Point needed someone they could trust to send money home, the rich soil was attracting immigrant farmers, and Galena was only a day's ride away. In addition, the federal government was beginning to sell land in Wisconsin, or to give it away in the form of warrants awarded to former soldiers. Many of these veterans were only interested in turning their awards into cash. Mineral Point was the location of the only federal land office in western Wisconsin. For a reliable agent who knew the country, there was opportunity here. If his clients had cash to pay for his services, Cadwallader for the first time had a way to take advantage of some of the opportunities he had been observing since he had first arrived on the banks of the Mississippi six years earlier.

This would be Cadwallader's pattern for the rest of his life. Always restless, always bursting with new ideas, he would earn money for the sole purpose of investing it elsewhere. For Cadwallader, the practice of law was the means to an end. Not for him were the niceties of courtroom debate, the intricacies of the legal code, or the camaraderie of the circuit. For this most restless and energetic Washburn, concentrated as he was on financial success, the law was the gateway to commercial opportunity.

Cad was particularly conscious of his obligation to pay back his creditors, especially those in his own family. In 1842 he wrote to his brother Sid, who had been financing him since his initial trip west, "I think I shall come out straight as a shingle by and by."[6] Neither could have known that within thirty years, Cad would be making more shingles than anyone else in the whole upper Mississippi River Valley.

As a lawyer, Cad was trusted to perform services such as land brokerage, rent collection, payment of taxes, and even foreign exchange. Congress steadily liberalized the land warrants it was now offering as incentives for army enlistment, and Washburn realized a lively trade in these as well. He typically earned a ten percent commission on each transaction. Lawyer and agent Washburn had an inside position as the deals were being made, especially the land deals. Having surveyed most of it, he knew where the best land was, he knew which mines were performing best, and he knew which government land was going to be sold. When he could afford it, or when he could persuade someone to invest with him, he did not hesitate to make his own investments.

He was a good persuader. His brothers Sidney and Elihu were early investors. So was Charles Stephenson, another Maine entrepreneur in Mineral Point who would soon become his brother-in-law. As the stakes got bigger, his brothers stayed with him. Through periods of boom and bust, through every peril and threat, through times when it seemed there was no escape from failure, bankruptcy, and disgrace, they stayed with him, and in the end, they were all rewarded. In 1846, for example, the state of Wisconsin put several million acres of pine lands out for sale to pay for new schools. At an average price of fifty cents per acre, both Cadwallader and Elihu bought as much as they could. Elihu held ten thousand acres until the 1880s, when he sold most of them for over $20 an acre. As a result of these and other investments through Cad, Sid had a comfortable income until he died, and Elihu retired a wealthy man. Cadwallader, pouring his proceeds into other projects, did best of all.

In 1844 Cadwallader got a big boost in his land dealings. That year he took on as partner another Mainer named Cyrus Woodman. Woodman, a graduate of Bowdoin College and Harvard Law School, had been the local agent for the Boston and Western Land Company. He had many contacts among investors and lenders back east. Not the least of these was his brother George Woodman, who would become the western Washburns' New York banker for many years. Cyrus Woodman was a hard worker, scrupulously honest, good with details, but conservative by nature. He would act as an important counterbalance to Cadwallader's enthusiasms. Their partnership would last eleven years and their friendship for life.

Access to East Coast investment and finance would prove critical to the success of the Washburn and Woodman firm, since Mineral Point, like Orono and Galena, was a place where there was little cash. The partners both made frequent trips east in search of capital to invest and land warrants to resell. Within a year of their partnership, Washburn and Woodman were also purchasing land in large lots for their own account.

Their land acquisitions gradually moved from farm lands to forest lands. They tried other enterprises: a shot tower on the Wisconsin River near Helena and a flooded lead mine in nearby Dodgeville. The results were mixed. The shot tower eventually broke even, but the drowned mine was a loser and

*The Washburn-Woodman office in Mineral Point, Wisconsin.
It was here that Cadwallader Washburn and Cyrus Woodman
built a fortune through land speculation, land management,
banking, shot-making, and lumbering.*
COURTESY OF MINERAL POINT HISTORICAL SOCIETY

never returned their expenses in pumping equipment. These
enterprises were characterized by Washburn's extensive use of
other people's money and his open mind toward the use of new
technology.

Overall, the partners did well enough to move into a new
building. It was located literally next door to the federal land
office that provided so much of their business.
Cadwallader, as interested in social cachet as was his brother
Elihu, also tried adding an *e* to his name, and the firm of
Washburne and Woodman became a major player in the land
boom in western Wisconsin. The extra *e* did not last long, however, and Cadwallader soon reverted to the spelling he had

been born with. He got proof of his reputation without the *e* when Wisconsin became a state in 1848. He ran a strong third in the election of delegates to the new state's constitutional convention that year.

There weren't many women in Mineral Point in the 1840s, but young Cadwallader Washburn managed to find a prize there. The local judge in town, Mortimer Jackson, who must have known Cadwallader well, had married a lady named Kate Garr from a prominent family in New York City. In 1847 his wife's beautiful sister Jeanette came out for a visit to experience the wild frontier. What she experienced was the rough-hewn entrepreneur from Maine. Cadwallader wooed and won, and on January 1, 1848, Miss Jeannette Garr of New York became Mrs. Cadwallader Washburn of Mineral Point.

Sadly, the storybook marriage ended in tragedy for them both. After producing two daughters in three years, "Nettie" became increasingly unwell. Cadwallader invited his sister Martha to come west to help with the children, but his lovely young wife did not improve. Depression turned into coma, and Cadwallader finally had to place his bride in an institution for the insane back in New York. Martha got married herself, was soon busy with her own babies, and Cadwallader had to ship his own two little girls back to their grandparents on the farm in Maine. Except for one or two business associates, he never again had a close personal relationship. From then on, Cadwallader Washburn's many business enterprises were his life.

Land values dropped in the wake of the California gold rush of 1849. Cad himself estimated that as much as a quarter of the area's male population was leaving or about to leave, and prices fell sharply as a result. However, for those like Washburn and Woodman who were able to hang on, the steady influx of new settlers drove land prices up again. The government was continuing to open up new lands for sale—the Mineral Point land office handled 400,000 acres in 1849 alone—but the supply was finite. Eventually most of the usable land was gone, and the new owners were planting, not selling. In addition, the lead mines were becoming exhausted. When the government opened up new land offices to the west in La Crosse and to the north in Stevens Point, the writing was on the wall for the land business in Mineral Point. Woodman even made a trip to California in 1850 to explore business possibilities there, but returned discouraged after five months.

The shrinking inventory of agricultural lands still left the timber lands, however. Washburn and Woodman invested increasingly in forest acreage all over northwest Wisconsin. They concentrated their holdings along the west-flowing rivers, where they could get their logs out most easily: the Wisconsin, the Black, the Chippewa, and the St. Croix. By 1854 they had committed to 83,000 acres in Wisconsin and Minnesota, and dreamed of monopolizing the entire forest. They were both familiar with the lumber business from their days in Maine, and before long they had their own crews out cutting in the vast pinery. As in Maine, cutting and hauling required the construction of lumber camps and facilities for getting logs to and down the rivers in the spring. In addition, crews had to be paid long before the logs could be sold, and the partners were faced by urgent needs for cash.

Washburn and Woodman tried another enterprise: In 1852 they became bankers. There had been no national currency since President Jackson had shut down the national bank in 1832. Commercial financing and issuance of currency had been carried out by state-chartered banks since that time. Briefly, if a local entity could guarantee to redeem its notes with gold on demand, it could print its own money. Despite a history of failed banks, in 1852 Wisconsin decided to allow "free banking." Washburn and Woodman succeeded in establishing banks in Mineral Point and back in Hallowell, Maine. The idea was that they would issue notes in Hallowell, use them along the Mississippi River Valley, and, until they "made their way home" for redemption in Maine, the partners would have the use of the float.

The bank required a lot of help to get started and an iron nerve to continue. Brother Sidney was persuaded to leave his merchandizing career in Boston and to return to Maine to run the operation in Hallowell. Old Artemus Leonard, now a leading citizen there, agreed to act as chairman. Brother Elihu bought stock, as did Sid. Elihu also persuaded the biggest bank in Galena, run by his friends the Corwith brothers, to redeem the new notes. Dorilus Morrison, a Maine cousin then active in the lumbering business in Minnesota, was persuaded to pay his crews with the new notes.

Essential to their operation was confidence by the public that the bank's notes were, in fact, good. At any time, competing banks could show up unannounced in Hallowell or at Galena or Mineral Point and present a stack of notes for redemption. While Woodman tended the office and worried, Washburn was on the road. He solicited investors in New York and Maine. Fighting back one redemption threat, he made at least two hazardous trips to pre-Civil War Atlanta to carry out preemptive strikes on a competing bank there. He also dealt with horrendous weather. In February 1855, blocked by twenty-foot snowdrifts, he spent a week fuming in Chicago, including twenty-four hours stranded on an unheated train outside the city.

Anxiety levels were high for both partners, for at one point over $45,000 worth of Hallowell notes were circulating up and down the Mississippi River Valley from Minnesota to St. Louis. In addition, Washburn's frequent travels added to Woodman's workload in Mineral Point. In one six-week period in early

*Trains caught in midwestern blizzards often required days
to dig out. C. C. Washburn spent twenty-four hours
stranded in a train like this one, outside Chicago in 1855.*
COURTESY MINNESOTA HISTORICAL SOCIETY

1853, the meticulous Woodman filled a letter book of nearly
five hundred pages.

No one had more experience with "wildcat" currencies cir-
culating along the river than the steamboat companies. In his
1909 memoirs, *Old Times on the Mississippi*, George Merrick,
serving as a clerk on a steamboat, remembered his tribulations
with wildcat money with wry humor:

> At McGregor we put off a lot of freight and were ten-
> dered money. We consulted our lists and cast into
> outer darkness that which had upon it the anathema
> of Mr. Jones, the secretary. We accepted all on the list

of the elect, and compromised on enough more to balance our freight account. The agent at McGregor had
a list of his own which partly coincided with ours but
in general disagreed. In the meantime another boat of
our line had arrived from up river, and we get from her
clerk fifteen or twenty lists of bills which would be
taken or rejected at as many landings above. This
helps somewhat, as we see our way clear to get rid of
some of our twenty-five percent stuff at par in
exchange for cord wood or stores on the upper river,
and we sort our stock out into packages which are
reported current at each landing. We also see an
opportunity to swap at Dunleith some bills which are
not current there at all, but which are taken at par at
Prescott or Stillwater, for other bills which they do
not want, but which will be taken at the company's
office in Dunleith in settlement of our trip.

It required a long head to figure it out. Mine was
long enough, but unfortunately it had the same
dimensions both ways, and was not to be depended
upon in these finer transactions. Mr. Hargus labored
with the problem, studying lists until he came nigh to
the point of insanity, with the result that when we
"cashed in" on our return, it was usually found that we
had from five hundred to a thousand dollars that was
not acceptable. On the next trip we would usually be
able to work off some of this stuff. At the end of one
season I recollect that we had some two thousand dollars, face estimate, of this paper on hand, which the
treasurer would not accept, for the banks on which
the bills were drawn had gone out of existence.[7]

In the end, the tension was too much, and Washburn and

Woodman decided that the advantages of banking were not worth the cost. In addition, Cadwallader was becoming steadily more interested in politics. The partners closed the doors of the Mineral Point Bank in 1855, and the Bank of Hallowell two years later. They redeemed most of the outstanding notes, ended their partnership, and emerged with their reputations intact. Cyrus Woodman wound up his affairs and took his family to Europe.

It was a near thing, however. They were just ahead of the Panic of 1857, which would cripple the market for lumber and greatly affect Cadwallader's commercial fortunes for the next several years. With over 40,000 acres of prime timber on the Black River alone—all of it involving borrowed money and anxious investors back east—Cad would miss the steady hand of Cyrus Woodman in the trying times ahead. At a low point in 1859, Cad wrote Sid, "I shall be able to pay none of my notes at present.... I am broken down in mind, body, and estate, whence I shall stand erect again, God only knows."[8]

Fortunately, however, the doors of a new career were opening for Cadwallader Washburn, as they were also opening for his brothers Israel and Elihu. Great new events were calling them.

1. The reader should note that in the 1840s, the Mississippi River marked what were considered the "western" and "northwestern" frontiers of the country.

2. Israel Washburn, Jr., remarks at Orono Centennial Celebration, March 3, 1874, privately printed. (Maine Historical Society Library, Portland).

3. Typescript of Washburn's argument can be found in the Portland Room Collection, Portland Public Library, and is titled "The Telos Canal: Evidence Before the Committee on Interior Waters."

4. Quotes are taken from "Early Recollections" paper.

5. Augustus L. Chetlain, *Recollections of Seventy Years* (Gazette Publishing Co., Galena 1899), 38.

6. CCW to ASW, March 31, 1842 (Washburn Library).

7. George Byron Merrick, *Old Times on the Mississippi*, reprinted University of

Minnesota Press (Minneapolis, 2001) 179–80.

8. CCW to ASW July 19, 1859, from ASW papers (Duke University Library).

FOUR

Changing the Country

ON NOVEMBER 6, 1860, ABRAHAM LINCOLN, a candidate hardly known in half the country and representing the Republican party, which hadn't even existed six years earlier, won election to the presidency of the United States. He did it with only forty percent of the popular vote. Small though this margin was, the election marked a profound revolution in the country's politics and in the country itself. Southern control of the central government was gone. Curbing slavery was a top national priority. The Democrats would be out of office for most of the next one hundred years. As an immediate consequence of this election, eleven states left the union. It took the bloodiest war in the nation's history to bring them back. When it was all over, as Shelby Foote observed, the United States was an "it" and not a "they."[1]

Driving this revolution were the energetic efforts in five states by five brothers from the Washburn family of Livermore.

Given their lifelong interest in politics, it was not surprising, perhaps, that so many of the Washburn brothers were interested in running for office. That so many of them achieved *national* office was remarkable in its own right; that they made such an impact after they got there was even more remarkable.

The dinner table at the Washburn farm was hardly a place of revolution. Whigs as a group were conservative, and the

Washburn family grew up in the quiet belief that existing political structures could accommodate the needs of the people very adequately. The family's political icons, John Quincy Adams and Henry Clay, were sanctified for their intelligence and political know-how—not for upsetting any apple carts.

During the fateful decade of the 1850s, however, it seemed that every resource designed to address the concerns of the people was either paralyzed or stacked against those concerns. For the Washburns, an immoral institution—slavery—was being foisted on the entire country. It seemed to them that neither the president, the Congress, the Supreme Court, nor either of the two major political parties wished, or was able, to do anything to stop it. Southern slaveholders were in control of the central government, and they were using this control to expand their "Peculiar Institution" into all of the western territories—despite their agreement under the Missouri Compromise of 1820 not to do so. A vast group in the middle, who wished only to avoid conflict, seemed paralyzed or intimidated by the southerners' threats to break up the country if they didn't get their way.

As the Washburn clan saw it, control of the national government was out-of-balance, and a great evil was being unleashed as a result. Difficult though it might be to accomplish, somehow the existing structures of government had to change. With a quiet determination, each of five different Washburn brothers, in five different parts of the country, put his considerable talent and energy into bringing that change about.

* * *

All politics, it has been said, is local politics. Although great events would soon catch them up and test them severely, each Washburn started his political career in the most parochial fashion.

For Israel and Elihu, it started with a vacation junket. In January 1848 Elihu was called to Washington on some court business, and Israel and Sidney decided to meet him there for the opening of Congress. For all of them, it was simply the most enjoyable thing they could think of doing, and enjoying it together made it even better. As it turned out, the trip included several experiences they never forgot.

They met at the Willard Hotel. The family's hero, John Quincy Adams, had just died, and the brothers joined in the crowd to view the body in the Capitol rotunda. In between the pomp and ceremony and speeches at the Capitol, Elihu brought his old Illinois friend Abraham Lincoln over for an afternoon of yarning in their room at the Willard—an afternoon of homespun wisdom and humor that all of them remembered with pleasure. Little did any of them realize how intertwined their lives would become twelve years later.

The upshot of the trip was that both Israel and Elihu went home with a serious case of "Potomac Fever." When they got home, both began to explore their respective chances for a seat in the Congress.

Each had reason to hope for success. For well over a decade each had been building a solid reputation for competence, honesty, and hard work across a wide area of his respective state. In addition, each had worked diligently to promote the Whig party. Each had honed his forensic skills in many a stump speech in many a campaign. So, at respective caucuses in Maine and Illinois, both let it be known that they would be interested, if their party saw fit to consider them for nomination to Congress. The results were mixed. In Maine, Israel won the nomination but lost the election. In Illinois, Elihu lost the nomination to the spellbinding Edward D. Baker, a recent arrival in Galena. Baker was a political veteran whose speaking skills not only won the election, but were later of great value to

Charles Washburn in winning the 1860 election for Lincoln in California.

Neither brother was discouraged by these setbacks. Both had become better known through the experience, and both would try again.

Their next chance would be in 1850. Although Baker ruled the roost in the first Illinois district, and the Penobscot district in Maine was still solidly Democrat, both Washburn brothers saw their chances improving. The restless Baker had tired of Washington and was deeply involved in a railroad-building scheme in Panama, and the Democrats in Maine were developing splits that would make them very vulnerable.

At the national level during the early 1850s, all three branches of the central government were firmly under the influence of the southern states. Since George Washington, slaveholders had held the presidency for fifty years, Speaker of the House for forty-one years, chairman of Ways and Means for forty-two years. Twenty-five out of thirty-six Senate presidents had been southerners, as had eighteen out of thirty-one Supreme Court justices. Neither national party could nominate a presidential candidate without the approval of their southern delegates.

However, with the great population shift from the northeast to the northwest—shifts epitomized by the Washburns themselves—rumblings of challenge and change were beginning to be heard across both sections of the country. At the center of the argument was the uniquely southern institution of slavery. Side-stepped by the founding fathers in order to get a constitution approved, and now the linchpin of the southern economy, slavery had always been anathema in pulpits across the North. As the country acquired new territory in the west, the question arose as to how, or if, slavery should be allowed to expand there.

In the past, antislavery rhetoric had gotten little political support in the North. Outright abolitionists repelled moderates with their vehemence, and they offered little in the way of answers as to how to provide for the blacks after they were freed. Competing with issues like temperance and nativism, abolition was slow to gain momentum in the North. However, some far-seeing figures like Israel Washburn, Jr., realized that stopping slavery would be the issue with the greatest long-term traction with the public.

The way toward a more moderate slavery position was opened in 1846 with the Wilmot Proviso regarding new territories acquired from Mexico. Newly acquired territories were administered by Congress, and Pennsylvania representative David Wilmot proposed prohibiting slavery from any of them. Although the proviso was never adopted, it had two profound effects: It introduced a huge qualifier into the nation's drive to expand westward, and it provided a way that northern moderates could stop slavery without interfering with it in the southern states themselves.

In 1850 things began to change. As part of a package of laws aimed at mitigating northern and southern differences over slavery, Congress passed a greatly strengthened Fugitive Slave Act. Northerners now had to watch as runaway blacks were hauled off in chains from their own backyards. Outrage at the institution, and at the southern political muscle that protected it, began to provoke serious opposition across the North. As both the national Whig and Democratic parties equivocated, it became harder and harder for mainstream northern politicians to avoid taking a stand. The equivocators became known as "doughfaces."

From a parsonage in Brunswick, Maine, came a little book in 1852 by Harriet Beecher Stowe called *Uncle Tom's Cabin*, an excoriating attack on what slavery did to black families.

Northern outrage mounted, and with it the beginnings of a new unity across northern and western sections of the country. This unity was personified by the three Washburn congressmen—representing east and west, elected separately in 1850, 1852, and 1854, from Maine, Illinois, and Wisconsin respectively. They were still brothers from the same womb, and in 1854 they were rooming together and entertaining constituents together in Washington. The unity grew as each was reelected, and it strengthened still further when they took the forefront of a new political movement.

* * *

There was nothing in their history to indicate a Washburn penchant for political revolution. On the contrary, they had all grown up with strict political orthodoxy. Their causes were the traditional Whig causes: federally funded internal improvements, protective tariffs, and a strong national bank. Henry Clay, the great compromiser between north and south, was their idol. They were early aware of the obligation to serve their neighbors. They were early attracted to the workings of a democratic government. They loved debates over great issues, and they accepted, albeit sometimes grumbling, whatever solutions emerged.

In Maine, Israel Washburn, Jr., had to tread carefully. On the one hand, he and his constituents shared a resentment of southern political influence that went back to the state's struggle for statehood in 1820. It simmered again after the Webster-Ashburton Treaty, as western states gained territory while Maine had to give it up. The Mexican War, seen as a southern-inspired conflict, was opposed all over New England. Maine declined to raise a single regiment of volunteers for that adventure.

* * *

On the other hand, Maine's commercial interests greatly benefited during the 1830s and 1940s from the cotton trade. Three-quarters of the world's cotton came from the southern states, and most of it was exported in Maine-owned or Maine-built ships. Conservative businessmen were most reluctant to interfere in the affairs of their southern customers and vendors.

There were also two other issues competing in the waters of Maine politics starting in the late 1840s. These were temperance and nativism. Along with slavery, each had the effect of splitting traditional party loyalties, creating either crossover voting or new party affiliations altogether. The splits went all the way up to national party level, and most candidates were on their own in picking their positions in the face of crowds of vehement partisans unwilling to hear compromise. Fortunately for them, neither temperance nor nativism played much of a part in Washburn political campaigns. The brothers were either abstemious or didn't drink liquor at all, and all were active in places where immigrant labor was welcome and the presence of liquor was not controversial. However, the third issue, slavery, had been arousing their strong feelings since they first heard it decried from the lectern of their Universalist meetinghouse back in Livermore.

Strong commercial ties with southern customers and southern vendors, both on the coast of Maine and the banks of the Mississippi, had kept the issue muffled until 1846. Then the Wilmot Proviso gave northerners a way to oppose the *expansion* of slavery without disturbing it in the southern states that depended on it. This went over well in Maine. By concentrating on stopping its growth, Israel Washburn, Jr., found an antislavery position which was palatable to the shipowners in Bangor, as well as attractive to churchgoing liberal Democrats and Free-Soilers throughout the Penobscot district. It wasn't quite enough to enable him to win election on his first try in 1848, but it did find enough supporters for him to win election to Congress in 1850.

Although they were Whigs, a minority party on the frontier, all the brothers enjoyed strong reputations through the districts where they operated. Thanks to his Telos Canal work, Israel was well known across the north woods, from the Canadian border to Bangor. In addition, he had steadily boosted Whig numbers in Orono and Bangor since he'd been there. In the west, thanks to his years on the circuit around Illinois, Elihu also enjoyed a good reputation through the courts in his area, as well as through his work for the Whigs at election time. In Wisconsin, Cadwallader had a reputation through his commercial activity, since there were few communities in western Wisconsin where the firm of Washburn and Woodman had not been active. People appreciated his honesty and straight talk, and they respected his record as a businessman. He was creating a lot of employment.

To win an election, you either have to win it, or your opponents have to lose it. In Maine, Israel's course would have been much more difficult if his Democrat opponents had been united. During the 1840s the slavery issue proved disastrous for Maine Democrats. Hannibal Hamlin, who had become strongly opposed to slavery during his several terms as a Democratic congressman, lost a heated campaign in the Maine legislature for a seat in the U.S. Senate in 1846. Because he took an antislavery stand which opposed the national Democratic platform, his loss split the Democratic party in Maine. The split was permanent. Antislavery Democrats, nicknamed "woolheads," split from their party and nominated their own ticket in future elections, running against both conservative Democrat candidates and Whig candidates. For Washburn in 1850, this meant he had two opponents, each of whom took half the Democratic vote. Thus, as he wrote his brother Elihu, in the September election, unlike most of the other Whig candidates, "I slid in like butter on two plates." He was the first

Whig ever elected in the hitherto Democratic Penobscot district of Maine, taking his seat in January of 1851.

* * *

Elihu's path was harder. As had his brother Israel in Maine, Elihu had enjoyed the Whig good times in 1840. William Henry Harrison won the presidency, and young Elihu was asked to speak at a Whig rally at the Tippecanoe Club in Galena that year. He thought he acquitted himself well, but the election did not make much of a dent on the town's political landscape.

Despite the redistricting that happened in 1852, Galena and Jo Daviess County were at the extreme northwestern corner of their congressional district. For any candidate from Galena, there was a problem of name recognition in the district, as well as the dominance of the opposition Democrats. Also, in both county and district, both before and after 1852, the Whigs were badly outnumbered. It would be twenty-four more years before Galena would change from its Democratic sympathies.

Nevertheless, Elihu continued to attract attention as a stump speaker for the Whigs. At the age of only twenty-seven, in 1840 he was selected as a delegate to the national Whig convention in Baltimore, which nominated Henry Clay for the presidency. As mentioned previously, in 1848 Elihu lost the Whig nomination for Congress from the northern district of Illinois. He was outmaneuvered by the charismatic Edward D. Baker, a veteran of the Mexican War and a brilliant stump speaker, who had already served in Congress from the Sangamon District. Baker got the Galena nomination only three weeks after he moved there in 1848.

He won the election, the only Whig in Illinois to do so, but only served part of one term. He got bored after a year, became attracted to building a railroad across the Isthmus of Panama, and declined re-nomination. It seemed as if Elihu had a fresh chance, but the Whigs turned elsewhere for their nominee. The candidate they preferred, a lawyer and sometime itinerant Methodist minister named Martin P. Sweet from Freeport, was defeated, and Galena returned to its Democrat ways. The mercurial Baker got sick in Panama, and moved to California in 1852, where he was very important to brother Charles Washburn and the nascent Republican party there.[2]

Elihu went on to be mentioned for the territorial governorship in Minnesota, and was again selected as a delegate to the national Whig convention in 1852, where he joined his brother Israel in opposing the southern effort to put pro-slavery planks in the national platform. They lost this effort, and the Whigs lost the next national election as a result, even though they had a national hero, General Winfield Scott, as their candidate for president.

Then in September 1852, while attending his sick brother Cadwallader in Mineral Point, Elihu got word that he had won the Whig nomination for Congress from the First District over Stephen A. Hurlbut of nearby Belvidere, Illinois. (This would be the first of five times that Washburne would win the nomination over Hurlbut. Perhaps out of compassion, Elihu would help Hurlbut get appointed as a brigadier general in 1861, which would result in his collision with another Washburn eleven years later— brother Cadwallader in Memphis.[3])

The First District had just been reconstituted. It extended across northern Illinois from the banks of the Mississippi to Lake Michigan—about 140 miles west to east. At the time, the new district included seven counties, and was regarded as solidly and safely Democrat. Washburne was best known in his home area of Jo Daviess County, tucked off in the westernmost corner of the district, and a particular Democratic stronghold. The further east in the district he went, the less he was known. In addition, his Democratic opponent, a fellow lawyer named

Thompson Campbell, was no pushover. He was the incumbent, and Washburne, as early as 1840, had described him to Sid as "a man of very decided talent...but a perfect drunkard and a gambler."4 Despite the long odds, the lure of Congress was strong. Elihu accepted the nomination and set out to do his best.

It was an epic campaign. Washburne traveled the district for ten solid weeks. The area was little served by public trans-portation, and, as he said later, he traveled in every conveyance from farm wagon to his own two feet. Night and day he spoke in taverns, in town squares, and on courthouse steps, to audi-ences from immigrant farmers to war veterans, teamsters to trappers, miners to merchants. He kissed babies, curried favor among the families of influential men, attended every church service in sight, donated to Sunday schools, danced with young ladies, and glad-handed his way through county fairs. In the end, after spending all of a rainy election day "looking after the voters" back at Galena, his coat completely covered with mud, he finally returned home and luxuriated in a bath and a clean shirt. Two days later he learned he had won. Of 17,000 votes cast across the district, the margin was just 286 votes. He was the only Whig victor in the state, and one of the only ones to come out in opposition to allowing slavery in the territories. Like his brother Israel two years before in Maine, he owed his victory to the disruption among his opponents, the crossover support of Free-Soilers, and a split in the normally Democratic Irish Catholic vote. Twenty years later, with a terrible civil war and a wrenching presidential impeachment trial behind him, and trapped amid Prussian artillery shells and rampaging mobs in Paris, he could still recite that 1852 tally in Illinois—county by county.

Elihu made the most of his victory. For the next eight elec-tions—a total of eighteen years—despite every tactic of his opponents, from redistricting to slander to physical attack to boycott—Elihu Washburne was repeatedly re-elected. In May of 1854, at the end of his first two-year term, he was present at the historic Washington gathering where his brother Israel proposed forming the Republican party. When he got home, he was the first candidate to be nominated for Congress by the new party in Illinois.

The new party depended on attracting refugees from a wide spectrum of groups—many of whom had a long history of antipathy to one another. Even Lincoln admitted that it was made up of "strange, discordant, and even hostile elements."[5] They included Free-Soilers, Liberal Democrats, former Whigs, Know-Nothings, radicals, abolitionists, and immigrants. Disparate they might be, but as Israel had foreseen, the cause of antislavery was enough to overcome all differences. In just six years, the Republicans would win the White House.

It was several years before Lincoln cautiously joined the party. When he did, Elihu enthusiastically supported his friend. During Lincoln's unsuccessful U.S. Senate campaign against Democrat Stephen Douglas in 1858, Washburne helped bring the most famous of their famous debates to his district, at nearby Freeport, Illinois.

Although always a teetotaler, Washburne was never afraid of a fight. During one campaign there was a story of Elihu wading into his audience to throw an inebriated heckler into the street.[6] In another incident recounted by his Illinois colleague Owen Lovejoy, he was part of a midnight shoving match on the floor of the House, involving Congressman Barksdale from Mississippi. Abolitionist Lovejoy was delivering an incendiary antislavery speech, which Barksdale interrupted to call Lovejoy a "black-hearted scoundrel and nigger-stealing thief," and congressmen on both sides of the aisle jumped to their feet and surged around the speaker's platform.[7] Amid the mob of enraged congressmen, Barksdale took a swing at brother

Cadwallader, who was trying to restrain him. The scuffle ended when Elihu reached over to grab Barksdale by the hair—and came up with his toupee instead. All three Washburn congressmen were involved that day. Besides Cadwallader and Elihu, brother Israel, temporarily doing duty in the Speaker's chair, frantically banged the gavel above the melee and tried to restore order.[8]

Despite the excitement in Congress, sentiment in the country about curbing the spread of slavery ranged from fear to apathy. Two things needed to happen in order for the issue to gain real political traction. On the one hand, there had to be a clear sign that the central government was in favor of spreading slavery. On the other hand, there had to be a coherent and legitimate political means by which to oppose its spread. Both of these things happened in 1854, though few realized their significance at the time.

Southern influence was strongest among the Democrats, but it was also strong enough among the Whigs in 1852 for them to adopt a national platform plank approving enforcement of the Fugitive Slave Act, despite the opposition of the two Washburn congressmen. After this experience, the brothers had to admit that the antislavery cause would get no help from the Whigs.

Then, in the spring of 1854, Democratic senator Stephen Douglas, backed by a coterie of southern colleagues, proposed a bill creating the territories of Kansas and Nebraska. The bill included a repeal of the prohibition against slavery in the northern territories that had been in place since the Missouri Compromise of 1820. By a combination of personal influence and power politics, Douglas sailed the bill through the Senate. Then, after a desperate fight against it led by Israel Washburn, Jr., the bill was approved in the House by eleven votes. President Franklin Pierce, deeply indebted to the South, promptly signed it. The first sign had been given: The national government was in favor of spreading slavery. A holocaust for both major parties followed.

The very morning after the passage of the Kansas-Nebraska Act in Washington, Israel Washburn, Jr., invited thirty moderate congressmen from every party to meet at a boardinghouse near the Capitol where two Massachusetts representatives had their rooms. This was more than mere wound-licking. The diminutive congressman from Maine voiced his opinion that neither national party was capable of blocking the drive of the "slave power" to push slavery into the territories, and from there ultimately into every state. The only solution, he proposed, was to form an entirely new party. He even suggested a name for it: the Republican party. This may not have been the first meeting proposing the idea, but it definitely was the first meeting of well-known national leaders. Moderate opponents to slave power were about to have a vehicle with which to carry their defiance to the ballot box. Moral and political outrage had joined together. In the face of rupture between the northern and southern sections of the country, a new means to unify the north and west was born, and the Washburn brothers were at the heart of it. This was the second sign. Simultaneously across the northern and western states a new political party would come to life, and it would provide the vehicle for political change.

Anti-Nebraska demonstrations roiled across the northern states in the spring and summer of 1854, reaching into every backwater—even East Livermore, Maine. On July 3 and 4, at a Methodist camp meeting ground not far from the Washburn farm, there was a huge gathering, "as probably never before had been in the interior of the state, estimated from six to ten thousand," stated one report.9 People had bounced and bumped over rough country roads from as far as sixty miles away to be there, and to hear no less a personage than Harriet Beecher Stowe boast that every word of *Uncle Tom's Cabin* had been written right there in Maine.

Out in Illinois, Elihu was renominated by the Whigs, while at the same time he was also named at a special "fusion" convention of Free-Soilers and Liberal Democrats in Rockford. This latter meeting, on September 30, 1854, was guided by his old rival Stephen Hurlbut, who himself hoped to be named as the candidate. The meeting adopted a series of radical anti-slavery resolutions, perhaps with the intention of scaring Washburne off. (In Galena, due to its heavy commercial relationship with St. Louis and New Orleans, pro-slavery feeling ran high.) However, Elihu supported every one of the resolutions, and was nominated by acclamation as a result. As had happened for Israel in Maine, anti-Nebraska Democrats split from their national party in Illinois. Elihu won re-election with three times the votes of either of his opponents—a whopping majority of 5,905 votes. It would, however, still be fourteen more years before his hometown of Galena would support him.

* * *

The third Washburn brother's rise to political prominence was not as issue-driven as were his brothers' triumphs in Maine and Illinois. True, the northern and western parts of Wisconsin, composed largely as they were of New England expatriates, were strong antislavery areas. In fact, the first-ever meeting to organize the new Republican party had taken place in Ripon, before the Kansas-Nebraska bill had even been passed. That cataclysmic event, and the uproar which followed it, stirred a lot of people during the summer of 1854, Cadwallader Washburn and Cyrus Woodman included.

Such was the reputation of the partners that each was approached regarding a congressional nomination. Woodman declined the Liberal Democrats, and Washburn accepted the

Republicans. The new party, eager for high-profile names for its first campaign, gave Washburn its nomination in the Second District without opposition—almost as a matter of course. With his years of prominence in western Wisconsin, both in business and as a lawyer, and thanks to his reputation for honest dealing, he didn't need to do much campaigning to get the nomination. Similarly, in the election, he rode the tide of anti-Nebraska feeling to an easy victory over his pro-slavery Democratic opponent, Dr. Otis Hoyt.

In fact, Cad was never much of a campaigner. He was not a good public speaker, hated glad-handing, and never allied himself with any group or power bloc. His political career in Wisconsin, which amazingly encompassed a total of five successful campaigns for Congress and one term in the governor's office, was accomplished on the strength of his commanding presence, his straight speaking, and his reputation in the western part of the state. After the war, with the issue of slavery off the table and public sentiment shifting away from the great cause of saving the Union, his bluntness and distaste for equivocation made him vulnerable. He served his district well but never achieved the debating prowess of his brother Israel nor the political influence of his brother Elihu. Despite a distinguished record, Cad was nowhere near the politician that his older brothers were.

* * *

The thirty-fourth session of the United States Congress opened in January 1855 with a unique phenomenon among its membership. For the first time, the House of Representatives included three brothers. The Washburns—representatives Israel Jr., of Maine, Elihu of Illinois, and Cadwallader of Wisconsin—had been chosen to help run the nation's government. This was no coordinated cabal, no grab for power by a ruling elite, no intrastate gerrymander. Each man had been elected on his own merits, separately and independently of his siblings. Furthermore, this was no cameo appearance. Over the next two decades, all three brothers would leave their mark.

Naturally, they all roomed together. They found a house that cost $100 a month for November through March. When Maud or Adele was in town, they entertained (although their lease did not allow them to use the landlord's silverplate). For their various visitors, their 12th Street establishment represented both a symbol and a model for the alliance between east and west that was forming against the South.

The center of influence represented by the three roommates was humorously noted by one of Israel's constituents who wrote seeking an appropriation for a pet project. "Can you help us?" asked the Reverend T. S. King. "The Washburns being at least a quorum of the House, of course can carry anything. The Executive, Judiciary, Senate and the *Washburns* constitute the government. Read or show this to the other fifty or sixty of your brothers, call a caucus of the Washbournes [sic] and see if the appropriation can't pass."[10]

Although they were entering the national stage at a time when great events were about to override local considerations, each of the Washburn nominations and campaigns happened in a context that was mostly local. The brothers were proud that they each had been elected as a result of their own individual efforts. As evidence of this, though their elections represented a unique phenomenon for the country, there is no record that the three congressmen ever sat to have a picture taken together.

As a brilliant lawyer in Maine, Israel had proved himself a staunch advocate for the right of the public to benefit from the natural resources of the woods. In Illinois, Elihu had also proved himself an articulate, hard-working attorney, scrupulously honest, an enthusiastic Whig, and a fighter for order on

The first three Washburn Congressmen: Israel Jr., Elihu, and...

the frontier. In Wisconsin, Cadwallader was simply the best known and most trusted figure in his district. Each won on his own merits, with little help or direction from his national political party. Once in Washington, however, their actions took on a more global dimension. Simply stated, they were elected to build post offices and take care of constituents, but the events of the 1850s forced them to do much more than that.

Normal behavior for a first-time congressman is to keep his mouth shut and his ears open and to take good care of his constituents. All three Washburns followed this pattern, but each gathered prestige and power as he was reelected and gained seniority.

Near the end of his first term, Israel, speaking partly to his

*...Cadwallader, in their formal Brady portraits during the 1850s.
In their shared lodging in Washington, ties between eastern and
western states grew stronger.*
COURTESY WASHBURN LIBRARY

party and partly to the folks back home, had made an appeal to
the Whigs not to include a plank supporting enforcement of
the Fugitive Slave Act in their 1852 platform. As previously
noted, the appeal was in vain, the plank was included, and the
Whigs were soundly defeated in that year's congressional elections—the beginning of the end for the party. Two years later,
Israel spoke against slavery again, this time previewing ideas
that would be at the heart of the new Republican party. That
was in April 1854, and the speech earned him leadership of the
great floor fight in the house to defeat the Kansas-Nebraska
Act in May. Again, it was a losing battle, but with significant
long-term consequences, as Israel became the first congressman
to speak out for the need for a new political party.

Later, as chairman of the Committee on Elections, he would have another opportunity to speak out against slave power in connection with the irregularities of the 1857 elections in Kansas. His final speech in Congress, later reprinted and distributed all over the country, was an explanation and justification for the Republican party in the run-up to Lincoln's victory in 1860. Besides lambasting his Democratic opposition, he was not afraid to take on the most respected institutions in government. He blasted President Pierce for his actions to support slave power in Kansas, and he blasted the Supreme Court for its Dred Scott decision, which legitimized an open door to slavery everywhere. Israel had come a long way since his days as a freshman.

Despite these forensic high points, Israel Jr.'s greatest political victory after his defeat over Kansas-Nebraska took place back home in Maine. In Maine, the awful surrender of 1820 still rankled. Now, with that very compromise repealed, it seemed that the 1820 disgrace had been even further aggravated. Slavery was on the verge of legalization everywhere.

Nowhere in the country did Israel have more fertile ground for growing new politics than in Maine, and within days of his Kansas-Nebraska defeat, he was doing just that. Amid huge rallies and great public excitement, the Republican party began to take shape across the state. As both major parties dithered and split, state leaders began to come over to the new party. The climax came when Israel persuaded leading Democrat Hannibal Hamlin—who was facing defeat by conservatives in the state legislature for reelection to his Senate seat—to head the Republican ticket in 1856 as its candidate for governor. The result was a win for Hamlin by 18,000 votes, a sweep of all six of the state's congressional seats, control of both houses of the state legislature, and no less than 10,500 brand-new voters—all voting Republican. It was a total victory for the new party, and a revolution in Maine. Not only that, but because Maine's election was held two months before the national election, it was a jump-start for Republicans across the country. As Israel wrote a colleague afterwards, "I think our state election the most remarkable of any in the whole record of the country."[11]

The new party did not win the national elections in November, but it did sweep across many of the northern states. It was a sweep that Israel Washburn, Jr., started, and it would culminate in Lincoln's victory four years later.

In full cry, and with the highest moral principles behind him, Israel was at his most effective. But off the podium, his unbending adherence to principle could get him into trouble. That is what happened the next year with that most *unprinci-pled* colleague, James G. Blaine. It was trouble that did not go away.

Blaine had come to Maine from western Pennsylvania. At the age of only twenty-four, he became co-owner of the *Kennebec Journal*, which he turned into the official Republican mouthpiece in Maine, and which he used to propel himself like a rocket across the political sky, first of the state and then of the nation. Blaine was everything that Washburn was not. He was tall, young, handsome, and magnetic—a consummate vote-getter with a brilliant mind and a photographic memory. As Washburn was driven by high moral purpose, Blaine was driven by whatever it took to win the next election. Politics was a great game for Blaine—and he relished the power it brought to him. With Blaine writing the editorials and doing the infighting, and Washburn supplying the high moral tone and logical argument, the Republicans achieved a political dominance in Maine in 1856 that was to last for a hundred years.

The trouble started in late 1857 when Blaine asked Washburn for a personal favor. It seemed that his wife had a nephew who wanted a place at the military academy at West Point. Since the young man was at the moment in Washburn's district in Maine (hunting and fishing at Moosehead Lake), would Washburn give him his congressional appointment? Israel, who had already given his appointment to another young man—a legitimate resident of his district—regretted that he could not. Blaine persisted, asking a second time and offering inducements. He would gladly pay Israel's constituent up to $400 to give up his place, and he would personally embrace "every opportunity to reciprocate, personally and politically" with Washburn himself in the years ahead.[12] Again Washburn declined, pleading that he had given his word, and rules were rules.

Blaine, whose casual regard for rules would make him rich after the war but would cost him the presidency on four different occasions, never forgot Washburn's rejection. He realized that he could never control the principled Washburn, and men he couldn't control, he didn't trust. As Blaine achieved dominance over Maine's legislature during the next thirty-five years, he thwarted Washburn's hopes for a U.S. Senate nomination no less than four times. In the end, in order to free up the Senate seat he wanted for himself, he even arranged Washburn's removal from the customs collectorship of Portland, a position Israel had held for fourteen years, to create a place for Lot Morrill, the man whose Senate seat he had taken for himself.

* * *

Elihu's climb to prominence in the U.S. House of Representatives was similar to Israel's. Just two years after the Kansas-Nebraska debacle in the House, and after an epic struggle that lasted two months, the Republicans won the leadership of that body, successfully electing Nathaniel Banks as Speaker. As a reward for his part in this fight, Elihu was named to the influential Commerce Committee, where he would serve as chairman for thirteen years. Later, during the war, he would be chairman of the critically important Committee on Contracts. During all this time, however, he never forgot his constituents. In 1859, reflecting the growth of Galena, Elihu saw to it that a handsome new post office was completed there, as well as a new courthouse for the county. Two years later that courthouse would be the scene of one of Elihu's greatest moments.

In his work exposing fraud and waste, Elihu would earn the nickname "Watchdog of the Treasury." His career differed from Israel's, however, in that as he gained power and influence, he exercised it behind the scenes rather than from the podium.

An early example of his hidden influence nearly cost Elihu his life. After Lincoln's election in 1860, the period between his victory and his inauguration was one of enormous uncertainty for the country. As hotheads persuaded Southern states to leave the Union and national leaders frantically scrambled to avoid war, rumors and threats of violence were everywhere. Accompanied by his bodyguards, the detective Alan Pinkerton and the hulking Ward Lamon, President-elect Lincoln was smuggled into Washington at six o'clock on a cold February morning for his inauguration. The only representative of the government to meet him at Union Station was his old friend Washburne. At first Lincoln didn't see Elihu, but the two guards did, and neither knew who he was. As the congressman reached out to touch Lincoln on the shoulder, both bodyguards drew their pistols. Although Lincoln was delighted to see his old friend, and quickly put his guards at ease, Lamon never forgot the incident. Writing much later, he observed, "It was a very close call for Mr. Washburne."13

Cadwallader was the least visible of the brothers in Congress. Always sturdily antislavery, he preferred to work quietly for his constituents. He brought daily mail service to communities along the Mississippi, and he worked hard to expose fraudulent damage claims against Indians resulting from the Creek wars back to 1820. Near the end of his third term in 1860 he was picked to be a member of the Committee of Thirty-three, a last-minute effort to patch up differences between the sections. The group caved in to southern demands to strike down personal liberty laws in the northern states, to approve a constitutional amendment perpetuating slavery, and to restore the southern domination of the Senate by admitting New Mexico and Arizona as new states. Washburn, along with Representative Mason Tappan of New Hampshire, broke with the majority. He was fully aware of the danger. "The Union of these States is a necessity," he wrote in the Minority Report, "and will be preserved long after the misguided men who seek its overthrow are dead and forgotten...."14 Ten days later he was blunter still. Speaking of the long-dominant southerners, he noted in remarks before the House, "They have so long been accustomed to regard themselves as specially appointed to rule this country that they have forgotten how to obey...." His language was hardly that of a compromiser. He faced the prospect of civil war the same way he faced everything else—squarely and without flinching. About slaves and the future, he concluded, "If this Union must be dissolved...we shall have the consolation of knowing that when the conflict is over, those who survive it will be what they never have been, inhabitants of a FREE COUNTRY."15

Cadwallader Washburn's political career in many ways defied logic. He was a solitary man, often seen as aloof, and seemed to disdain the everyday necessities of getting elected. Yet at the same time, he was deeply ambitious. In 1860 Wisconsin was about to have a vacancy in the U.S. Senate. As he neared the end of his third term in the House, with the national government nearly paralyzed, but Republican fortunes steadily rising, Washburn resigned his seat to return to Madison to promote his candidacy before the state legislature for the U.S. Senate. Although he was an early leader, he did not have a majority of votes when the first ballot was taken on January 18. The legislature, perhaps influenced by the heavily populated eastern part of the state, and perhaps by Governor Alexander Randall, went a different way. They picked Timothy Howe, a young attorney from Green Bay who had once taught school back in Livermore and who would serve in the seat for eighteen years. Cadwallader's political career seemed—for the moment, anyway—to be abruptly over.

As the momentous 1860 national convention of the Republicans approached, all three Washburns preferred Senator William H. Seward of New York for the presidential nomination. He was a good friend and ally of theirs in Washington, and had been a frequent guest in their rooms. He was so close to Israel that he even gave the oldest Washburn access to his money to pay bills when he wasn't in town. Seward, an early convert to the Republicans, had been a moderate antislavery leader since the 1840s. In the run-up to the convention, he was an early favorite for the nomination. However, Seward's abolitionism was a little too vehement for the party rank and file. The convention was held in Chicago, and the more moderate Abraham Lincoln, thanks to some impressive management by his supporters, won the nomination. Elihu quickly persuaded his brothers to swing into line behind the little-known Lincoln.

Shortly after this, the Republicans in Maine held their gubernatorial nominating convention in Bangor, not far down the road from Israel's house in Orono. It, too, was a momentous meeting. It started joyfully, because Lincoln had just picked the popular senator from Maine, Hannibal Hamlin, to be his vice presidential running mate. But a crisis was brewing. The party went into the meeting with three huge challenges. First, because Maine's state election was held in September, it was the first state election after the national convention—fully two months before the national election. Maine's Republicans were in a unique position to establish momentum for Lincoln—if they won. Secondly, a defalcation in the state treasurer's office had just been discovered that had cost the state $94,000, and the Republicans' current state administration was in disgrace. Third, the leading candidate for nomination as governor was the wealthy but inarticulate Abner Coburn, who was disinclined to campaign.

There is no record of where the idea came from, but suddenly Israel Washburn, Jr., was seen as the one man who could solve all the party's problems. As a friend noted, the party's nomination came to Washburn "wholly unsought by him and entirely unexpected."[16] Thunderstruck, but realizing the importance of Maine putting on a good show for the country, Israel accepted the nomination. With Norumbega Hall roaring its approval, he gave up all his power and seniority in Congress to come home to head his party's ticket for the governor's chair. If he won, he also thought he stood a good chance with the legislature for a U.S. Senate seat later.

It was a spectacular campaign, the likes of which Maine had not seen before. For the first time funding came in from the national party. There were torchlight parades, illuminations, tableaux, and colorfully uniformed groups of first-time voters called "Wide-awakes." Even brother Sidney, still smarting from the closure of the Bank of Hallowell, was pressed into political service as head of the Hallowell Wide-awakes. He was probably present at a rally in the tiny town of Pittston, across the river, where more than 5,000 people showed up to whoop and holler.

True to his word, Israel campaigned vigorously from one

end of the state to the other. He delivered twenty-eight major speeches in thirty days, from Berwick on the New Hampshire border to Eastport on the Canadian border. When the votes were counted, his personal margin of victory was a grand 18,000 votes, and he had led his party to a sweep of all six congressional districts as well as comfortable control of the legislature. It was enough to cause Hannibal Hamlin to write to Lincoln on September 11, "Washburn will have some 20,000 over Smart [his opponent] and some 17,000 to 18,000 over all. We have carried all our congressmen and swept the state like a prairie on fire."[17]

Israel had started a bandwagon that was everything national party leaders had hoped for. In the November election, with the northern and southern Democrats so split that they had two separate candidates on the national ballot (Stephen Douglas for the north and John C. Breckenridge for the south), Lincoln was elected with just forty percent of the national vote. The party that was only a gleam in Israel's eye just six years earlier had now won the White House. On top of that, almost twenty-five percent more Maine voters had turned out than ever before. As Israel had foreseen, antislavery, anti-Southern feelings had dominated all other issues across the north. For him, it meant that his ten-year career of leadership in Congress was now to be exchanged for a new career of leadership as the governor of Maine. It was a position that his mother had predicted for him when he was only ten years old.

* * *

There were many miracles behind Lincoln's victory in 1860. Among them was his razor-thin margin of 711 votes in the state of California. California had been admitted to the Union as a free state, but anti-Republican sentiment there was high. Forty percent of the state's 370,000 residents were from the south, and anger against both abolitionists and blacks was high in all quarters. Pro-southern Democrats had won a decisive victory in the 1859 state elections, and generous federal appointments followed. In San Francisco, the building that housed most of the federal agencies was so filled with southerners that it was known as "The Virginia Poorhouse."[18]

Only seven out of fifty-three newspapers in California supported Lincoln. One of them was the *San Francisco Daily Times*. Its co-owner and editor was Charles Ames Washburn, the fifth son of the Livermore Washburns. His journey to this position had been circuitous and quixotic.

Growing up on the farm, Charles had been the introspective son. Usually to be found with his nose in a book, he was fond of writing long and flowery letters to his brothers, who worried about his dreaminess and lack of direction. He was certainly creative, and his mother loved him for it, but there was weakness there, and an inability to stick with any one thing for long. Born nine years after Israel, by the time Charles was seventeen his brothers were making enough money to subsidize higher education for him. A clerical snafu cost him a place at West Point, so he went down the road to Bowdoin College in Brunswick, Maine, instead. He stuck with that, and in 1848 became the first Washburn sibling to complete a college education. Upon his graduation, Israel promptly took Charles under his wing in Orono to study the law.

However, Charles was not going to be poured into that particular mold. For whatever reason, Charles didn't care for the study of law in Maine, so he moved out to Wisconsin to try it with Cadwallader. That didn't work either. Cadwallader was unusually benign about it—and about the money he advanced to subsidize Charles. He wrote Israel, "Charles has his weak points as well as the rest of us, and a principal one is his disposition to deal in moonshine [dreaming] rather than in substance more substantial.... What he owes me I almost consider as so much given, never to be asked for, unless an event should happen which I never expected, and that is that he should be able to pay it."[19]

Israel got Charles a good job at the Treasury Department in Washington, but that didn't work either. Desperate to follow the beat of his own drummer, the self-proclaimed vagabond of the Washburn family decided to take advantage of that year's escape of choice—the California gold rush. Using money borrowed from friends (which outraged his brothers), Charles headed west. After spending six weeks of hard work panning for gold near Mariposa, he wrote his brother Cadwallader (who had probably financed him again) with a long list of can't-fail financial schemes to make money off the gold miners. The list included teamstering supplies, raising beef cattle, operating a toll ferry, and catching salmon. However, he did none of these. He spent a couple of weeks as reporter and editor for a little newspaper in nearby Sonora, and then struck out for San Francisco—on foot. Once there, he tried newspapering again. He found that he liked it—he could give full expression to his political ideas without having to get involved. He could preach without having to *do*. In 1853 he partnered with Reverend S. D. Symonds to edit a religious antislavery newspaper called the *Alta California*.

Politics is no field for the supersensitive, and Charles nearly did himself in during 1854. That was the year of southern triumph in Washington with the successful passage of the Kansas-Nebraska bill, and the first stirrings of the Republican party as a result. Having lost advertisers because of his political editorials in the *Alta California*, Charles changed newspapers and joined the *Evening Chronicle*, also in San Francisco.

The city was full of vigilantes and violence, and politics was more a hurly-burly between personalities than a debate of opposing philosophies. Charles jumped into the fray, lambasting various prominent Democrats, especially the collector of customs, a southern "chivalric" with the red-white-and-blue name of Benjamin Franklin Washington. Charles referred to him, in print, as "Bombastes Furioso" Washington. The newspaper's insults so outraged the collector's pride that he challenged Charles to a duel. Charles unwisely obliged him.

It was a classic confrontation of different codes. The Southerner was driven by the chivalric code of honor, where all personal insults must be avenged. The Yankee was driven by the moral outrage over his opponent's affiliation with slavery. Unfortunately for Washburn, Washington was far more competent with weapons. Charles wound up getting shot for his efforts—the first Washburn to shed blood in the antislavery cause. Afterwards, Mr. Washington was supposed to have commented that "It was like shooting a tied bird."[20]

Charles suffered more than a gunshot wound from this incident. He also picked up a most unwelcome reputation. "Washburn is a duelist!" went the whispers, which were instrumental in snuffing out Charles's congressional ambitions later.

An unrepentant Charles, perhaps inspired by his brothers' successes in Maine and Illinois, spearheaded the first effort to organize a Republican party in California. He helped arrange a meeting of influential leaders in Sacramento on April 19, 1856. Though the meeting was broken up by Democrat rowdies, two weeks later a formal organization was established, with Charles listed as secretary. Not only did the party successfully organize that year, but it saw a former Californian, John Charles Frémont, picked as the first Republican nominee for president. Charles was a member of the California delegation at the Philadelphia convention that nominated the dashing "Pathfinder." Unfortunately, the party was brand-new, Frémont was an inept campaigner, and southern sympathy was long and loud in California. With none other than B. F. Washington as Democratic party chairman, the Democrats won the state handily.

Charles, who had called Frémont "an ass" in a letter to Elihu the previous year, was himself passed over for a nomination to Congress in 1856. (For history's sake, this was too bad. Had he been elected, he would have been the fourth Washburn brother serving in Congress at the same time, from four different states, and the fifth to serve there in all.) Referring to his tarred reputation as a duelist, he wrote Elihu that "the vigilant and pious San Franciscans [were] dead against me."[21]

A disappointed Charles left the *Chronicle* and returned to Wisconsin, where again his brother Cadwallader gave him a loan. The amount was a generous $3,000, which Charles took to Chicago. He used part of the money to start another paper there. Unfortunately, his timing was bad. Caught up in the bank crash of 1857, the *Saturday Evening Chronotype* shut down after just one issue.

But Charles was still an enthusiastic preacher of the Republican cause. Fueled by what was left of Cad's loan, he returned to San Francisco determined to resurrect the party there. His means would once again be his pen. With a partner named Alvan Flanders, a former governor of the Oregon Territory, he bought the *San Francisco Daily Times* and prepared to do more battle with the Democrats who dominated the state's political scene. For two years, in more than a thousand editorials and opinion pieces, Washburn labored to change the political sentiment of the voters in California. Outspoken, feisty, giving offense and taking it, he battled southern "chivalrics" at every level.

He championed U.S. senator David Broderick and did his best to turn him into a martyr after Broderick was killed in a duel with Democratic California Supreme Court chief justice

David S. Terry in 1859. Charles reported the encounter in detail—including a front page emblazoned with epithets such as "contemptible doughfaces...white livered, thin blooded, cringing wretches...craven sycophants...."[22]

Charles discovered that he could get away with almost anything. He repeatedly called California's other senator, a Mississippian named William Gwinn, a liar. Democratic presidential candidate Stephen A. Douglas was an "ingrained demagogue" and later, "a whiffling, treacherous whiffet." His warfare with James Simonton, editor of the competing *San Francisco Bulletin*, featured endless vitriol on both sides, which may have provided much entertainment for Bay Area readers, and sold newspapers as well. However, it didn't help Charles gain support for any of the federal appointments he later sought.

Newspapers were an important element of politics in nineteenth-century America. They had access to telegraph lines and were the main source of information about the latest events. They were a vital outlet for political parties to broadcast platforms and circulate key speeches, and to expose the real and imagined sins of the opposition. Virtually free of any constraints beyond the ill-defined limits of common decency, newspapers were a key arm of every political party. For the brand-new Republicans in California, the *Times* was an important component of their campaigns, regardless of its hard-working editor's occasional instability.

Of course, the editors of newspapers all had their own ambitions. Always in the shadow of his three older brother congressmen, Charles dreamed of a political career of his own. As James G. Blaine was riding the *Kennebec Journal* to a career of political dominance back in Maine, Charles aspired to do the same in California. Alas, he had none of Blaine's administrative or social skills, to say nothing of political competence.

His rhetoric by itself would not be enough. On the contrary, his intemperate journalism and arrogant air caused his fellow party-builders to shy away from him, despite his tireless efforts on behalf of the party. In 1860 he was again denied a congressional nomination.

As the 1860 national election approached, Washburn organized a Wide Awakes Club in San Francisco, and presided over a meeting that drew 5,000 people. This included a grand torchlight procession and a stirring speech by Edward Baker, the silver-tongued orator who had triumphed for the Whigs back in Galena in 1848. Baker, who had been practicing law in the city for eight years, had made a name for himself among the Republicans with a spectacular funeral oration for the martyred Senator Broderick in 1859.

On election day, against all expectations, Lincoln carried the state. It was an enormous upset: Just the year before, the Democrats had carried the state by 60,000 votes. Now, however, they were badly split over Kansas and the Broderick murder, and the Republicans triumphed by the narrowest of margins.

Charles got a gold watch and a gold-headed cane from his party, but no public office. Distrusted and probably disliked by most of the veteran political figures in the state, he was not admitted to the Republican State Committee. He was blocked from appointment as director of the San Francisco mint, and was unable to dislodge B. F. Washington from the collectorship. Almost as if to get rid of him, the Committee named Charles a presidential elector, and sent him off to Washington to cast the state's vote in the Electoral College. It was probably a one-way ticket.

* * *

The final piece of Washburn revolutionary activity before the war was supplied by brothers Samuel and William Drew. Two more different individuals can hardly be imagined. Sam fled from the family aura; William embraced it. Sam liked to operate against the elements with his hands, William with his head. Sam was a plugger; William was a skyrocket. Sam was blue collar; William was white. Sam could see as far as the bow of his ship; William's visions were Olympian. Sam quit school as soon as he could and went to sea as an ordinary seaman before the mast. William was college educated and became a polished professional. Sam didn't marry until he was forty, and met his wife in the Wisconsin woods. William married when he was twenty-eight, and won his wife from one of Bangor's wealthiest families. Sam moved in a world made up of the rough-hewn owners and crews of his ships and his lumber camp. William moved among the power elite of his state and the nation. Sam was the only Washburn who actually spilled blood in the war. William was carefully protected from having to serve and actually used the war years to lay the groundwork for his commercial activities afterwards. Sam was seven years older, but when they were in their fifties, Sam would be out in the fields at Norlands picking potatoes in his shirtsleeves, while William entertained on the great veranda or raced his buggy around the neighborhood at breakneck speed.

Yet, in their different ways, they were both leaders. When Sam was eighteen, he showed up at Sid's door in Boston, quietly determined to go to sea. Sid tried to talk him out of it without success. So Sid made a few inquiries among his commercial friends, and got Sam a berth on the bark *Huntress*, bound for New York, New Orleans, and Liverpool. It was a bare-knuckle life but Sam stuck with it. He loved the foreign ports and the opportunity to be well clear of his overachieving brothers. His correspondence was intermittent, but his progression to command was steady. Serving on several ships, mostly barks and mostly in the cotton trade, all of them in the range of three hundred tons and a hundred feet in length, he moved from deckhand to third mate, then to second mate, to first mate, and finally to captain, in about six years. It was not an intellectual life, but Sam knew who he was and what he could do, and he was well away from the lengthening shadows of his brothers.

Similarly William, after he graduated from Bowdoin and passed the bar in Bangor, gave up his comfortable prospects in the east and staked his future in the northwest, with the burgeoning city of Minneapolis. His brother Cadwallader gave him responsibility for completing construction of the dam and canal he was developing there, on the west shore of the falls at St. Anthony. By the time the war was over, William, in spite of desperate financial problems, had the dam up and seven tenant sawmills perched across it, one of which was his own. In addition, the canal was well underway next door, and several factories were under construction there.

Probably in 1855, while Bowdoin graduate William was just undertaking his law studies in Bangor, Sam grew tired of the sailor's life. Like a modern-day trucker navigating his eighteen-wheeler back and forth on the nation's interstate highways, Sam had been driving his vessels back and forth across the oceans of the world for twelve years. His performance had been steady, if not spectacular. He had never lost a ship, and he had made money for his employers. On the personal side, his creature comforts had been few, his compensation poor, and he was still a bachelor. He was ready for something new.

If Sam was looking to get away from the sea, Cadwallader had an opportunity for him that was about as far away from the ocean as it could be. He was looking for a tough man to oversee a lumber camp he was planning at a place called Waubeek on the Chippewa River in western Wisconsin. It was in the middle of ten thousand acres of prime Wisconsin pinery that Cad owned. If Sam took the job, the worst things nature could throw at him there were frozen darkness in the winter and black flies in the summer. Of course, Cad probably didn't tell him about the logjams and forest fires.

Sam had saved up some money, and Cad let him buy a half-interest in the camp. It was a move that Cad later had cause to regret.

Sam was supposed to manage the operation, but forces outside the woods were about to put a huge crimp in the lumber business. Always subject to volatile demand, the price of lumber took one of its periodic drops in 1856. The following year came the great Panic of 1857, and Cadwallader was caught between low demand for his product, low profits when he did find a buyer, and high anxiety among his creditors. Sam was apparently oblivious, but Cadwallader was furious over his brother's management of the operation. He brought in other people, but he was still unhappy that Sam seemed so easily distracted.

One of the things that pulled Sam's attention away from cutting lumber was a woman named Lorette May Thompson. (It took a couple of years and a military uniform, but Sam eventually married Lorette.) Another distraction was the 1860 election. Sam got picked to represent the camp at a district Republican convention that summer, but he was back to tending his vegetable garden and swatting flies right afterward. The following March, cutting and hauling logs for the seventh season, he was frustrated that he was the only Washburn brother not present at Lincoln's inauguration in Washington. It was small consolation to be elected chairman of the board of supervisors and justice of the peace for Waubeek, which now had— when they were sober—thirty-five voting residents. His role was modest, but Sam definitely played a part in swinging some votes for the Republicans in remotest Wisconsin in 1860.

Up in Minneapolis, the year 1860 found William and his

beautiful new bride Lizzie setting up house in the heat and dust of the new city. He had also been politically active and was not short on public spirit. He led a variety of initiatives to bring Minneapolis up to the level of nearby St. Paul. He even got himself elected to the Territorial Legislature, but lost his seat to redistricting when Minnesota became a state. He was an eager Republican like his brothers and lost no opportunity to promote the cause during the November election.

William's efforts, which included raising a company of infantry when the war broke out, resulted in his being named by President Lincoln as surveyor general of Minnesota. This position had the twin benefits of protecting him from the necessity of serving in the army while enabling him to become personally familiar with hundreds of thousands of acres of prime land all over the new state. Far from shot and shell, William was able to use this knowledge to jump-start his career as a lumberman.

* * *

It was no accident that six of the seven Washburn brothers made their way to Washington in March of 1861 to see the event that they had all worked so hard for—the inauguration of President Lincoln. For them, it was a celebration of the biggest political victory of their lives, and a triumph of moral principle over political expediency, apathy, and fear. And it was turning point for the country. Six years after they had helped create it, their new party was in charge of the central government.

Despite the long list of defeats they had suffered—the original Missouri Compromise that gave Maine its statehood, the Fugitive Slave Act of 1850, the paralysis and death of their beloved Whig party, the Kansas-Nebraska Act which gave the Republicans their birth, the upheavals in Kansas, and the Dred Scott Decision—despite it all, the Southern hegemony, domi-

Lincoln's election victory in 1860 culminated almost seven years of work by all the Washburn brothers. Six of the seven were excited enough to journey to Washington to attend Lincoln's inauguration, shown here.
COURTESY LIBRARY OF CONGRESS

nant since the Revolution, was ended at last.

Similarly, across the South, Lincoln's victory was the single event that caused the tide of secession to move from threat to reality. One by one, Southern states began to hold secession conventions. And right behind their votes to leave the Union, Southern "fire-eaters" began to appropriate federal property within their borders. Prominent among their targets was the bastion of Fort Sumter that squatted in the middle of the harbor at Charleston, South Carolina. This somewhat anachronistic pile would provide the flashpoint for a terrible war.

* * *

As men in North and South prepared to answer great questions with cold steel, their women prepared to support them.

1. From the Ken Burns television series *The Civil War*.
2. Described later in this chapter.
3. See Chapter Six.
4. EBW to ASW, May 20 and October 27, 1840 (Washburn Library).
5. Doris Kearns Goodwin, *Team of Rivals* (NY, 2005); quote from Lincoln's "House Divided" speech of June 16, 1858.
6. Mark Washburne, A *Biography of Elihu Washburne* (privately published), vol. 3, 136.
7. The writer is fully sensitive as to how offensive the n-word is to all our readers, both black and white. I have retained it as it was spoken (or yelled) 148 years ago without sugar-coating. When, before or since, have there been words that so enraged the leaders of our government that they literally lept into physical combat with one another?
8. There are several versions of this contretemps. The ones I have used are from a letter by Lovejoy to his wife, quoted in Edward Magdol, *Owen Lovejoy; Abolitionist in Congress* (New Brunswick, NJ: 1967), 233–35, and the congressional record as quoted in William F. and Jane Ann Moore, eds., *His Brothers Blood*, (Urbana, 2004), 195.
9. Austin Willey, *The History of the Antislavery Cause in State and Nation* (Portland, 1895), 443.
10. To IW from Rev. T. S. King, July 17, 1856 (Israel Washburn, Jr., Collection, LC). The good minister, like many Washburn constituents, was a little uncertain how to spell the last name.
11. IW to Charles Chandler, September 14, 1856 (Maine Historical Society).
12. Blaine to IW, December 16, 1857 (IW Collection, Washburn Library).
13. Included in Marie Fowler's *Reminiscences* (Washburn Library) 55.
14. 36th Congress, 2nd Session, House of Representatives Report #31 (in GS 1104), dated January 14, 1861.
15. Reported in the *Congressional Globe*, January 24, 1861 (2nd Session, 36th Congress, Part 1), 513.
16. From comments by Albert W. Paine, *In Memoriam* (Maine Historical Society, 1883), 102–03.
17. Hamlin to Lincoln, September 11, 1860 (Lincoln Papers, Series 1, LC).
18. Alvin M. Josephy, *The Civil War in the American West* (New York: 1992), 233.
19. CCW to IW, December 15, 1854 (Washburn Library).
20. James O'Meara, "Early Editors of California," *Overland Monthly*, vol. XV, no. 83, November 1889, 498.
21. CAW to EBW, October 5, 1856 (Washburn Library).
22. Theodore A. Webb, *Impassioned Brothers* (Lanham, MD: 2002), 20.

FIVE

Sod Roofs to Crystal Chandeliers

So far, this book has been a story about growth and accomplishment in the professions, in business, and in politics. The chapters that follow this one will be about war and diplomacy. This chapter is about a completely different subject: growth and accomplishment at home. It is the story of the Washburn women, who were on the periphery of every victory and defeat experienced by the Washburn men.

The story of the Washburn women, though not nearly as well documented as that of the men, is visible, at least in its outline form, through genealogical records, references in the men's correspondence, and the few records—sadly few—of the women that have survived. Their story is presented here, from first marriage to last death, as a single story. It is surrounded by the chronology of the men's stories, but is separate from that chronology. It is, in fact, a separate story.

As the women knew little or nothing about their men's commercial, political, or military affairs, so the men were only vaguely aware of what their women were going through at home. As the women accepted whatever worlds their men's careers opened for them, so the men came home to whatever worlds the women had made in those homes.

In the nineteenth century, most women had the same strength and courage as the men, but not the exposure. Few records were kept. Compared with the mountains of correspondence carefully preserved from the Washburn men, there is almost nothing left from the women. It is not that they couldn't write. They all received enough education to write very well. And they did write—coherently, and with beautiful, schoolmarm penmanship.

The sad truth is that almost none of what they wrote has been preserved. We have dates of birth and death for each of them and for their children, and we have occasional references to them in their brothers' letters, but precious little can be found today that is in their own voices. They were loved and appreciated for their devotion to their spouses and their children, and for their creation and maintenance of happy homes, but not for their writing.

The women were there, but out of sight. Except for the births and deaths of their children, their stories were little noted. Memories about them by their contemporaries were all laudatory—and therefore suspect. What we know is, through most of the varied adventures and accomplishments of the Washburn men, there were women close by. They were the sisters, the wives, and the daughters—and most of them were as strong as the men.

From the brothers' earliest years, there were three Washburn sisters—three female siblings who shared the same hardships and joys of the farm in Livermore. By 1861, as the war broke out, in addition to the three sisters there were also five wives, and two more would soon appear. Later, two of the first wives would die and be succeeded by second wives. Thus there are twelve Washburn women who are part of the family story. Although they were never allowed by law to vote, their presence, or absence, was a powerful factor in their husbands' fortunes.

The Washburn sisters: (left to right) Martha, Mary...

Three Washburn sisters also led to three Washburn broth-ers-in-law. In addition, by 1861, there were twenty-one living children. Twenty-four more children were still to be born, of whom only thirteen would survive. Of the ten Washburn sib-lings, only the oldest and the youngest, Israel and Caroline, would not lose at least one child. Ironically, each of these two would suffer a still greater loss, when each had a spouse die prematurely.

These heartbreaking numbers, not unusual for the nine-teenth century, say a lot about the role and fate of women in that age. The women's lives were filled with just as much uncertainty and challenge as most of their male counterparts. With regard to childbirth, they faced real physical peril. Their babies could and did die, and often they took their mothers with them. Such was the fate of two of the twelve Washburn women. A third wife was permanently hospitalized. It was

...and Caroline. Though not in the public eye like their brothers, they too found new lives away from Maine. COURTESY WASHBURN LIBRARY

perilous to be a mother, especially on the frontiers where their Washburn husbands preferred to go.

From their earliest years, every woman in nineteenth-century America faced a basic challenge: She had to find a husband. This was not only an economic necessity; it was essential to her entire mission in life. If she found no husband, then she had no family to raise, no household to maintain, nothing to show she was ever there.

If she was successful in finding a mate, then another great challenge still lay ahead. She was expected to bear children. It was best if she had lots of children, in order to make up for the ones who died. After that, she was supposed to raise those children and run her household through every crisis. For most of the Washburn women, they had to do this alone, for their husbands were away much of the time. This was a big reason these women preferred to have relatives close by. Starting with Mother Patty, most of the Washburn women were not only built of strong stuff; they were also rarely alone.

From what evidence there is comes a picture of strength, fortitude, loyalty, pride, and courage. The Washburn women, in the manner of their time, devoted themselves to their homes and families. Their accomplishments *were* their families. In this, they were typical for their time. Compared to the roles of their husbands, their roles were restricted geographically to home and hearth. Being Washburns, however, these women still managed to fill their lives with a broad range of experiences.

Here, in roughly chronological order, are the stories of those of their experiences that were recorded and kept.

* * *

To repeat, their first mission in life was the job of finding husbands. In this task there was a considerable difference between the experience of the Washburn sisters and that of the Washburn sisters-in-law. For the three Washburn sisters, finding husbands took a considerable effort, for they were not beautiful girls. For their sisters-in-law, the job was much easier. Most of them came from important families, and had been raised with some degree of comfort, crinoline, and connections. Life was gay and suitors plentiful. There is every reason to believe that all the sisters-in-law had suitors to pick from besides the rough-hewn Washburn men they chose.

Mary Maud Webster became the first Washburn spouse—at Orono, Maine, in October 1841. Daughter of one of the town's leading citizens, Colonel Ebenezer Webster, she made an excellent partner for the rising young attorney, Israel Washburn, Jr. They were a nicely matched couple, because she was even shorter than he was. They were undoubtedly married in the Universalist meetinghouse that her father and husband had helped build in Orono.

For the next eighteen years, Maud put up with a succession of younger Washburn sisters and brothers visiting in Orono, and gave birth to four children of her own. She was well prepared through her own upbringing to handle the additional responsibility of entertaining for her husband, and this grew more important as Israel's political career progressed. She was a popular hostess in Washington and Augusta, as well as in Orono. During Israel's frequent absences, she had plenty of both Websters and Washburns to keep her company. She was much loved by her husband—and by his brothers, as well. She was always welcome to stay with them when she chose to travel west. When her second son, Charles Fox Washburn, became critically ill in Minneapolis, both were happily received at William Drew Washburn's home. Charles Fox got better, but Maud caught typhoid fever. After months of uncertainty, during which her husband made several trips across the country to be at her bedside, Maud died there in 1873.

All the brothers were devastated. Normally they were reticent with one another about their marriages, but Maud's untimely death hit them all hard, especially Israel and Cadwallader. Her husband filled eleven pages of his journal with his anguish over the loss. Young William wrote Elihu in Paris to give him the sad news, referring to Maud as "our dearly beloved sister."

* * *

Four years after Israel had married Maud, Adele Gratiot, only eighteen years of age, entered the Washburn family as Elihu's bride. Once again, it was a match between the town's leading family and a rising young lawyer. Adele's grandfather, Charles Gratiot, a French Huguenot expatriate and revolutionary war veteran, had been the first to raise the American flag in St. Louis after the Louisiana Purchase in 1804. Adele's father and brother had come to Galena to get away from Missouri's slavery and to open up the lead mines in 1823. They had endured starvation, floods, cholera, and the Blackhawk Indian War. In 1826, in a sod-roofed log cabin with a clay floor, Adele was probably the first white child born in Galena. She weighed only three pounds, and family legend held that she was placed in a cigar box over the fireplace—the warmest spot in the cabin.

Adele's mother and father were greatly trusted by the Winnebago Indians who lived all around them. He acted as their representative with the federal government, and she treated their illnesses and became a much-respected medicine woman. When Adele was six or seven, she was taken off without notice by some braves to go on a hunt. After a week—which must have seemed much longer than that to her parents—she came back "wild with delight at the escapade," but so dirty that her head had to be shaved and her clothes burned before her parents would let her back in the cabin.

When her father died in Washington on Indian business, Adele was sent back to St. Louis to be educated by Mme. Pierre Chouteau, her father's sister, who combined great wealth from the fur trade with old-world elegance from France. She was described as "the grande dame of St. Louis," and Adele was in her charge for most of four years, including two in a convent at nearby Kaskaskia. By the time she was sixteen, Adele spoke fluent French as well as English and Winnebago. She had just returned to Galena when Elihu met and fell in love with her.

Adele would follow a long and varied road with Elihu. As a bride she had to endure the disapproval of her stern mother-in-law, who thought she was too young and too frivolous. On her first visit to Livermore Adele was terrified by Patty's austere figure. Her French trousseau also caused much consternation, especially the lace lingerie with pink and blue ribbons. She overcame it all, however, and Patty "learned to love her in spite of being a 'foreigner.'"[1]

Adele would bear eight children with Elihu between 1846 and 1868. They would bury two of them, including her first, when Adele was only nineteen, and she was still sick from it ten months later. She would endure the long absences of her husband. One historian estimated that during the first five years of their marriage, Elihu was away from home about five months a year, which increased to ten months a year during most of the 1850s.[2] Adele had the comfort of multiple Gratiot relatives during much of this time, but she also had to endure the deaths of many of these—including her mother, an uncle, and a sister within six months of one another in 1854. She and her children also had the company of Elihu's sister Martha and her family just next door during much of this time.

Having to be with her babies prevented Adele from sharing many of the highs and lows of Elihu's eighteen years in Washington. The journeys back and forth were remembered as "Herculean" and "a nightmare" because of the size of the party, the primitive accommodations, and the long delays between trains. Her duties in entertaining as her husband grew in influence were "strenuous."

One year in Washington they lived at a house on Lafayette Square across from the park, which was maintained by a watchman who also locked it up after sundown. Their daughter Susan remembered the story of one late night when an unnamed young diplomat and a prominent young lady were inadvertently locked in the park. Neither the watchman nor the key could be found. Susan recalled President Lincoln in his carpet slippers and Secretary of State Seward at two o'clock in the morning lugging a ladder to rescue the young couple and avoid an international incident.

Adele handled it all. Later, after her husband found them a pleasant residence in Paris, she brought her family there. As wife of the American minister to France, she was invited to sit at the right hand of the emperor during a formal visit to his vast country palace at Compeigne. Louis Napoleon was delighted by her command of the French language and her stories of growing up among the Indians.

Quite suddenly, Adele and Elihu found themselves caught up in the Franco-Prussian War. Just ahead of the encircling Prussian armies, Adele moved the family to the friendlier city of Brussels. There she gained the attention of Queen Maria Henrietta of Belgium for her efforts to aid refugees trying to contact relatives trapped and under siege in Paris. Again she endured months of anxious separation from her husband and from her oldest son Gratiot, both of whom stayed at their posts in the American legation in the French capital.

As soon as an armistice was signed, Adele took the family back to rejoin Elihu in Paris. It was too soon. They were surrounded by the violence of the Commune, and the national government's vengeful retribution. Her daughter Marie recalled her fear when they were caught on the wrong side of the barricades outside the railroad station upon their arrival from Brussels. She remembered watching and listening from their residence as artillery shells passed directly overhead from the batteries at Mont Valerien. One morning, after Elihu found a spent shell on his bed that had come in through an open window, they decided to move out. In constant fear of the famous "petroleuses" who were burning down the most beautiful buildings in the city, they shuttled from one place to another before settling into a small cottage in the suburb of Rambouillet outside the city. To get there, Marie noted that they had to pass through "crowds of fierce-looking men and women...so disheveled they looked like wild beasts."

After the bloody carnage of the Commune's fall, the Washburnes reclaimed their Paris residence and enjoyed several quiet and comfortable years there. The family was heartbroken when Elihu's term was up in 1877 and they had to return to America. Marie thought that the children had become more French than American.3

Upon their return to America, Elihu was able to procure a lovely mansion in Chicago, where they soon became part of another social world. They threw a gala coming-out party for their daughter Susie, and then her wedding in 1882, and they saw their brilliant son Hempstead elected city attorney for Chicago. Adele and Elihu enjoyed years of contented retirement there together. She died first in 1887, and her heartbroken husband followed her only six months later. Adele had come a long way from that sod-roofed cabin back among the Indians on the Fever River in Galena.

* * *

The third lady to enter the Washburn family differed from the first two in that her family might have been the most prominent of all of the Washburn spouses. Jeannette Garr was part of a large brood of children of one of the most distinguished lawyers in New York City. She was on an adventure—a visit to her sister on the wild frontier—when she met young attorney Cadwallader Washburn. She arrived in dusty Mineral Point, Wisconsin, in the summer of 1848. Undoubtedly her brother-in-law, Mortimer Jackson, who was a judge there, knew Cadwallader well and was able to speak well of him, both to Jeanette and to her father in New York. Cad wooed and won, and Nettie, as she was called, married him on New Year's Day, 1849. Unfortunately, the adventure turned into tragedy for the beautiful young woman with impeccable credentials in the East. Although she bore her husband two daughters in the next three years, Jeanette grew progressively more depressed. On the way back from a visit to her family in New York in 1852, she became catatonic. Cad had to hospitalize, and finally institutionalize, her. For the rest of their lives, although Cad occasionally worked hard at it, without a wife and mother, all resemblance to a normal family life was forever gone for him and the two children.

Jeanette's absence was a reminder of just how important was the woman's role behind the scenes for all the Washburn brothers. Her removal from Cad's side not only removed her nurturing from their daughters, it also drastically affected *his* life. Cad had always been a serious person, impatient, and with a powerful ambition to make something of himself. Now he was alone, and blocked by convention and his own code of honor from partnering with another woman. Without the mediating presence of a woman, he became more serious, more reserved, and more driven. Never one for glad-handing or light conversation, Cad distanced himself from close relationships with anyone beyond his siblings. He became a distant and imperious figure to his daughters and was often viewed by strangers as aloof or even arrogant. Many years later, when his daughters had to choose between him and their husbands, they unhesitatingly chose their husbands and fiercely stood by them.

* * *

Close at hand to Cad's tragedy was the oldest Washburn sister, Martha Benjamin Washburn. She had been named for her mother, but never, as far as we can determine, tagged with her mother's nickname of Patty. Apart from a brief reference to her by the nickname "Goose" in the family journal on her fifty-second birthday, among the family documents that have survived there are no nicknames for this most serious sister.

Martha Washburn was born in 1820. As soon as she was able, she helped her mother with the endless work that had to be done around a hardscrabble farm with ten hungry children to feed. When it was open, she attended the local school. She was fifteen when she described the "agreeable discord" of the busy farmhouse mentioned earlier (see Chapter Two).

Martha was to have years of responsibility for creating order out of uproar. She was sent for a few terms of "finishing" at the Waterville Liberal Institute. After that, she came home to Livermore and undertook to try to support herself. Like her father and her brothers Elihu and Cadwallader, she earned a few dollars by teaching in the local country schools. She was tough and determined. In 1839 she wrote her brother Sid that she had charge of thirty young people. Despite the fact that many of them were bigger than she was, "I make them toe the crack, I can assure you," she wrote. In 1842 she was keeping a school at Haines Corner in East Livermore, on the opposite side of the Androscoggin River from the family's farm. Like her brothers Cadwallader and Elihu, her experiences in controlling remote and rowdy country schoolhouses also left Martha a serious, and even severe, person. Years later in Mineral Point, Cad's two little girls, remembering the beautiful gifts and clothes they used to get from their Garr family aunts, thought that Aunt Martha was jealous and mean. They blamed her for their being "taken away" to the old folks in Livermore after their mother was hospitalized.4

There was no doubt that Cad felt badly about this. As the girls grew up, he made many efforts on their behalf—even if from a distance. He paid for a year of schooling at Westbrook Seminary for his daughter Jeanette, and even sent a neighborhood girl named Julia Chase to Westbrook with her. Julia Chase had a brilliant career at the school, came home to marry Uncle Reuel's son Seth, and wound up writing an almost flawless genealogy of the family, from their progenitors in Massachusetts to their situation in 1898.

School terms were short, rarely longer than twelve weeks,

and eligible young men were few. Martha's best chance at meeting new people would come through the efforts of her brothers. Her oldest brother Israel had a thriving law practice amid the lumberjacks of Orono and Bangor. His new wife Maud was pregnant, and they had a house under construction. Martha made a quick visit there in 1842, enjoyed a succession of "assemblies, parties, and jams," and determined to return. This was the first of at least four visits she made to Orono, where she helped with Israel's new house and growing family, and where she was introduced to the rough-and-tumble society of New England's last frontier. Her husband-hunt had begun. She was in Orono again for three months in 1843, and because of the low pay she got as a teacher, she feared for her financial future. "Unless I get longer and more profitable schools, I don't know but I shall have to go to the factory," she wrote her brother Cad—certainly the only such reference by any Washburn female. She returned to Orono again for several months in 1845, and yet again for more months in 1846, but all in vain. She wrote Cad that she spent the time "quite pleasantly, but I fear not profitably."5

Rescue and a fresh opportunity came with an invitation from her favorite brother. Cadwallader needed someone to come out to Wisconsin and keep house for him. There were a lot more men than women on the western frontier, and so Martha decided to go west. If all else failed, she figured, the lead miners in Mineral Point could always use a new schoolmarm.

She arrived in September, and in a few months things took a turn for the better. Cad's business partner, Cyrus Woodman, had an old childhood friend in town named Charles L. Stephenson. He was from Gorham, Maine, was five years older than Martha, and had been engaged in various businesses in the west for even longer than her brother Cad had been. At about the same time that Cad took an interest in Jeanette Garr,

Martha attracted the attention of Charles Stephenson. When Cad won Jeanette, Martha acted as a witness at their wedding in January of 1849. Then for the next six months, Martha wrote her brother Elihu, she "trembled lest she do something censurable" in the eyes of Mr. Stephenson. Happily, in June, Martha became Mrs. Charles L. Stephenson. She was twenty-eight years old, and she never had to tend school again.

Following this, as things fell apart for Cad's family, the Stephensons began to prosper. The couple set up house in Mineral Point, and children soon followed. A daughter, Elizabeth, was born in May 1850, and a son, Frederic, in February 1853. Martha had her hands full with her own children and couldn't, or wouldn't, take on Cadwallader's, whom she thought had been spoiled by their Garr aunts and uncles.

The oldest of Cad's girls, Jeanette, did not have happy memories of Martha. She wrote that Martha "had inherited a certain masculine strength of character, but she never found any time for the cultivation of the graces. She made my mother very uncomfortable and unhappy by her jealous interference and had neither kindness or sympathy for the delicately nurtured girl who came from a house in New York to the rough little settlement...."[6] After her mother was hospitalized, young Nettie was kept for a while with the Jacksons, who had no children, but there was trouble between Martha and the Jacksons over how she was being brought up.

Cadwallader reluctantly sent his baby girls back to Maine to their grandparents and plunged into his own burgeoning business and political affairs. Always on the move, unable and unwilling to give up hope for his wife, he lived a restless and solitary life. During all of their growing up, Nettie and her sister Fanny saw their father no more than two or thee times a year.

In the meantime, Martha grew close to another family

member. Thirty-five miles down the road from Mineral Point, in Galena, Illinois, her brother Elihu and his wife Adele by 1854 had four children. Elihu was often away, and Adele, who had plenty of her own family members in the area, welcomed Martha's company. Adele, in turn, came to Mineral Point for the birth of Martha's second child in 1853.

By the mid-1850s, the writing was on the wall for Mineral Point. Both the mines and the land business in southern Wisconsin were playing out. The prospects for Charles Stephenson were better in the midst of the busy commerce along the Mississippi River at Galena. Brother Cad, who was closing up his bank and dissolving his partnership with Cyrus Woodman, was elected to Congress in 1854, and he would soon be away in Washington for many months each year. Probably that winter, the Stephensons left Mineral Point and moved down to Galena.

For the next five years, as war clouds gathered, Charles engaged in various enterprises in and around Galena. He leased a small flour mill in town, the War Eagle Mill, and brought in a miller from St. Louis to run it for him. He invested in Cad's unsuccessful effort to revive an abandoned lead mine near Dodgeville, Wisconsin.

In 1860 the federal census listed him as a steamboat captain, and in January 1862 he received an acting officer's appointment in the navy. (This was later revoked—perhaps for reasons of health.) In 1863 the flour mill was listed for sale, described as a five-story-high stone building, 40 feet by 60 feet, including six acres, a storehouse and a dwelling house. The reason Charles sold his flour mill was that in June of 1862 his influential next-door neighbor and brother-in-law Elihu had secured for him the federal position as supervising inspector of steamboats. Charles held this position for almost twenty years, until he died in 1880. It was a job not without peril: At least one steamboat blew up while Charles was inspecting it.

As the years passed Martha had three more children—one of whom died—and the family filled up its comfortable house on Second Street in Galena, which backed up to Elihu and Adele's impressive home. As the Civil War swirled in the background, the two families contributed at least nine children to enliven the neighborhood.

* * *

About the time that his three brothers were taking their seats in congress, and the Stephensons were pulling up stakes from Mineral Point, back in Maine the treasurer of the Bank of Hallowell, forty-year-old Algernon Sidney Washburn, brought his long bachelorhood to an end, and a fourth Washburn sister-in-law joined the family. She was Sarah A. Moore of Bangor, and she must have enjoyed laughter as much as Sid did. For the next twelve years she and her husband and their sons made their house on Middle Street in Hallowell a favorite destination for all the Washburn siblings. The visitors nicknamed it "Blythe House," in honor of their easygoing and generous hosts. Despite financial panics and alarms, the upheavals of war, investment reverses, and political crises, Sid and Sarah's happy times in Blythe House lasted until 1866.

That year unimaginable tragedy struck them. Sarah died giving birth to their fourth son, and he died less than a month after he was born. To cap Sid's sadness, his oldest son James died from a fever three months later in the same year. Within four months, Sid's family went from six people to three—the lonely father and two boys, ages eight and five. For solace, Sid and the boys began to make lengthy visits back to the home place in Livermore.

* * *

Two years after Sid and Sarah had tied the knot, the youngest and most vivacious of the three Washburn sisters took a husband. This was Caroline, who was called both Callie and Carrie by her brothers. Eight years younger than Mary, and thirteen years younger than Martha, she was the darling of the family. Pert and vivacious, she, too, was sent to Waterville Liberal Institute, and then to Gorham Seminary for a year after that. Then, like her sisters before her, she went off to Orono for a lengthy visit with her oldest brother Israel, by now a well-established lawyer and congressman, and his family. As with her sisters, the purpose of the visit was for her to be introduced around—in an area where, thanks to lumbering, there was now more wealth per capita than anywhere else in Maine.

Israel introduced Callie to society in Orono and Bangor, and it wasn't long before she caught the eye of a young doctor just out of Bowdoin College and medical school in Washington, D.C. His name was Freeland Holmes, and he was establishing a practice in the nearby town of Foxcroft. Dr. Holmes was successful in his suit for Callie, and the couple was married in the parlor at the Washburn home in Livermore in 1857. Together they set up house in Foxcroft. When the war broke out in 1861, they had a two-year-old daughter, and Carrie was expecting her second child.

Their domestic tranquility was short-lived, however. Doctors were badly needed by the regiments that brother Israel, now governor, was raising, and Freeland signed up. He was sent to northern Virginia as a surgeon with the Sixth Regiment of Maine Volunteers. In camp at Germantown a year later, he came down with the dreaded "camp fever"—probably diphtheria—which was a far greater killer than any of the battles. Freeland died there on June 23, 1863. Callie was visiting with her sisters and brothers in the west when she got the word. At the age of thirty, she was a widow with two small children.

All her brothers offered to take her in, but it was brother William, two years older than she (compared to Israel, who was twenty years older), to whom she turned. She elected to join him in Minnesota. With Bill and Cad's help, Caroline found a little house there, and she and her children spent the next fifty years in Minneapolis. Perhaps out of loyalty to the memory of her spouse or perhaps out of disinclination to go through another traumatic experience, like her brothers Cadwallader and Sidney she never remarried.

* * *

Less than a year after Callie's wedding, the parlor at Livermore saw another Washburn wedding. There, in March 1858, her older sister Mary triumphantly became Mrs. Gustavus Buffum. This simple ceremony capped what had been an epic effort.

None of the Washburn sisters could be considered a dazzling beauty, but Mary was perhaps the plainest. The search for a husband was hardest for her. Like Martha, Mary was sent off for a few terms at the Waterville Liberal Institute, and, like Martha, she engaged in lengthy visits with her oldest brother, Israel, in Orono. Details are skimpy, but there is a reference to Mary teaching school at Livermore in 1842, when she was seventeen, and to her visiting Orono three years later in 1845. In the hot summer of 1846, her no-nonsense older sister Martha was sweating in the little schoolhouse at Haines Corner and wrote Cad that Mary was "at Stillwater [Orono] until she gets a beau."

It was a full four years after that when Mary finally got her beau. Young Gustavus A. Buffum, an adventurous carpenter from Palermo, Maine, was on his way around the Horn to the gold fields of California. Passing through Orono, he put a ring on Mary's finger before he left. The engagement was to last for eight long years. In the meantime, Mary helped out with Israel's family in Orono and in Washington after he was elected to Congress in 1850. The years went by unrecorded, but Gus came back at last in 1858. He had no gold, but family legend

Solid Gustavus Buffum early earned the trust of
his brother-in-law, Cadwallader Washburn.
Under Buffum's and his descendants'
management and later ownership, Washburn's
lumberyards flourish to this day.

has it that he presented Mary with yards and yards of brocaded
satin for a dress for her trousseau, and brought the family a
trunk full of oranges. They were married at the farm in
Livermore on March 29, 1858. Within a year, the Buffums, too,
headed west, settling in Wisconsin near Mineral Point at a
farm settlement called Monroe. Their first child was born
there.

Mary's brothers liked Gus Buffum a lot. Brother Sid called
him "remarkable." Brother Cad hired him in Wisconsin, and
sent him off to manage a lumberyard he owned in Iowa City,

Iowa. Later, Cad transferred him to bring order out of chaos at his lumber camp in the Wisconsin woods at Waubeek. Brother Sam was supposedly in charge at Waubeek, but Cad was far from happy with the situation. So Gus Buffum went up to take over and "infuse some energy into the concern." There were clashes with Sam shortly after he arrived, and Gus threatened to quit. Cad was furious at Sam and backed Buffum over his brother without hesitation.

An uneasy peace was restored, and Mary, now with a new baby, joined the little settlement in the spring of 1860. Shortly after that, Cad brought in another outsider to run Waubeek. At the same time, brother Elihu—who had also invested in the operation—succeeded in getting Sam a commission in the navy, thereby removing him from the scene. Then Cad promoted Gus to take charge of his big lumberyard at Lyons (now part of Clinton), Iowa. Probably in 1862, Mary and their daughter moved there with him. The family flourished. Mary produced two more children, in 1862 and 1865, and took them all back for a visit to Livermore in 1866.

Then Mary became pregnant with twins, and tragedy struck. There were complications in the delivery, and she died at Lyons in March 1867 with Martha at her bedside. The twins, both boys, also died a few months later. Mary, the second daughter and eighth Washburn sibling, thus became the first of her generation to go.

Gus Buffum remained in charge of Cad's Lyons operation, and later moved down the river to manage the even bigger lumberyard they had established at Louisiana, Missouri, seventy miles north of St. Louis. For five years after Cad's death, Gus and his two sons, plus a new wife he had gone back to Orono to find, continued at Louisiana, managing the operation for Cadwallader's estate. His relations with the Washburns remained good, and when Cad's estate was at last settled in

William Drew Washburn,
nicknamed Young Rapid by his family
COURTESY OF ANN GAMLIN

1888, his executors sold the Louisiana operation to the
Buffums. All of them, including Gus's new wife, were beneficiaries in Cad's will, and were always welcomed back for visits to
the Washburn homestead in Livermore.

* * *

The eighth Washburn marriage, and probably the biggest, took
place amidst almost royal circumstances in Bangor in April of
1859. There, youngest brother William, the restless Prince
Charming of the family, took as his bride Elizabeth Little
Muzzy, one of the three beautiful daughters of a leading Bangor
businessman, Franklin Muzzy. The wedding attracted Ralph
Waldo Emerson as one of the guests, and he was so impressed
by Lizzie's beauty that he supposedly dedicated one of his books
to her.

Elizabeth Muzzy Washburn, with her son Stanley
COURTESY OF WASHBURN LIBRARY

Though raised in comfort and an elegant social whirl, Lizzie was of an adventurous as well as courageous nature. Right after the wedding, she allowed herself to be carried off from her comfortable surroundings to the primitive environment of the Nicollet Hotel, the first public hostelry in Minneapolis. On her way there, traveling up the river from St. Louis, she had to run a gauntlet of critical Washburn eyes in Galena. Stopping off for a few days, she successfully passed muster with two Washburn brothers (Cad and Elihu), two Washburn sisters (Mary and Martha), and three Washburn in-laws (Charles Stephenson, Augustus Buffum, and Adele Washburne).

Lizzie loved early Minneapolis. From its summer dust to its endless winters, she loved the prairie, which began literally at her door. Her enthusiasm some years later may have influenced one of her sisters, Olive, to take on a similar adventure of her own. Olive Muzzy married a Bangor businessman named John Crosby, who had been recently widowed. When Cadwallader picked Crosby to be his new partner in the flour business in 1877, no doubt Lizzie's presence in Minneapolis made the prospect of leaving Bangor easier for Olive.

Lizzie produced no fewer than nine children with William, of whom six survived. She kept the peace in the family, as they all grew to be as opinionated as her husband. She graciously managed larger and larger quarters as the family grew, William's many enterprises flourished, and his preferred lifestyle grew more and more elaborate. They were famous hosts during William's twelve years in Washington, and in Minneapolis they wound up in an eighty-room castle called Fair Oaks, which was the wonder of the city. Their marriage lasted fifty-three years, until William's death in 1912, and their children, though not fitting into the molds their father expected for them, all made impressive records.

* * *

In contrast to Lizzie Muzzy's dazzling Washburn match, Lorette Thompson's entry into the Washburn family was far more modest. She had seen a lot of Sam Washburn while she was on a visit to her sister near Waubeek in the woods of Wisconsin in 1861.

Sam Washburn turned thirty-eight in January 1862. He was still a bachelor, out of the Wisconsin woods at last, but in deep trouble with the U.S. Navy. He had misinterpreted his leave, gone AWOL in the navy's eyes, and been ignominiously dismissed for disobedience—less than two weeks after receiving a commission. At the heart of his trouble was the same Lorette Thompson who had distracted him in Wisconsin, causing Cad's frustration with his performance. Sam, his new brass buttons in peril, nevertheless pursued Lorette to her home in

LeRoy, in western New York State.

Brother Elihu intervened to get Sam reinstated with the navy, and Lorette reconsidered her reluctance. They were married at LeRoy at the end of March 1862, shortly before Sam went to sea as acting master on the gunboat *Galena*. Their first child was born in December.

When the war finally ended and Sam came home a partial invalid, the couple took the proceeds from the sale of Sam's stake in the Waubeek lumber camp and moved fifty miles west, across the Mississippi into Minnesota, to start a lumberyard in the town of Owatonna. It was a difficult period for both of them. Sam was popular in the town but had trouble with his business. Lorette gave birth to a second son in 1866, but they lost him the following year. Another son was born in 1868 but died shortly afterwards, and Lorette herself didn't survive much longer. The end for her came in February 1869. Sam sold out soon after that, and he and his surviving son Bennie came home to Livermore, where his aged and blind father needed caring for, as did the family farm. As the new mansion the brothers built for their father (and for themselves) rose on the foundations of the old, Sam labored to keep the fields productive around it.

* * *

New Jersey socialite Sallie Catherine Cleaveland was twenty-three when she agreed to become Mrs. Charles Ames Washburn and end the bachelorhood of the last Washburn brother. This was in May of 1865. Since Charles was serving as the American minister to Paraguay at the time, theirs was the most long-distance of all the Washburn courtships. No doubt taken by the ambassador's tales of an easy life in a tropical paradise, Sallie was ill prepared for what awaited her in South America.

It was good thing that Mother Patty didn't live long enough

to meet Sallie. If she thought Adele was frivolous, no doubt she would have thought Sallie much more so. Used to a gay whirl in New York, Sallie would be plunged into quite a different life in Asunción, Paraguay. A four-way war had just broken out when Charles left his post to come to New York to marry her. After the wedding, the happy couple blithely returned to South America. For eighteen months they wandered about Argentina waiting for each of the belligerents, plus the U.S. Navy, to allow them passage back to Paraguay. When they finally got there, things were so bad that they were virtually besieged in their own residence. As their friends were being tortured and killed, and their mission was filling up with refugees, Sallie gave birth to a daughter. At last, the navy reappeared to rescue them. Sallie, half-mad from fear and tension, returned with her husband and baby to Livermore, where she gave birth to a second child in 1869. Sallie was not happy at Norlands, nor at any of the many other places they tried to live, including Reading, Pennsylvania, where a third child and second daughter was born. As Charles stumbled in and out of different job situations, nothing was quite right. There was not much communication or understanding between them. They eventually settled in Morristown, New Jersey, and, in the end, Sallie would outlive Charles by twenty-five years.

* * *

In 1872, also at Livermore, brother Sam became the first Washburn to remarry, and twenty-six-year-old Addie Brown Reade of Lewiston became the second Mrs. Samuel Washburn. The couple had two children, one of whom died in Sam's arms at Livermore in 1875. The following year, Israel Washburn, Sr., died at the age of ninety-one. Sam and Addie continued to operate the farm, but Sam's health deteriorated steadily. They left Livermore and moved to Portland, where Sam had a major operation in 1881 that rendered one leg virtually unusable.

After that, he received a disability pension from the government, and two years later was admitted to a sanitarium in Avon Springs, not far from Lorette's hometown of LeRoy, New York. Addie buried him back in Livermore in 1890.

* * *

The final lady to join the Washburn brothers was also a second wife. Thirty-seven-year-old Robina Napier Brown agreed to become the second Mrs. Israel Washburn, Jr., at Boston in January of 1876. She was the daughter of two of Israel's oldest friends in Aroostook County, and evidently had no qualms about joining with a man twenty-six years older than she was. After an exhausting honeymoon trip all over Europe, the happy couple returned to Israel's home in Portland, where she and his two unmarried daughters helped make Israel's last seven years busy and productive. Following his death, Robina and her mother left Maine for San Diego, California, where Robina lived until her death in 1919.

* * *

By 1870, with Elihu serving in France, the number of Washburn siblings along the upper Mississippi was reduced to four, including the two surviving Washburn sisters, Martha (still married) and Callie (widowed), both half a continent away from where they had grown up. Fortunately, brothers Cadwallader and William were getting steadily richer. In 1870, with Elihu's help, Callie had a comfortable house of her own in Minneapolis. When Cad died in 1882, he left a generous bequest for an orphan asylum in the city of Minneapolis, and stipulated that Callie and William serve on its board. They did just that for the rest of their lives. One of Israel's sons, Charles Fox Washburn, came to Minneapolis to work for William, and Israel's beloved wife Maud died there during a visit in 1873. Although she paid regular summer visits back to Maine, Callie was to live in Minneapolis until her death in 1920. The last of the siblings to be born, she was also the last to die.

Martha and her family stayed on in Galena. Charles Stephenson was inspecting steamboats up and down the river until his death in St. Paul in 1880. Martha's brothers and sisters thought enough of him to name him in 1876 as trustee responsible for the maintenance and repair of all the buildings at the Washburn property in Livermore. After Charles died, Martha and her widowed daughter Martha joined her married son Benjamin in North Dakota. The elder Martha died in Mandan in 1909, having been a widow for twenty-nine years.

It is always dangerous to generalize about twelve different people. However, the truth is that, of the twelve Washburn women, no less than six followed their husbands to new places immediately after they were married. The remaining six all moved to new places in later life. Not one died anywhere near where she had been born. They were all clearly open to new experiences and not afraid of change. Through the dangers of childbirth, through premature deaths of children, and often through long periods alone, they put down roots, faced the perils of frontier life, and raised their surviving children in environments far different from those in which they themselves had been born.

They probably didn't have much choice about it, for they wanted to establish homes and families of their own and were attracted to an adventurous group of spouses. They made the best of it. Like their illustrious siblings, all of the sisters and sisters-in-law, with the possible exception of Sallie Cleaveland, were apparently happy in their new environments, and all had the satisfaction of raising respectable families and seeing their children grow and prosper. As their brothers and husbands were devoted to their political and business careers, so the Washburn women were devoted to their unsung roles as keepers of the hearth. Where political, business, or charitable necessities required them to be gregarious, they were—from backwoods lumber camps to embassies abroad. They reflected the popularity of their spouses.

They proved remarkably adaptable and flexible. Although never in rags, during their eventful marriages to their adventurous husbands, they experienced huge changes in financial fortune, in location, in social circle, and in culture. Adaptation was easier for some than for others, but adapt they did. In remote outposts from fleabag hotels to flyblown lumber camps, they endured loneliness, fear, and physical hardship. In state and national capitals, they managed huge households, learned new cultures, charmed dignitaries and politicians of every stripe, and through a variety of real perils, they won respect and admiration from heads of state on several continents. They endured literally years of separation from their husbands, handling every kind of crisis as their own individual judgments dictated.

They made no speeches and won no elections. They weren't even allowed to vote. They founded no great enterprises and made no changes in the landscape. However, the Washburn women all did what they were expected to do. They found respectable husbands, bore children for these husbands, and, with the sad exception of Cadwallader's wife Jeanette, they established warm and comfortable households in which to raise their families and provide their husbands with both platforms of support and justification for their strivings. In the roles that were open to them, and in the roles they desired, the Washburn women left a record of accomplishment that, though quieter, was equal to that of their brothers and husbands.

Most of the Washburn women were fortunate to live long enough to enjoy comfortable final years with their spouses and to take satisfaction from both their spouses' accomplishments and their own. The great trauma of the Civil War brushed them and preoccupied their men, but their experiences with childbirth proved far more lethal.

1. Quotes taken from Fowler, pp. 9, 18, and 20.
2. Timothy R. Mahoney, *Provincial Lives, Middle Class Experience in the Antibellum Middle West* (New York: 1999), 156.
3. Fowler, 32, 35
4. Jeanette Washburn Kelsey (Washburn Library), 43.
5. MBW to CCW, March 26, 1842, September 17, 1845, December 7, 1848 (Washburn Library).
6. Jeanette Kelsey (Washburn Library), 29.

Six

To Save the Union

BEFORE DAWN ON APRIL 12, 1861, the United States of America broke in two. The break had actually started earlier, but the exploding artillery shells and flying masonry at Fort Sumter made it official. Southerners, their long control of the central government gone, felt they could take no more. They not only left the country; they determined to fight to stay apart. Northerners like the Washburns were stunned, but determined to bring them back. The worst nightmare for any nation, a civil war, was at hand.

From a historical perspective, for the Washburns the timing of this national disaster was propitious. It came at a moment when many of them were at a peak of power and influence. The Republican movement, which they had all worked long and hard to nurture, had just won the highest political office in the land. At a time when the frontier states in the west were tipping the balance of power in the country westward, no less than five of the seven brothers and two of the three sisters were on that frontier. The drive to limit the expansion of slavery, and the drive to curb the power of the southern states that was behind it, had been the cause for which every Washburn man had devoted most of his political energy for the past ten years. They accepted that their cause had now resulted in war. Their long fight for principle would now have to be conducted with untold expenditure of the nation's blood and treasure. This was an awful realization—and one that did not come until the first battles had been lost.

However, the terrible cost did not cause any one of the brothers to waver. Throughout the next four years of suffering and occasional despair, they never lost their certainty. Their cause was right. It would reestablish the high moral precepts of the founding fathers. It would confirm the status of their country as a beacon of light for the world. It would remove a sin against man. They would see the struggle through.

Though separated geographically, they were united in sentiment. Oldest brother Israel had fought the "southern oligarchs" for over a decade in Congress. He had led the movement to counter their power, and he had paved the way for Lincoln's national victory by leading another unprecedented Republican sweep of state offices in Maine two months before the national election of 1860. Now he sat in the governor's chair in Augusta, stunned that the southerners had actually made good on threats they had been making for fifty years, and sobered by the enormous task ahead.

One thing was clear to him: The fate of the Union would only be settled by the efforts of the states that wished to preserve it. He was in no doubt about the desperate work at state level that would be needed immediately. The governors held the real power; the governors were closest to the people; the governors could raise the troops. The governors would have to save the country. With his back stiffened by moral certainty, and the unprecedented mandate of his recent landslide election to the governor's office, Israel Washburn was grimly ready to take on the job in Maine.

Banker Sid was with his family just down the road from Augusta in Hallowell, probably wondering what the financial impact of the fight would be, and grateful that his children were too young to serve. Perhaps he was also secretly glad that it was Israel, and not he, who had the tiger by the tail up in the governor's office.

Elihu was in Galena, on recess from his congressional duties in Washington. He, too, was grimly determined to see the struggle through with his old friend Lincoln. As he set about organizing the first rally in town to support the Union, he was filled with great anxiety. Would the Democrats, who controlled Galena and most of the Mississippi River Valley, give up their long history of sympathy with the South and support sending troops to save the Union?

His sister Martha, along with her steamboat captain husband, Charles L. Stephenson, were also in Galena. Thankful that their children were too young to be caught up in the fighting, she and her husband were all too aware that the great river that flowed by their doorstep was the main route to the southern heartland. That river was bound to become an important military objective for both sides. The coming conflict would be closer to them than to many.

Brother Cad was up the river in La Crosse, calculating how the war could affect his tattered political fortunes, to say nothing of his business enterprises. His experience with managing people and resources gave him a realistic idea of the size of the task ahead.

Younger brother Sam, stuck at the Waubeek lumbercamp, may have wondered whether or not the war might give him an opportunity to get out of the woods at last. His journal reveals none of the global concerns of his older brothers. His concern was much closer and more immediate. He had just met a lady named Lorette Thompson, and she had him hoping that at last he might be able to end his long bachelorhood.

Sister Mary and her husband Gus Buffum were downstream in Iowa, she taking care of the children, and he trying to find buyers for Cad's lumber.

Young William and his bride were up in the new town of Minneapolis, he supervising construction and drumming up tenants for Cad's new dam and canal there. Both were young and eager for whatever new adventure lay ahead.

Elsewhere, California brother Charles was in Washington, now in his fourth month of trying to coax a job out of the Lincoln administration. His intemperate newspaper support in California had helped contribute to the Republicans' narrow victory there, but the power brokers behind the new party did not trust him. He was not receiving their support for any federal position in the west.

Youngest sister Caroline was happy with her new babies and her young doctor husband Freeland Holmes back in Foxcroft, Maine. Within a year, the war would radically change their lives forever. Though her life seemed the furthest removed from the war, of all the siblings she would pay the greatest price.

* * *

The events in Charleston Harbor put an end to the debate that had raged across the country since its founding. It was now fact that a federal installation was under attack by the military forces of several rebellious states. In an instant, for every citizen of the republic, the long years of talk had turned into action.

The reluctant forces at the center—across Pennsylvania, New Jersey, Ohio, and Illinois—ambivalent about slavery in the territories, shocked over the split in the Democratic party and the defeat of Stephen Douglas for the presidency, still desperately seeking compromise, and terrified by the awful prospect of a civil war—watched appalled as the shells fell on Fort Sumter. The die was cast, and the time to choose sides was at hand.

The niceties of argument over the nature of property, the

Though seven rebel forts combined,
Set Sumter's Fort in flame,
They in each freeman's heart enshrined
Brave *Anderson's* bright name.

Fort Sumter, and its commander, Major Robert Anderson, became symbols that ignited Northern passion to preserve the Union. Even postal envelopes like this one became tools to whip up public fervor for the war.
Courtesy New York Historical Society

relative rights of states and the central government, the expansion of slavery into the territories, and—above all—control of the central government, would now have to be settled by cold steel. With a terrible clarity, across every shade of the political spectrum, across every northern and western state, there was only one cause; the Union was under attack. The Union must be saved.

The Washburns would fight in the war in many different ways, both in and out of uniform. Some would dodge shot and shell at the front lines, and others would use their leadership and integrity to keep the cause on track behind the armies. Many would quietly endure trials at home. Unlike many of their neighbors, however, none of the Washburns ever doubted the cause. No matter how grim the news, none of them ever wavered. In the end, after four of the most terrible years in the nation's history, the group, in all its different locations, was as resolute as it had been at the beginning, sure that the Union cause was right, and confident that the country would emerge stronger for all the suffering it had endured.

* * *

Following the surrender of Fort Sumter, the deluge of war caught Israel and Elihu first. Lincoln's call for troops was the catalyst. In Maine, when Lincoln's request for a regiment arrived in Augusta, Governor Washburn called an immediate special session of the state's legislature. He gave the far-flung lawmakers six days to gather in Augusta, and 117 of them managed to make it.

For more than a decade, although pulpits across Maine had rung with antislavery rhetoric, abolitionism's very intensity had worked against it. Thoughtful moderates were reluctant to interfere in the affairs of other states, and noted that the wild-eyed antislavery leaders had little in the way of practical ideas for dealing with the slaves *after* they were freed. Palatable though it might be politically, even Wilmot's position was not enough for men to die for, and Israel Washburn, Jr., who had been against slavery since his first Universalist church service, knew it.

The attack on Sumter brought the abstractions home. After Sumter, the issue was no longer just about slavery. The crisis was about saving the country from those southern states which had left it and then attacked it. This was a cause for which Maine farm boys would gladly give their lives. In fact, during the next four years more than ten thousand of them would do just that.

The lawmakers' response to the governor's appeal in Augusta was dramatic. Putting their historic fractiousness aside, in three days they passed the most revolutionary legislation in the state's forty-one-year history. In rapid succession, they approved funding for ships to guard the state's lengthy coastline, they revised the state's statutes to allow local militia to be mustered into federal service, and they authorized borrowings that tripled the state's debt—debt that Israel had just been elected to reduce. Each move was unprecedented. When Israel signed the new militia law, for example, with a stroke of his pen he gave up a power that had been central to state governors since colonial times—the control of their troops.

Governor Washburn had been nominated to clean up a bad mess in the state treasurer's office. He had campaigned on a promise to do that and to reduce the state's debt as well. Now, just four months into office, the legislature was giving him more than one hundred times as much money as was missing. Along with it, they authorized him to raise ten times as many troops as Lincoln had asked for. With almost no infrastructure in place and no precedent to follow, and working almost without rest, he did the job—finding men, finding officers, finding clothing, weapons, tents, horses, and even band instruments, for ten regiments in just six months. Even after the initial appropriation was spent, he kept on raising regiments. All but seven of the regiments that Maine sent to the war would be raised during Israel's two years in office. And, through it all, not one dollar was unaccounted for.

During the nineteenth century, Maine's governors served one-year terms. Although sheer physical exhaustion led Israel to decline to run again after two terms, he could have had the office for as long as he wanted it. Besides a spotless financial record, he left an impressive record of political leadership. Behind his diminutive, bespectacled figure, the state's notoriously quarrelsome legislature became united. Overwhelmed by the great cause of saving the country, factions driven by local rivalries grew quiet. Despite incompetent, disorganized, unrealistic, or outright fraudulent direction from the War Department in Washington during the first months, Washburn got almost thirty regiments gathered, equipped, and at least partly trained. He silenced or outmaneuvered his political opposition—from nativists, to temperance activists, to Peace Democrats. As the fortunes of the Union Army waxed and waned, he continued to inspire Maine's young men to turn out to serve their country. Fifty years afterwards, Portland's leading newspaper still called Israel Washburn, Jr., Maine's "War Governor."[1]

When the final numbers were at last available, it would be seen that no other Northern state would equal tiny Maine in percentage of eligible population who served in the war.[2] By 1864 in most of the towns across the state, there was hardly a healthy male between the age of eighteen and thirty-five to be found. Accordingly, by the end of the century, there were few towns that hadn't erected some kind of monument to those who had fallen.

Governor Washburn's spectacular performance was driven by more than energy, honesty, and political acumen. Of course he was certain that the cause was right—morally as well as politically—but his perspective was also global. From his modest office in the capitol of one of the country's most remote states, as he struggled with details from harnesses for horses to buttons for overcoats, the Livermore farm boy clearly saw the task at hand for its global significance. He summed it up in a letter to an American consul in London who was trying to obtain rifles for the Maine troops. He wrote, "The hundreds of millions that the rebellion will make us pay will be the best investment the country has made since the beginning. It will be shown, thank God, that we are a nation; a nation to be respected by all others, as well as by our own people."[3]

* * *

Out in western Illinois, the situation was as murky as the waters of the Mississippi that lapped at Galena's waterfront. Here in this riverfront town, most of the commerce, culture, and communication originated with the traffic on the river. That trade was substantial. One observer felt that, in the mid-1850s, Galena's total commerce exceeded even that of Chicago.4 The town's dependence on the river meant that there was a lot of local sympathy with Southern interests downstream. In addition, reflecting the long-time power of the Democratic party along the river, there was much sympathy for the lately defeated Illinoisian candidate for president, Stephen A. Douglas. There was also the ingrown resistance to central authority common to any frontier. In Galena, Congressman Elihu Washburne held his breath to see which way the town would react to the news from Sumter. The key moment arrived with Lincoln's first call for troops. Despite his friend's victory in 1860, Elihu knew that the town had long resisted the Republicans. He knew that ties to the new government were weak among disaffected Democrats, independent-minded frontiersmen, and those who were sympathetic to the slaveholders.

The day before Lincoln's first call for volunteers actually arrived in Galena, Washburne helped organize a patriotic rally at the local courthouse. The excited meeting started out poorly when the town's mayor, newly elected Democrat Robert Brand, spoke against the war and in favor of compromise and peace. However, the crowd shouted him down. To Elihu's great relief, John A. Rawlins, a fellow lawyer and Democratic leader in the community, rose to say that the time for compromising was over and it was time to "stand by the flag and appeal to the God of Battles" to defend the Union.5 The Union cause was safe in Galena.6

This was important because of Galena's importance. Located at the halfway point between St. Louis and Minneapolis, on virtually the only north-south thoroughfare in the country, Galena was one of the biggest towns in the northwest. Galena's army volunteers were the first ones enrolled west of Chicago. Its first company was filled on April 21 and for a few days drilled with pine laths for rifles in Elihu's side yard. It left for Springfield on April 25, to become part of the 45th Illinois Infantry, nicknamed "The Lead Mine Regiment."7

At another rally, a day or two after the Rawlins speech, Elihu was introduced to a somewhat scruffy-looking individual named Ulysses S. Grant, an ex-army officer who had only been in town a few months, clerking in a family harness shop. Realizing that the unimpressive Grant was one of his few constituents who had both West Point training and combat experience in Mexico, Elihu urged the man to go down to Springfield and seek a commission from Governor Yates. Yates, like brother Israel in Maine, was frantically raising regiments. Though the hard-drinking and excitable Yates was no friend of teetotaler Congressman Washburne, Grant followed Elihu's advice and went down to camp outside the governor's door. Grant was neither a politician nor a salesman, and it took some time, but eventually Yates gave Grant a colonel's commission and sent him off to try his luck straightening out a particularly troublesome regiment. In just two months, Grant quietly brought order to the unit. The rumpled leather clerk's moribund military career was reborn, and Congressman Washburne was the midwife. The two would soon cross paths again.

After ensuring that recruiting was off to a smooth start in Galena, Elihu returned to Washington to provide congressional support for Lincoln, the untried and largely unknown president. Two months later, Elihu became the first Washburn sibling to see action in the war.

The frontier lawyer had never been one to miss a good fight. In July, seeking to assess the state of the Union Army personally, and eager to see an early action close-up, Congressman Washburne took a buggy out to Centreville, Virginia, to observe what was to become the first Battle of Bull Run. In a confused three days, he proudly watched the new regiments march into battle, cheered at their early success, and got caught in the melee of their retreat. He came under fire with the troops, and, moving from one observation point to another, just missed being captured in an enemy cavalry charge.

From his description to Adele, we can visualize the scene. With Minié balls whistling by his ears, he gives up his buggy seat to a wounded soldier. Then suddenly, on foot and unarmed, he is overrun by a huge tide of panicked Union soldiers. In his shirtsleeves, he tries to stem the Union rout. His sturdy frame and stentorian voice are no match for the terrified men, and he is overwhelmed and carried off in the mob. Finally, around midnight on July 21, he struggles back to the capital to report to the president. Bloodied but unbowed, the next day he ends a letter to his wife with grim determination. "We will whip the traitors yet," he promises. However, no one now knows better than Elihu Washburne that it will be a long and dirty business.

By August, recruiting in Illinois had gone so well that the state had earned the right to have several brigadier generals appointed. Lincoln owed his army to the states, so he asked the Illinois congressional delegation to make recommendations for officers to fill the new places. Meeting with his colleagues in Springfield, Elihu was able to get one of the slots for Grant, and to have the commission backdated to provide his constituent with seniority. Thus it was that Ulysses S. Grant, future general of the armies and president of the United States, and one of the finest military leaders America has ever produced, owed his first star to a roomful—no doubt smoke-filled—of Illinois politicians. Once again, his chief advocate was Congressman Washburne.

Thanks to Elihu Washburne, Grant now had a chance at significant military leadership. But dozens of other smoke-filled rooms were producing dozens of other generals, only a few of whom could claim either military experience or competence. Grant would need Washburne's protection many more times before he finally emerged as the North's most decisive general.

Washburne, critical of shoddy purchasing by the War Department, was made chairman of the special House Committee on Government Contracts. This was the beginning of the sharp-eyed congressman's reputation as "Watchdog of the Treasury." Looking for trouble, the committee visited St. Louis and southern Illinois during the 1861 congressional recess to investigate irregularities among contractors supplying the western armies. They found plenty. The congressman was shocked by the stew of cronyism and malfeasance that his committee uncovered. There were overpayments to California contractors for fortifications around St. Louis. Hundreds of horses were bought for $130 each, but only one in six could be used. There was one shipment of muskets bought from the government for $17,406 and sold back the next day for $109,912. Washburne wrote Lincoln in October that, "the robberies, the frauds, the peculation in the gov't which have already come to our knowledge are absolutely frightful."[8]

At the top of the army's chain of command in the west was an important and popular political figure. Major Gen. John C. Frémont, the dashing "Pathfinder" who had been the Republicans' first choice for the presidency in 1856, was now commander of the Western Department of the Army. His premature efforts to free the slaves in Missouri delighted the radicals, but almost lost several wavering border states to the

Confederacy. Now Elihu's findings, which named the names of some of Frémont's closest California cronies, gave Lincoln further reason to replace Frémont. This move was an early example of the steel that lay beneath Lincoln's homespun exterior. Despite all the pressure that Frémont's politically well-connected wife could exert on his behalf, the handsome but careless general spent most of the rest of the war in New York City "awaiting orders." He would come to Washburne's attention again after the war.

Some of Washburne's committee hearings took place at Union Army Headquarters in southern Illinois at Cairo, at the junction of the Ohio and Mississippi rivers, where a military force was being organized for a drive south into Kentucky and Tennessee. There, Washburne had an opportunity to observe Grant in action. He became further impressed by his constituent's integrity and quiet efficiency, which strengthened his support of the general. However, aware of rumors concerning Grant's drinking, he helped arrange for John Rawlins to come down from Galena to join Grant's staff for the main purpose of keeping the new general away from temptation. At the same time, Washburne became a fierce defender of the general's interests in Congress.

His influence was needed almost immediately. Unlike many of the "political" generals, Grant lacked connections in Washington. He was quite innocent of the necessities of political protection in a democratic government. Despite early victories at Forts Henry and Donelson, in Congress and at the White House Grant was virtually unknown. In the uproar that followed the inconclusive but bloody battle at Shiloh, Elihu was all that stood between Grant and dismissal. It took all his political muscle to save Grant's career.

Later, he had to do it again. The problem this time was the horde of civilian traders that Cadwallader himself would have to battle later on in Memphis. Despite prohibitions against trading with the enemy by both Union and Confederate governments, the mounting stocks of unsold Southern cotton presented a lucrative target for entrepreneurs on both sides. Grant, building up for the Vicksburg campaign, was camped at Holly Springs in Mississippi. Driven to distraction by the swarms of peddlers and hangers-on, he issued the infamous Order #11, the order that expelled Jewish (and other) cotton speculators from the Department of Tennessee. Though not as politically incorrect then as it would be today, the order raised an immediate uproar in Washington. Lincoln had to reverse the order, and Elihu had to intervene to protect Grant in the Congress. By a single vote, he got a bill to censure Grant tabled, and he probably intervened again to keep Grant in command of the Vicksburg campaign. Thus, Elihu Washburne not only started Grant's career in the Civil War, he intervened to save that career on probably three critical occasions. And his greatest intervention was still to come.

Since so much of Elihu's contribution to the Union war effort happened because of his proximity to Lincoln, it is worth a moment to examine the relationship between these two country lawyers from Illinois.

To begin with, they honestly liked one another. Long before the afternoon he brought Lincoln to the Willard Hotel to swap yarns with his brothers, Washburne and Lincoln had shared courtroom experiences in Springfield, had shared the political challenges of being minority Whigs in Illinois, and had together enjoyed the camaraderie of the afternoon gatherings among colleagues at the state law library. There was a strong element of trust between them. Both were rawboned country boys, not afraid of a fight or of hard physical labor. They had known each other on Illinois law circuits and campaign trails for more than twenty years.

Lincoln owed Washburne for his support during the debates with Douglas, for making it easier to sidetrack potential competitor John C. Frémont in St. Louis, for his protection of Grant—the one Union general who appeared to win battles—and for his ferocious defense of the government's purse strings during a period of unprecedented federal spending. Later in the war, Lincoln also owed his most important military decision to Elihu's advice.

In February 1864, with the Union Army floundering once again, Washburne introduced a bill in the House to give new impetus to the war effort by creating the position of general of the armies and authorizing the reestablishment of the rank of lieutenant general to fill the position. He of course had Grant in mind for the post. Lincoln, however, having never met Grant, was afraid the general would use the new position to run for president in 1864. He'd already had to remove two other generals—Frémont and McClellan—who were potential aspirants for the office. Washburne needed to prove to his old friend that he had nothing to fear from Grant.

To do this, Elihu found an independent third party whom Lincoln knew and trusted, and who also knew Grant well. The man was Russell Jones, his old friend from Galena, now an investment banker in Chicago. Elihu wired Jones to come to Washington to assure the president that Grant had no political ambitions. Jones did just this, the bill and the appointment went through, and the North got the military leader who finally won the war for them.

* * *

The Washburn siblings, though separated by physical distance, had long made it a habit to watch out for one another. As the prospect of a long and bloody war became more evident, the older siblings were concerned about protecting their younger brothers, Charles and William, from its violence. With financial help from their older siblings, Charles and William were the first of the generation to go to college. Both graduated from Bowdoin College, Charles in 1847 and William in 1854. Both were of an age to serve in the military, but Charles was hardly one to fit into a military hierarchy. He had already been turned down at West Point, and during his newspaper days in California had developed an intemperate tongue that had made him few friends there. William's immense energy and charm were needed to keep Cadwallader's enterprises on track in Minnesota, where William had already performed the civic duty of raising a company of infantry.

The extent of Elihu's involvement will never be known, but in 1861, Lincoln appointed the thirty-nine-year-old Charles as U.S. commissioner to Paraguay and thirty-year-old William as federal surveyor general for Minnesota.

Charles had come to Washington as a presidential elector in 1860, sent there by influential California Republicans as a reward for his journalistic services to the party—and no doubt in the hope that he would not return. His assignment to Paraguay would not only keep him well clear of the war at home, but, it was hoped, well clear of embarrassment for his political brothers as well.

In his new state position, young William had to move from Minneapolis over to the state capital at St. Paul, but he was still able to keep an eye on Cad's enterprises at the falls while also becoming familiar with townships and timberlands across Minnesota. The surveyor job also gave him a title, and William relished being called "the General" for the rest of his life.

These appointments did not go unnoticed. On Charles's appointment, the acerbic secretary of the navy, Gideon Welles, noted in his diary that "the mission [to Paraguay] disposed of one of the troublesome family of Washburns who are now all provided for." Poor Mr.Welles. He didn't know it, but he was far from finished with the Washburns.

* * *

Two more Washburn brothers were fated to serve their country in the war, both of them in Union uniforms. Their paths, and their motives, could hardly have been more different.

That Cadwallader Colden Washburn would submit his formidable energy and independence to the service of the Union Army deserves note in itself. This was not a man who was used to reporting to others. This was not a man who suffered fools easily. This was a man already balancing vast business enterprises with a political career. Literally hundreds of men across two states looked to him for their livelihood—despite the fact that, at the moment, buyers for his lumber were few and far between.

In sharp contrast to C. C. Washburn's world of unfettered capitalism, the world of the military was narrow, resistant to change, woefully under-funded, and bitterly opposed to civilian interference. When the war broke out, the military establishment was better prepared for bureaucratic infighting than it was for a shooting war to save the country.

Washburn's motives in stepping forward were not altogether altruistic. He needed to rebuild his badly damaged political career in Wisconsin, and his businesses needed protection from creditors. Besides that, Cad had always wanted to be a soldier.

Ever since he had been unable to get into West Point as a young man, Washburn had admired soldiering. Now, with Wisconsin's Governor Randall handing out commissions to men who could raise regiments, and with hundreds of Washburn's lumberjacks and other constituents across western Wisconsin willing to sign up, he saw a new chance for the military career that had always fascinated him.

These things pulled him, and bigger things pushed him. He had just suffered a smarting political defeat. He had resigned his seat in Congress in 1860 to campaign for a seat in the U.S. Senate and had been defeated in this effort. In a state legislature dominated by representatives from the eastern part of the state, he didn't have the support he needed. As Washburn saw it, military service might be just the thing to restore his tattered political capital.

In addition, for three years Cadwallader Washburn had been juggling unpaid creditors. Millions of feet of unsold Washburn logs lay in booms along the Mississippi River, and desperate negotiations were underway to sell his precious timberlands along the Chippewa River. On top of this, Washburn was committed to major expenditures on dam and canal construction at Minneapolis, to say nothing about repaying earlier obligations. No one, including Washburn, thought that the war would last long. If precious timberlands had to be sold, Washburn thought he could transact these sales just as well from an army billet as from his office in La Crosse.

Washburn cut the deal with Governor Randall, who owed him one for supporting Timothy Howe in the recent Senate debacle, and the Second Wisconsin Regiment of Cavalry was born. Colonel C. C. Washburn, ex-congressman and entrepreneur extraordinaire, was its commander. He reported for duty October 10, and by the end of the year had some 1,150 troopers drilling at Camp Washburn in Milwaukee, waiting for equipment, and thirsting for action. This brought to four the number of Camp Washburns where Union recruits were being trained by the end of 1861. The others were in Maine, Illinois, and Minnesota.9 For the next three and a half years, thanks to almost daily correspondence with brother Elihu, and thanks to Elihu's considerable influence in Washington, Cadwallader would be one of the most political of the many political officers in the Union Army.

* * *

In sharp contrast was the military career of former sea captain brother Sam Washburn, now in his sixth year of moldering in the wilds of Wisconsin at Cad's Waubeek lumbercamp. Sam was probably the physically toughest Washburn, less ambitious and less cerebral than his brothers, but just as independent and strong-minded. Whether hammering a square-rigged ship through an Atlantic gale or hammering a crew of hungover lumberjacks through the frozen woods, Sam carved his own path.

He is an enigma to the historian. He left far fewer papers than his siblings—perhaps because he did not wish to be compared with them, was not running for office, or was just too modest to believe that anything he did was worth memorializing. Sam did start a journal in 1860, but it was only a partial record of his experiences. In keeping with the habit of every sea captain to leave a log that was as pleasing as possible to the ship's owners, he omitted any reference to anything unhappy.

There were problems at Waubeek, and, beset by creditors and the depressed lumber market, brother Cadwallader was greatly frustrated over the camp's management and production—supposedly Sam's area of responsibility. He shared his feelings with brother Elihu, who had also invested in the operation. In the summer of 1860, Sam took a few days off to go down to Galena and discuss his prospects with Elihu. When the war broke out, Sam's seagoing qualifications made him an obvious candidate for the navy, and so Elihu made another approach to Secretary Welles. The result was a commission for Sam, which came through in November of 1861. Sam was to report to the Brooklyn Navy Yard in December. He left the lumber camp immediately, and made a beeline for LeRoy, New

York, to show off his new buttons to Lorette Thompson.

On the way, he followed a family tradition and managed to stop over in Washington, where he met Mary Todd Lincoln. He was terse and direct in his opinion of her. "I don't like her a bit," he recorded. "She is a d———- Sesesh in my opinion."[10] As we have already learned, almost immediately after reporting to Brooklyn, Sam misinterpreted his leave, inadvertently went AWOL, and was actually dismissed from the navy. He had to be rescued by another Elihu intervention with Secretary Welles. Finally, Sam was assigned to the brand-new experimental gunboat *Galena*, then under construction at Mystic, Connecticut. He had the title of acting master, with responsibility for navigation and for the two forward deck guns, the biggest guns on the ship.

A design compromise from the beginning, the *Galena* was an abomination in the open sea. It was hoped she would do better in sheltered waters such as Chesapeake Bay and the James River. After fitting out in Brooklyn, the ship was found to be dangerously top-heavy. She nearly sank with all hands in a moderate sea on the way down to Norfolk—Sam wrote that she rolled so much that she took water in through her funnel. Nevertheless, except for the maverick *Monitor*, she was the newest thing the navy had seen in fifty years. She was even shown off to President Lincoln. On May 13, 1862, not long after the fall of Norfolk and the destruction of the Confederate naval base there, *Galena* was assigned to lead a flotilla up the James River toward Richmond, in a naval expedition loosely in support of General George McClellan's Peninsula Campaign.

It was an ill-starred trip. Probably undertaken mainly to show off the navy's might, the mission had little strategic justification and no military objective, other than to sow panic among the enemy civilian population—which it did. However,

Wash drawing of the gunboat Galena *as she appeared at Hampton Roads in 1862, before the action at Drewry's Bluff.* Galena *and* Monitor *were the first ironclad experiments undertaken by the U.S. Navy.* U. S. Naval Historical Center Photograph

the army never gave it any support from the land—probably was not even aware of its presence.

The first couple of days went well. With Sam plotting her path between the mudflats—all the buoys having been removed by the Confederates—*Galena* led the little fleet up the river, using her guns to scatter occasional artillery batteries and snipers on both banks. This was long before it occurred to anyone to coordinate operations between the army and the navy, and with every mile the little flotilla was another mile farther away from any support. It was not nearly as invincible as it looked.

Only seven miles short of Richmond, at a place called Drewry's Bluff, *Galena* met her judgment day and Sam had his appointment with hell. Just the night before the Union ships got there, the Confederates managed to block a narrow bend in the river with two sunken ships. They also managed to place a large battery of naval guns on the bluff commanding the site. They called it Fort Darling. Ironically, both the guns and the men operating them were battle-hardened veterans from the Confederate ironclad *Virginia*, recently scuttled near Norfolk to keep her out of Union hands. As *Galena* stopped to deal with the obstructions in the river, the big guns at the top of the hill opened fire. In minutes they had the range. Many of the Union guns could not be sufficiently elevated, and for four hours the two sides thundered away at each other. *Galena* definitely got the worst of it. Her armor plating, the weight of which had nearly caused her to capsize in the open sea, was not nearly thick enough to ward off the fire of the enemy's heavy guns. Hit forty-six times, her main deck was a shambles, and many men went down, including Sam, who took a glancing eight-inch solid shot off his hip and was briefly knocked into the scuppers. In his official report of the action, Admiral David Porter wrote, "The *Galena* was simply a slaughterhouse."[11] Finally, when ammunition ran low, the Union force had to back off and retreat down the river. *Galena*'s funnel looked like a nutmeg grater, and she had dozens of men dead and wounded. In addition, the ship's hull had suffered. Plates had been sprung, framing cracked in several places, and she was leaking.

Despite his pain, Sam was still on his feet and still full of fight. The nerve damage he suffered would eventually put him on crutches for the rest of his life, but for the moment he was able to stay at his post, and stay fighting mad, too. It showed in the hasty letter he scribbled to Elihu a few days later. During the battles of Glendale and Malvern Hill, he reported in an undated letter that "we shelled the sons of bitches for four hours yesterday afternoon and are all ready to give it to them again today."[12]

Despite the fact that Union soldiers and sailors were eager

Cleaned up for a visit by Matthew Brady shortly after the actions on the James River, Galena *still shows holes in her stack from Confederate cannonballs.* Courtesy Library of Congress

to fight, their general-in-chief was not. Beset by nameless fears and uncertainties, and recently trounced by Robert E. Lee at the Battle of Gaines Mill, Union commander George B. McClellan was a beaten man. Although Union forces actually repulsed Lee at Malvern Hill, McClellan's entire Peninsula Campaign was sinking, thanks to the psychological state of its commander. Sam Washburn was a personal witness.

In the middle of the battle of Malvern Hill, General McClellan signaled to be taken on board the *Galena*. For several hours, the general cruised the river, away from his headquarters, leaving his army to fend for itself. Awed and flattered by the presence of their overall commander, Sam and his shipmates did not at first realize the significance of McClellan's extraordinary visit. As was his habit from long years spent pleasing his owners in the merchant trade, Sam's official entries in *Galena*'s log were quite circumspect.

Given a few days to reflect, however, in private communications with both Elihu and Israel later, Sam left no doubt as to what he thought—that the general was terrified. Modern historians have been even less charitable, and McClellan's absence from the battlefield that day has recently been described as dereliction of duty worthy of court-martial.[13]

It is not known if Elihu passed Sam's incendiary information on to Lincoln, but all of the Washburns were glad when Lincoln removed McClellan from his command four months later. Following Antietam, Israel went to a meeting of rebellious Northern governors in Altoona, Pennsylvania, aimed at forcing Lincoln to replace the popular general with someone more effective. He later went to Washington to make this argument personally with Lincoln, when he learned from Stanton and Seward that the order was going out to relieve the general that very evening. Israel wrote that the news made him feel "like one raised from the dead."[14] The next day, en route to a last visit with Maine troops in Virginia, Israel watched without comment as the departing general's train passed by on the other track.

* * *

As the war ground on and the casualties mounted, most civilians were far more resolute than were the military professionals in charge of their armies.

No one was more resolute than Cadwallader Washburn— or more frustrated by his commanding officers. He turned down an opportunity to join Grant's staff right after Grant's brilliant victory at Fort Donelson, because he was disgusted by the political infighting he saw there. "You can see contemptible jeal-

Extracts from Log Book of U.S.S. Galena.
June 30th 1862.

From 12 to 4.— Laying at anchor at Carter's Wharf. At 1 o'clock P.M. several army officers came on board. At 3 P.M. heard heavy firing near and to windward, and sent boat with army officer on shore, which returned immediately. _Loring._

From 4 to 6 P.M.— At 4.45 weighed anchor and steamed up river with Gen. McClellan and Staff on board. Heard heavy cannonading up river. At 5 o'clock got under weigh and steamed up river and commenced shelling the enemy. S. B. Washburn.

* * * * * * *

July 1st 1862.

From 12 to 4 A.M.— Commenced with light breeze and clear weather. At 3.45 Gen. McClellan sent for a boat, which was sent on shore immediately. At 4 o'clock Commander Rodgers went on shore in Gig. S. B. Washburn.

* * * * * From

Two entries from the logbook of Galena by Sam Washburn for June 30 and July 1 noted the presence of General McClellan on board but tactfully omitted any reason for his being there.

COURTESY LIBRARY OF CONGRESS

Colonel C. C. Washburn and his staff of the 2nd Wisconsin Cavalry
Regiment. The picture was taken while they were waiting for
horses at Benton Barracks, St. Louis. Washburn had just declined
an invitation to join Grant's staff.
Courtesy Washburn Library

ousy sticking out all around," he wrote Elihu.[15] Colonel
Washburn preferred to stay with his regiment, despite the unre-
lenting animosity of the new department commander, Major
General Henry W. Halleck, who hated all political officers.
The Second Wisconsin was shuffled off to several ill-conceived
and incompetently led campaigns in Arkansas, Louisiana, and
Texas. Although these campaigns produced great frustration,
anger, and illness for Cadwallader, his honest and efficient
management eventually came to the notice of two important
figures, Ulysses S. Grant and William T. Sherman.

Cad's stream of confidential reports to his brother Elihu

may have been responsible for the removal of many incompetent or corrupt commanders in the Union's western armies. In Halleck's eyes, this was meddling of the highest order. For the straightforward Cad Washburn, as for his brothers, wrongs had to be corrected, no matter whose ox got gored in the process.

Cad's three and a half years of letters to Elihu during the war form a fiery trail—in front of, at, and behind the front lines. In them, the reader can follow the businessman's stubborn struggle for efficiency, his resoluteness, and his honesty. The reader can also feel the author's impatience, frustration, rage, and despair. As the months pass, and Cad gets promoted to successively greater responsibilities, one can also sense an increasing sense of accomplishment and pride, as well as a growing political wisdom about picking his battles. Here are some excerpts: From Grant's headquarters at Fort Donelson, "All that is wanted is vigor and common sense to end this war. I see little of either." On the march in Missouri, "Any man that keeps a keg of brandy in his tent is not in my opinion a fit man for commander." After a cavalry raid across Mississippi, "I stampeded the entire rebel army." Requesting a certain lieutenant he wanted as quartermaster, "I feel very anxious to get a man appointed who has some *snap* to him, one who will not lie in bed one half the day and drink whiskey the other half." In his whole life, never did Cadwallader Washburn leave a better summation of himself than in this single line. To his dying day, no one had more "snap to him" than C. C. Washburn himself.

As months of isolation and physical illness combined to wear him down, his patience grew ever shorter. From the swamps of northern Arkansas, he wrote, "It was a crime to send General Gorman here. [He has] not a grain of common sense...utter incompetency..." and, "His staff officers among whom are two sons, are openly charged with bribery and corruption of the basest kind." After the fall of Vicksburg, he wrote, "the delays among the powers that be try me beyond measure. I have no expectations that any man not a West Pointer will have any but a subordinate position in this war. Many things make me sick, but none more so than the contemptible imbecility that characterizes the management of this whole army…. The public are constantly deceived." From a sandbar off the coast of Texas, he wrote of the "incompetent management of transportation" and "I am vexed at the want of push in this army." Of General Banks's Department of the Gulf, "the truth is that no one can conceive of the imbecility and profligacy of that department." In command at last in Memphis, he called his predecessor, General Stephen Hurlbut, Elihu's old rival from northern Illinois, "a drunken, corrupt scoundrel." The day after almost being captured in one of General Nathan Bedford Forrest's most audacious cavalry raids, he passed off the incident with the comment, "It was a miracle I was not killed." He then went on for two pages about what he thought much more important: his battles with corrupt cotton buyers, that he was "in constant hot water fighting rascals," and Treasury Secretary Salmon P. Chase had "the biggest lot of scalawags the world affords." Later he wrote, "I tell you that there is not to exceed one honest man connected with the Treasury Department in the Mississippi Valley." Regarding another commander, he wrote, "I never knew a man who was such an infernal stench in the nostrils of all men as this man [General N. J. T.] Dana…a petty tyrant without principal or ability…corruption in high places…oppressive misuse of military power."[16]

We will never know the full impact of these diatribes, because both Elihu and Lincoln were discreet when it came to politically charged personnel decisions. But we know that Cadwallader did escape Bank's disastrous Red River campaign, that Hurlbut was removed, that Dana was transferred, and that, five weeks after Cad wrote Elihu about the abovementioned "scalawags," Lincoln finally accepted Treasury Secretary Chase's resignation from his cabinet.[17]

Because of Elihu's proximity to Lincoln, most of Cad's notes probably produced removals and transfers that justified General Halleck's worst fears about political appointees. They also no doubt added immensely to the efficiency and integrity of the Military District of Western Tennessee.

Although he missed the heat of a major battle, Cad Washburn's first two years in the war did have some high points. He missed the Shiloh battle as his Second Wisconsin Cavalry was getting equipped in St. Louis. They just missed the Pea Ridge battle in southwest Missouri, and their invasion of Arkansas fizzled due to bad weather, poor roads, supply mix-ups, and feisty Confederate opposition. Cad and his troopers straggled into Helena, on the Mississippi River south of Memphis, after weeks in the Arkansas backcountry. After getting the supply stream running smoothly again, he found himself promoted to brigadier general. Cad led a big cavalry raid across the river into Mississippi, taking 2,000 troopers across the Tallahatchie and leaving a wide trail of burned cotton, torn-up railroad track, and scattered Confederate opposition all the way to Abbeville.

With Halleck promoted to Washington, General Washburn took part in some of the frustrating early stages of Grant's campaign against Vicksburg. Despite his own illness and exhaustion, during the spring of 1863 his Wisconsin lumberjacks cleared miles of obstructions from the Yazoo Pass, but were frustrated by poor naval support and well-placed Confederate defenses. Washburn was promoted to major general and commanded a blocking force during the final stages of the siege of Vicksburg. Though he saw no action, he succeeded in keeping Confederate General Joseph Johnson from

Washburn statue at Vicksburg
COURTESY OF THE NATIONAL PARK SERVICE

making any effort to relieve the besieged city. Immediately after Vicksburg, in the wake of Grant's removal of General John McClernand, Washburn was given temporary command of the XIII Corps and transferred to Banks's Department of the Gulf. In recognition of his service, a statue of Major General Washburn stands on the Vicksburg battlefield today.

After the Vicksburg victory, although hoping for a campaign against Mobile, General Washburn was instead redirected to two poorly conceived, poorly supplied, and poorly led expeditions in Louisiana and Texas. Both efforts provided classic confrontations between incompetent Union leadership and extremely competent, if outnumbered, Confederate opposition. In the first, the so-called Bayou Teche Campaign, Union commander Nathaniel P. Banks (who has been called the second most important politician after Lincoln himself) was humiliated by Confederate Richard Taylor (a son of former president Zachary Taylor) in several actions across the bayou country of southern Louisiana. In one of them, the timely arrival of Washburn's troops at Grand Coteau, south of Opelousas, probably saved Banks's Fourth Division under General Burbridge from a serious defeat.

Following that effort, Washburn spent pointless weeks in blowing sand and biting fleas along the coast of Texas. This was a second assignment under Banks—one that wound up on Matagorda Island off the Texas coast in the wake of a spectacular Union repulse at Sabine Pass. This adventure was marked by huge supply foul-ups, timid naval support, and absolutely no action against the enemy. Alternately battling swamp fever, cotton speculators, and corrupt or incompetent commanding officers, Cad was finally granted some leave in 1864. He used it to attend to business affairs in Wisconsin, to come East to put his two daughters into school, and to campaign for a better assignment. He came up with a good one.

With Grant's blessing, Sherman put Washburn in charge of the District of Western Tennessee, with headquarters in Memphis. His predecessor, Stephen Hurlbut, had proved ineffective, but Washburn was the right man for the job. His major assignment was to confront the Confederacy's legendary cavalryman, Nathan Bedford Forrest, and to keep him away from the right flank of Sherman's new campaign, just then starting south toward Atlanta.

Five days before Washburn's arrival, Forrest's Confederates had carried out the bloody capture of the Union bastion at Fort Pillow fifty miles above Memphis, during which the casualties among black Union defenders were unnaturally high. Accusations and counter-accusations sprinkled a fiery correspondence between Washburn and Forrest all that summer.

For most of the next eighteen months, although never to command troops in battle, Washburn carried out his mission.

Despite a setback at the battle of Brice's Crossroads, and a mixed result the following month at Tupelo, Washburn's forces kept Forrest's Confederate cavalry away from Sherman's right flank in Georgia. Even more important, Washburn brought to a halt the huge and illegal cotton-for-supplies trade that was flourishing across the lines up and down the Mississippi.

As Elihu had found out in his investigations into crooked contractors in St. Louis, not every Northerner shared either the Washburns' integrity or their devotion to the high ideals of the Union cause. Many viewed the war as an unparalleled opportunity for profit. Thanks to the Union blockade of Southern ports, in warehouses and on wharves all along the Mississippi and its tributaries, thousands of unsold bales of Southern cotton continued to pile up. If not appropriated outright as spoils of war, a single bale could be bought for less than $50, or swapped for that amount in military stores. It could then be sold for ten times that much to eager buyers all over the North. All that stood between these bales and the profits that could be made from them were a few unsupervised Union military officers. The occupying army was the law. Often accompanied by unscrupulous relatives, many Union commanders and Treasury officials up and down the Mississippi were unable to withstand the temptation. The fact that they were trading with the enemy at the same time that the enemy was shooting at their soldiers seemed to escape their attention. It did not escape the attention of either Cadwallader or Sam Washburn, however.

Stopping this trade in Memphis was Cadwallader's greatest contribution to the Union war effort. There is a great irony in this, because no Washburn spent his life in the search for business opportunity the way Cadwallader did. Indeed, as he took command, his business eye saw plenty of opportunity all around him. Shortly after his arrival at Memphis in 1864, he wrote

Elihu that "I have taken pains to ascertain the probable amount of trade from here that goes into rebel lines, and I am satisfied that it will reach $36,000,000 a year."[18] This was far more than the total of what supplies a few Confederate blockade runners were still able to get through the tightening Union blockade of Southern ports. Just two years earlier, brother Israel had been able to raise, train, equip, and send off ten whole regiments in Maine for $10 million. The significance of $36 million in critical stores and equipment for the Confederacy in 1864 was enormous. If the trade could be stopped, it would add materially to the hardships across all the Southern states, to say nothing of the shortages plaguing the Confederate army.

However, this trade was also important to businesses in the North. The burgeoning textile industry in New York and New England was in desperate need of this cotton, and they were well represented in Washington. To cut the trade off would require not only resolute and incorruptible leadership on the ground, but also significant political influence in the Congress.

General Washburn had all of this. On May 8, 1864, he wrote Elihu, "I will send a copy of the trade order as soon as issued. Ben Wade [outspoken senator from Ohio] said he would back me. I shall hear a howl that will rend the welkin when the order comes out. Get Wade to offer a resolution, if you can, approving it as the policy to be pursued."[19]

The order went out May 10, to be effective five days later. Four days after that, Cad issued a second order, closing the Mississippi to trade in the region and backing it up by ordering a federal gunboat to arrest anyone on the river found trading with the enemy. There were immediate howls of protest from "certain merchants" in town, and immediate pressure was brought to bear in Washington to override the general's order. Elihu got letters that the order "has been like a bombshell in the enemy's camp."[20]

Congress followed up Cad's orders with a bill that Lincoln signed on June 28, but unfortunately it included a big loophole for special permits to be issued to certain Treasury agents. This wasn't closed until Elihu's Commerce Committee heard testimony that one Treasury agent had purchased some 930,000 bales of cotton from sixty-one different persons in less than three months, and that ships loaded with meat, salt, and sugar had sailed from New York directly to regions in Virginia and North Carolina nearest to the Confederate armies. Largely due to Elihu's pressure, both Treasury Secretary Chase and the politically powerful Union general Benjamin F. Butler resigned or were removed by January 1865.

As a result, the South's major source of supplies was shut off, and a new moral tone was brought to the Union command along the Mississippi. It was a triumph of Yankee rectitude, and a body blow to Southern logistics—and morale. Within ten months of the order, staring at starvation, the last forces of the Confederacy surrendered.

The trade order did not bring a happy result for its author— at least not right away. Probably at Halleck's urging, Cadwallader was replaced at Memphis by the hated General N. J. T. Dana. Cad, however, accepted the transfer and reported quietly back to Vicksburg. He was full of criticism for Dana, but wisely willing to bide his time. In less than two months, Grant reversed Halleck, transferred Dana out of Memphis, and brought Washburn back in. In a note to Halleck, he described Washburn as "one of the best administrative officers we have" and noted that he "will effectually stop supplies being sent through our lines to the enemy wherever he is."[21] Grant's mind was on winning the war, and he fully appreciated the contributions Cadwallader could make behind the lines to this end.

Cad's final months in Memphis were his finest. Trade with the enemy was halted, and he was even able to score a victory against the Treasury Department. The *New York Times* reported on March 9 that he had "ordered the arrest of the Chief Clerk in the office of Mr. Ellert, Treasury Agent, for the purchase of cotton."[22]

When the war ended in April, Washburn was feted at banquets in both Vicksburg and Memphis. At La Grange, forty miles east of Memphis, he gave a farewell address that was attended by 10,000 people. A year later, Elihu visited Memphis on congressional business in connection with the Memphis riots of 1866. He found that his brother was still universally praised and admired on all sides for his even-handed administration there. As with Israel's governorship of Maine, and Elihu's increasing fiscal responsibilities in Congress, Cadwallader's wartime career ended with public praise, no hint of shady dealing, and no missing money.

* * *

Two additional stories about Cadwallader Washburn's war should be told. During his daring raid on Memphis in August 1864, Forrest's cavalry came within seconds of capturing General Washburn one night—he was forced to flee in his nightshirt, so the story went. Later, Steven Hurlbut, the political general Washburn had replaced, famously groused, "At least I was able to keep Forrest out of Tennessee. Washburn couldn't keep him out of his bedroom." As this untrue remark circulated, so did the story that Hurlbut himself escaped capture that night only because he was visiting a certain widow lady in the town.[23]

All this furnished local laughs, but Cadwallader must have been much more satisfied by something else that was passed on to him. Forrest's boss, Confederate general Steven D. Lee, was rumored to have said that Washburn was the only federal commander in Memphis that he couldn't buy.

Even after the war ended, Cadwallader fought injustice in

the army. Some of his old troopers from the Second Wisconsin, with a few more months of their original enlistments left to run, were caught up in a bizarre expedition to dusty Texas during the summer of 1865 under flamboyant George Armstrong Custer, the already-famous "Boy General." One history of the regiment called the trip "a great picnic expedition for General Custer, his wife, his father, his brother, his staff, and the wives of one or two of the officers." 24 The men, who had been fighting across Mississippi and Arkansas since 1862, and whose enlistments were to expire in the fall, were not enthusiastic enough for the twenty-five-year-old major general. His treatment of them included public punishments, drumhead court-martials, and even a public execution. The troops thought it verged on the inhuman. When their reports got back to Cad, now a civilian in La Crosse, he immediately informed Elihu. Grant, still commander of all the Union armies, ordered that Custer be court-martialed. Custer escaped—one of his many escapes—thanks to the protection of his regional commander, General Philip Sheridan, another impetuous cavalryman with a volatile temper.

Eleven years later, when word came of Custer's death at Little Bighorn, in some quarters of western Wisconsin there was little regret at the news.

* * *

Brother Sam was transferred from the shot-up and leaky *Galena* in 1863 to Admiral Farragut's blockading fleet in the Gulf. There he was at last promoted to acting lieutenant and put in charge of a small squadron to interdict cotton and sugar smuggling along the Louisiana bayous. It was an independent command—the kind of situation where all the Washburns flourished—and Sam's little group broke up several smuggling operations in the backcountry. Oblivious to the fact that he was deep in enemy territory, he, too, expressed moral outrage at

Acting Lieutenant Samuel B. Washburn
COURTESY WASHBURN LIBRARY

the attitudes of the locals. In a rare letter to Elihu, he observed that not one man in ten along the whole Atchafalaya basin was an honest man—a ratio about the same as Cadwallader was finding among treasury agents in Memphis. From the halls of Congress, down the wide Mississippi, to the bayous of Louisiana, the Washburns never lost their moral compass. Through a combination of willpower and military might, they slowly brought begrudging order to their unruly surroundings.

With hostilities ended, Cad resigned his commission and returned to Wisconsin in May 1865 to resume his business affairs. The revival of his political fortunes, as well as the high regard of his fellow citizens, was demonstrated when they easily reelected him to his old seat in Congress the following year.

Sam's discharge came a little later, in October, and he, too, returned to Wisconsin. With the payments he received from

Cad for his share of the Waubeek operation, Sam and his family went west into Minnesota to try the lumber business there. Alone of the Washburns, Sam carried a permanent physical reminder of his war service. The nerve damage to his hip would grow progressively worse—a constant source of pain that would eventually cripple him.

* * *

Like Cadwallader, Elihu also ended the war with many satisfactions. None was greater than persuading Lincoln and the Congress to make Grant a three-star general and put him in charge of all the Union armies. Largely due to Elihu's tenacity and unwavering faith in his protégé, the Union Army finally got a commander who was as determined as were the governors who provided the troops. The war would now be firmly directed—from the field rather than from the capital—until it was won.

Elihu was in on both the beginning of the end and the actual end of the war in Virginia. He was present in May 1864 as Grant kicked off his final great effort at the Battles of the Wilderness and Spotsylvania Courthouse. At Grant's invitation, he accompanied the general for seven days amid the crash of battle in the smoking and bloody thickets of this epic struggle. When he returned to Washington, Washburne delivered to General Halleck Grant's famous letter proposing "to fight it out on this line if it takes all summer."

Elihu himself returned to the political battlefields. All that summer, he worked hard for Lincoln's, and his own, successful reelections. Part of this effort included getting furloughs for the troops to go home and vote. Sherman's military successes on the ground around Atlanta, made possible in part by brother Cad's actions against Forrest in Tennessee, also contributed to the critical support that the election provided for the Lincoln administration.

As the war approached its final days, Elihu wanted to be in on the end of it, and Grant gave him a blanket pass that would allow this. Word reached Elihu in Galena of the unexpected fall of Richmond on April 3, 1865, and he left immediately for Washington. By train and ship and train he arrived at the end of the rails south of Petersburg. In a downpour, he pushed on by horse for six hours through the mud to Burkeville. Exhausted, he made thirty more miles in an ambulance to Farmville, arriving at 10:30 P.M. A final heroic journey in terrible weather put him at Grant's tent just before 10:00 P.M. on April 10, near Appomattox. There he learned that Lee had signed a surrender document at noontime that day. Grant, Sherman, and Meade did not wait around for the actual surrender of the army, but Grant provided a cavalry escort so that Washburne could go the MacLean House to see that ceremony, which began at 6:00 A.M. on the 12th. Thus it was that Elihu, after an incredible trip halfway across the country, was the only civilian to stand with Maine's General Joshua Chamberlain as Lee's army stacked its arms.

Afterwards, he spent the long ride back toward Richmond persuading Confederate general John B. Gordon of Lincoln's moderate intentions for dealing with the South after the war. No sooner did they reach the former Confederate capital, however, than there came the tragic news of Lincoln's assassination.

Of all the tragedies of the war, this was the most far-reaching in its effect. All plans about moderate reconstruction were suddenly off. The radicals, eventually including Washburne himself, set about a fifteen-year course of revenge. This course included the near-impeachment of Lincoln's Tennessee-born successor, Andrew Johnson, and the imposition of "carpetbagger" rule on the Southern states, which in turn sparked a white racial backlash that isolated the region politically and economically from the rest of the country for more than a century.

Elihu's Civil War ended with him in the long cortege accompanying Lincoln's body across a shocked and grieving country. The magnificent administration that had started with six out of seven brothers in Washington ended with a single brother at a graveside in Illinois. Elihu was a pallbearer as the assassinated president was laid to rest in Springfield.

* * *

Back in Maine, the war's end found oldest brother Israel in a completely different job. Exhausted by his tumultuous years as governor—between raising an army, doing battle with government bureaucrats, and keeping peace in the legislature—he had declined his party's nomination for a third term in the governor's office, though he could have won it easily.

He left office in January 1863, and later that spring a grateful Lincoln appointed him collector of customs in the city of Portland—the highest-paying federal job in the state. Israel felt ill-qualified for the job and at first declined it. But friends like Senator William Pitt Fessenden urged him to try it, and eventually Israel accepted.

Israel Jr.'s elevation to the Portland collectorship had several happy outcomes. The post paid three times as much as had the governorship, and so for the first time he began to enjoy financial comfort, as well as build important connections across the commercial world of northern New England. He moved to Portland, built a lovely home in the Western Promenade section of town, and wound up overseeing the greatest period of commercial growth in the city's history. Sid was there with him to celebrate the surrender at Appomattox. Sid wrote that "there was such a hurrah all night that we did not get to bed till almost morning."[25]

With the support of friends such as Senator Fessenden and Secretary of State William H. Seward, to say nothing of his

John Stobart's painting of the bark Halcyon *leaving Portland Harbor in 1876 has Washburn significance in two ways. First,* Halcyon *is about the size of the many vessels that Samuel sailed back and forth across the Atlantic in the 1850s; second, the customhouse, shown on the right with its two cupolas, was completed in 1872 and was Israel Jr.'s greatest achievement during his fourteen years as collector at Portland.*
COURTESY JOHN STOBART

brother Elihu and his own competent record, Israel served as Portland's collector of customs for an unprecedented fourteen years. During his administration, the port of Portland experienced an explosion in activity. By 1875, his last year, trade through the port topped $50 million, and he had sixty-one people working for him.[26]

Behind him in Augusta, Israel left a political vacuum that was immediately filled by that formidable operator, James G. Blaine. Blaine had never trusted Washburn, mainly because the principled War Governor would not be controlled by any political "boss." Blaine had a long memory, and the cadet incident of 1857, as well as the embarrassments of 1860, still rankled.

It wasn't long before Blaine was able to exact his revenge. His absolute control of the Republican-dominated legislature in Maine after the war enabled him to crush Israel's hopes for a seat in the U.S. Senate on several occasions—the same fate suffered by his equally principled brothers Elihu in Illinois and Cadwallader in Wisconsin. Blaine's power also led to Israel's losing the Portland collector's job in 1876. Washburn, whose inclination was not to "make a fuss," privately thought that Blaine was unfit for any of the jobs Blaine was later given. Perhaps it was fortunate that Israel died in 1883. He never had to watch as Blaine—then mired in controversy—cost Washburn's beloved Republicans the presidency in 1884.

* * *

The price that Maine paid in the war was more than the men she lost and the power she gave up. The war also accelerated the flow of emigration out of the state. In the Washburns' hometown of Livermore, the 1890 census revealed a population of only 1,151. Ten years later, it was still decreasing, and the 1909 Town Register listed the 1900 population of the town as 1,125.

Looking back on the Washburns in the war, one sees them, in and out of uniform, at many key junctures in the struggle. Their weapons ranged from political oratory to naval cannon, their troops from lumberjacks to jack-tars, their influence from congressional strong arm to Yankee moral integrity.

At the beginning, they worked hard to bring about the political revolution that brought on the war. Then, from the dusty streets of Minneapolis to the woods of Aroostook County, they labored to raise the troops that provided the Union with its army. They took advantage of political appointments that resulted from that troop-raising, and at the same time worked tirelessly to root out the incompetents and the corrupt from these same political appointments. With Lincoln, they saw early that Union success would depend on military competence as well as moral high principle, and from Altoona to Vicksburg they never ceased striving toward both these goals. In the end, from Augusta to Appomattox, they saw the struggle through to victory and a new dawn for a united country.

Much has been said and written about unbending, sober Yankee pilgrims who imposed their will on an unruly nineteenth-century world. The Washburns were prototypical of this breed, bringing a stamp of certainty and steadfast integrity wherever they went, both before and during the Civil War.

Some of them, particularly the two youngest sons, Charles and William, did this with more than a little arrogance and much less consistency than their older siblings. However, in a time of unprecedented crisis and confusion for the country, this Washburn certainty was precisely what was most needed.

The war, with all the pain and cost it brought to the nation, was the right time for the Washburns. Looking back on them from the perspective of 150 years, one can see wisdom in their integrity, and value in their unwavering confidence that they and the country were on the right track.

With the war over, the Union saved, the question of slavery settled, and a much-empowered central government in place, the needs and priorities of the country changed. Economic opportunity replaced the desire for strong government leadership. For many, economic opportunity relaxed the standards of personal behavior as well. Some of the Washburns would find themselves out of step with this new world. For them, there would be great highs and great lows. Some, like Israel, Elihu, Cadwallader, and William, would flourish. Some, like Sam, Charles, and Sid, would not.

Before the most successful commercial experiences of the clan, however, unexpected adventures overtook two of the Washburn brothers in foreign lands. With little preparation and no relevant experience, they found themselves alone and isolated in the midst of unexpected war, siege, and famine, many thousands of miles away from all that was familiar to them. Their stubbornness had greatly different effects in two very different environments.

1. *Maine Sunday Telegram*, May 28, 1911.

2. William B. Jordan, *Maine in the Civil War* (Portland, ME: Maine Historical Society, 1976), 72.

3. Washburn to Consul P.M. Moore, June 8, 1861, Maine State Archives, Washburn Collection, Folder 3.

4. Chetlain, 278.

5. Webb, *Impassioned Brothers*, 61.

6. An excellent description of this pivotal meeting is contained in Lloyd Lewis's, *Captain Sam Grant* (Boston: 1950), 394–400.

7. Chetlain, 65, 70.

8. Washburne to Lincoln, October 17, 1861 (Lincoln Papers, LC).

9. Mark Washburne, vol. 2, 14.

10. SBW journal for December 14, 1861 (Washburn Library).

11. David D. Porter, *The Naval History of the Civil War* (New York:1886), 357 ff.

12. SBW to EBW, dated only 1862 (Washburn Library).

13. Stephen W. Sears, *Controversies and Commanders* (Boston: 1999), 17.

14. IW personal journal, vol. 2, (Washburn Library), 121–25.

15. CCW to EBW, March 5, 1862 (Washburne Papers, LC).

16. Quoted from EBW, March 1862 through February 1865 (Washburn Papers, LC).

17. Doris Kearns Goodwin, *Team of Rivals*, (New York: 2005), 621, 631. Cad's letter to EBW was dated May 16, 1864 (EBW Papers, vol. 1, LC)

18. CCW to EBW, May 16, 1864 (from EBW Papers, LC)

19. CCW to EBW, May 8, 1864 (From EBW Papers, LC)

20. Russell K. Nelson, "Early Life and Congressional Career of Elihu B. Washburne," PhD dissertation for the University of North Dakota, 1953, 391–96.

21. Grant to Halleck, February 4, 1865, from Mark Washburne, 436.

22. Mark Washburne, vol. 2, 439.

23. Brian Steele Wills, *Nathan Bedford Forrest: The Convederacy's Greatest Calvaryman* (University of Kansas Press, 1992), 242.

24. Emmet C. West, *History and Reminiscences of the Second Wisconsin Cavalry Regiment* (Wisconsin State Register Print, 1904), 31.

25. ASW to Gratiot Washburne, April 10, 1865 (Washburn Library).
26. Kerck Kelsey, *Israel Washburn, Maine's Little Known Giant of the Civil War*, (Rockport, ME: 2004), 158.

———•—•———

SEVEN

Under Siege in
Paraguay and Paris

IN THE SIX YEARS THAT FOLLOWED the American Civil War, there were two other bloody conflicts on opposite sides of the globe. One was in the remote interior of South America, the other in the middle of Europe. As it turned out, a Washburn brother was squarely in the center of each. The reasons for these two far-flung Washburns being where they were when they were, and their performance while there, varied considerably.

As with military appointments, the appointment of most American representatives to foreign countries was part of a system of political rewards that had been in place for many years. There were important differences between political appointments to the military and political appointments to the diplomatic corps, however. With a war on, military appointments carried with them the prestige of military rank, and a hoped-for chance at military glory. Recipients such as Cadwallader Washburn were able to use them to revive sagging fortunes at home.

Diplomatic appointments, on the other hand, provided the party in power with the opportunity to repay political debts or promises, as well as to banish unwanted stalwarts to places where they could do little harm, and where they would be well away from causing further damage or embarrassment for their patrons. On the other hand, for some recipients, these assignments provided positions of comfort and prestige, rest for the weary, and an opportunity for family adventure. Lincoln's 1862 removal of the corrupt and incompetent Simon Cameron as secretary of war to be minister to Russia in far-off St. Petersburg was a famous example of the former. Grant's appointment of Elihu Washburne to France was an example of the latter. Less well known was Lincoln's appointment of Charles Ames Washburn to Paraguay.

Charles had been in Washington since December 1860. His ceremonial duty as a presidential elector completed, he put aside his earlier disdain for governmental employment and joined the army of office-seekers that swarmed over the new administration. He was not too proud to ask his brothers for help. Israel's good friend William E. Seward was now secretary of state, and Elihu was close to the new president. However, there was serious opposition to Charles from Californians who feared he was untrustworthy to the point of instability, and who had blocked his previous efforts to obtain appointments as collector of customs or as director of the federal mint back in San Francisco.

Growing increasingly frustrated and impatient, Charles waited in the capital for five long months. Finally, Lincoln, who had little concern about South America but a very keen concern about how much he would need Elihu Washburne's support in the House in the months ahead, appointed Charles as U.S. commissioner to the South American country of Paraguay. Although no paper trail was left to mark the connections, that appointment, and brother William's appointment as Minnesota surveyor general in St. Paul a few weeks earlier, were the first indications of brother Elihu's influence with Lincoln. Elihu's trail behind the scenes, often encouraged by brother Cadwallader's incendiary letters from the front, would end with General Grant's election to the presidency and his own appointment to France.

Charles was commissioned by Secretary of State William H. Seward on June 13, 1861, six weeks before the first Battle of Bull Run. Gideon Welles made his spiteful diary entry, and Charles Ames Washburn had a job at last. He, with his brothers Elihu and Sam and their friend Seward, would all come back to bedevil Secretary of the Navy Welles in the years ahead.

Who was this Washburn who inspired so much antipathy and mistrust among his freewheeling California colleagues? Now almost forty years of age and still unhappily a bachelor, Charles Ames Washburn was shorter than his brother Elihu but shared his most impressive feature: a pair of light blue eyes. He looked out upon the world from behind a full beard with an attitude both innocent and suspicious. He was the only Washburn sibling who was not cleanshaven. Ever quick to take offense, he was a Puritan idealist with little tolerance for human imperfection. To strangers, he came across as much too sure of himself, and much too sure of his moral superiority in a world of scoundrels. In fact, he was deeply sensitive to personal attack. When challenged, his habit was to fill the world with words—some well chosen and some not so well chosen. Children loved him, but as his nation's representative to a country run by one of the world's most absolute dictators, he would be a disaster.

Probably the only reason that Secretary of State Seward felt he needed a representative in Paraguay at all was to continue trying to collect a $500,000 debt the country owed to the influential Sprague family of Rhode Island. This was the price tag for several manufacturing enterprises built in Paraguay during the 1850s by Sprague's United States and Paraguay Navigation Company. They had been seized by Paraguayan dictator Carlos

Antonio López without compensation in 1858. A previous effort by President Buchanan in 1859 to collect the debt—an early "big stick" expedition that involved twenty-three U.S. Navy ships—had been frustrated by low water on the Paraguay River. Arbitrators meeting in Washington in 1860 had decided that Paraguay owed the United States nothing. Adding to the tension, in 1854 a U.S. Navy survey vessel had been fired on by a Paraguayan fort, and an American sailor had been killed. The U.S. Congress had taken six years to recognize Paraguay's independence, and Washburn was to be the first American representative there since that recognition. It was a murky situation, and Charles was ill prepared to make it anything but murkier.

Paraguay in the 1860s was one of the more remote countries on earth. It had a subtropical climate and was verdant and forested, with a chain of hills to the east and a mighty river down the middle. To the south, along this river, there was a considerable area of lagoons and marshes. The country's only access to and from the outside world was via a long trip down the Paraña and Paraguay rivers through territory controlled by three other countries: Argentina, Uruguay, and Brazil. A hundred miles below Paraguay's capital, Asunción, the marshes began. There, at a sharp bend where the river narrowed, at a place called Humaitá, British engineers had assisted the Paraguayans in constructing a mile-long complex of artillery batteries for the purpose of controlling all access from the south. Navigation rights on the river were vital to all four countries that depended on it. In the 1860s there was literally no practical way of getting to Paraguay, or to Brazil's Mato Grosso province above it, except by the river. Use of the river was therefore a subject of continuing tension between the two countries. Since declaring independence in 1811, Paraguay had been characterized by one-man rule and isolation. Paraguayan society was more cohesive than its larger neighbors, thanks to the constant fear of being swallowed up—a fear which Paraguayan leadership had used to build up its military. In Paraguay, the president was the state, and by 1862, Paraguay's army was by far the largest in the region.

Charles's diplomatic career started with a rap on the knuckles. Shortly after he was appointed, he made an unauthorized trip up to Rhode Island to talk to the investors there about their claim in Paraguay. As a result, he was late in leaving for his post and was fined by the State Department. This incident was similar to his brother Sam's unauthorized disappearance six months later—right after he reported for duty with the navy. Both these independent-minded Washburns were sure they knew better than the government that had just hired them.

The most common route to Paraguay was via London and Buenos Aires. Charles finally arrived in Buenos Aires in October 1861, and shortly afterwards was taken up the river on the U.S. gunboat *Pulaski* to Asunción. The U.S. Navy would not again be so cooperative with him.

The thousand-mile trip took two weeks. When Charles at last stepped ashore in the capital, he found it a dusty town with a population of about 20,000. Its adobe houses sat in sharp contract with several modern stone buildings: a cathedral, an arsenal, a shipyard, a roofless opera house, an impressive railroad station, and an enormous presidential palace. Most were unfinished. The roads were unpaved and there was no drainage—perhaps the rainy climate made sewer systems a low priority. The country had two languages, Spanish and Guarani, and there is no evidence that Minister Washburn on his arrival spoke either.

The people of Paraguay were mostly *mestizos*, a blend of native Guaranis and Spanish colonials. Most of the population tended farms and ranches in the countryside while an elite of landowners and businessmen was centered in Asunción. The main products of the country were cattle and yerba matte tea.

Paraguay's neighbors were in various stages of violent nation-building. To the north and east, the enormous Portuguese-speaking empire of Brazil was made up of a highly stratified society governed by an entrenched elite that still sponsored, and depended upon, slavery. The government was centered around this elite, in the person of the emperor, Dom Pedro the Second. To the south and west, the Spanish-speaking Republic of Argentina was a loose grouping of provinces whose recent history had been full of civil wars between the *porteño* forces of Buenos Aires, who had the money, and the fiercely independent caudillos of the pampas.

Further to the south, along the north shore of the River Plate estuary, most of the Banda Oriental area had been granted its independence as the nation of Uruguay in 1828, but remained a subject of contest between its two giant neighbors, Argentina and Brazil. Like Argentina, Uruguay was torn between town and country—represented by its two rival political parties, the Colorados (based in Montevideo—liberal and nationalist) and the Blancos (representing the country—conservative and independent). The ongoing rivalry between these two parties featured armed conflict more often than elections. Its violence was often sponsored by, and accompanied by the interference of, the two giant neighboring states.

Paraguay was in a bad neighborhood. It was a neighborhood that required sensitive leadership and careful diplomacy. What it got instead was suicidal leadership and bumbling diplomacy.

Historians, many weighed down with national biases, have not been kind to Charles Ames Washburn. Objective interpretation of his time in Paraguay is as difficult now as it was then. It is true that he was poorly suited for the furnace of sensitive egos, fiery tempers, arrogance, and pride among the newly born nation-states into which he was thrown. He could not be objective, had no finesse, and his kindnesses were clumsy and indiscreet. In his struggles to reach personal happiness in a miasma of fear and misunderstanding, he exhibited many all-too-human weaknesses. However, as a perceptive writer marooned in a foreign and hostile land, he also left a vivid record of a time and place where few Americans had ventured and little was known. And, as a stiff-backed Yankee like his brothers, he sometimes stuck out like a sore thumb.

Charles settled into a legation compound that resembled a large barracks. After a two-week wait, he had his first meeting with the dictator Carlos Antonio López. He apparently got off to a bad start with the Paraguayan leader. The corpulent presidente used the occasion to give the new commissioner a long list of complaints about the United States and Paraguay Navigation Company and its former agent. This individual was a colorful flim-flam man named Edward A. Hopkins, who had been expelled in 1854 due to romantic indiscretions with the wife of a prominent citizen of Asunción. López also felt resentful about the threats against him from the U.S. Navy. He warned Washburn that he, too, might be expelled unless a favorable outcome of the claim was reached.

Washburn reported the interview in a long letter—the first of many—to Secretary Seward. In it, he said that he thought López was prejudiced against Americans in the country. In a nation already subjected to more than a few arrogant Yankee adventurers, Washburn had an uphill climb from the start.

López now refused to discuss the subject of the navigation company at all, and Charles received word from the State Department to stay put to await developments. López became increasingly unavailable to Minister Washburn. Within three months, in letters to his brother Elihu, Charles was alternately hinting at gunboat diplomacy and inquiring about getting transferred to another country, perhaps neighboring Argentina.

With nothing much to do, and with his own country absorbed in its own great civil war at home, the months in Asunción slipped away uneventfully for the American representative. Despite the difficulties with López, the weather was for the most part pleasant, as were his associations with the people of Asunción.

He grew bored and lonely and susceptible to local liaisons, one of which may have even produced an illegitimate child. In 1871, after Charles had returned home in a flurry of controversy, his successor, General Martin T. McMahon, replied to one of Charles's intemperate letters to the newspapers about him. The general reported that, after Charles had left Paraguay, one day a woman brought a three-year-old child to the mission claiming that Charles was the father. Furthermore, when McMahon later asked Charles about it, he did not deny the accusation.[1]

Charles did spend a lot of his time during this period writing. By the time he left the country, he had completed one novel, started another, and was well underway with the first-ever national history of Paraguay.

In September 1862 Carlos López died. He was succeeded by his son, Francisco Solano López, who would be an even greater despot than his father. Charles's relations with Francisco were even worse than they had been with his father Carlos. Seventy years later, Charles's oldest daughter, Hester Howell, born during his appointment in Paraguay, wrote a description of Francisco that no doubt reflected family lore, since she had been only an infant when they left Paraguay. She described Francisco as "ignorant, vulgar, gross, a fat pot-bellied little man, who wanted to be a second Napoleon and rode a white horse, looking like a toad on a chopping block."[2]

The first months under Francisco were quiet. As the new
leader solidified his power in Paraguay, he continued a significant buildup of his military. He had agents purchasing arma-
ments in Europe, and even discussed the purchase of arms with
the American commissioner, which probably did nothing to
endear Washburn to any of Paraguay's neighbors.

Tensions increased steadily. War in Uruguay between
Argentina and Brazil was narrowly averted in 1863, but a
Brazilian naval invasion in 1864 resulted in a massacre of
Blanco forces at the Uruguayan city of Paysandu at year's end.
Another Brazilian force had occupied the capital of the
Uruguayan department of Cerro Largo in October. Alarmed at
these Brazilian incursions, and at the massacre of the forces he
wished to support, López sent a Paraguayan force of 10,000
men south and east across the upper Paraña and established a
camp in Missiones Province, an empty area claimed by both
Paraguay and Brazil.

The area was barely under the control of its respective governments. The borders were in dispute, and local caudillos were
loyal to the central governments only if they could control
them. Recent history had been full of revolutions and counter-
revolutions and struggles to the death between fiercely independent ranchers in the interior and nation-builders from the
coast. López, all too aware of the expansionist enthusiasms of
his neighbors, had been wooing individual caudillos in an effort
to encourage their ambitions in case Paraguay came under the
Brazilian gun and needed their support.

López was also sympathetic to the Blanco government that
was then running Uruguay. That government was the target of
threats by Brazil over Uruguay's efforts to tax Brazilians living
along their common border. Tensions were also long-running
between Paraguay and both Brazil and Argentina over use of
the river system that connected them.

Argentina was involved, too, in the Uruguayan imbroglio. She supported the Colorado opposition in Uruguay, the recent victors at Paysandu. This caused Brazil further concern about growing Argentine influence in the border areas. As the two behemoths jockeyed, Paraguay grew increasingly uneasy about its own security.

Rarely has an American representative appeared to be so unaware, or unwilling to admit, what was going on around him. Unlike his siblings, Charles seemed to have little appreciation of the "big picture." Perhaps lulled by the languid pace of life around him, he seemed to be oblivious of the power struggle between Brazil and Argentina, and of the roles of both Uruguay and Paraguay as buffer states between them. In addition, right there in Paraguay, he greatly underestimated López's hold on the Paraguayan people.

He seemed quite unaware that the most confusing, senseless, and merciless war that the hemisphere had ever seen was about to break out all around him.

When Brazilian cavalry invaded Uruguayan territory in October, López saw an opportunity to strengthen Paraguay's situation. Wishing to support the Blancos by distracting the Brazilians in Uruguay, and wanting to snatch various stockpiles of much-needed arms and stores, the president decided to attack Brazil in a completely different quarter. He sent his own armed force upstream from Asunción into the Brazilian province of Mato Grosso. On November 12 he also seized the Brazilian vessel *Marques de Olinda* on one of its regular trips up the river, and jailed the newly appointed Brazilian governor of Mato Grosso, who happened to be a passenger. He also sought to expel into the jungle the Brazilian ambassador to Paraguay, as well as the steamer's crew.

Charles's superiors at the State Department were as ignorant of the situation as he was and their attention was focused elsewhere—on keeping the British from recognizing the Confederacy. Communication was as slow as it was uninformed. On his own initiative, and with only humanitarian motives, Charles put off a scheduled home leave to intervene on behalf of the exiled Brazilian. He pleaded that the ambassador be allowed to leave by steamboat down the river. This was granted, but Charles earned the Paraguayan leader's resentment for meddling.

Charles's main attention now fixed on a more personal objective elsewhere. Despite the separation of over six thousand miles, he engaged in a determined effort to an end his long bachelorhood. The object of his attention was a somewhat vacuous young socialite he had met in New York named Sallie Cleaveland.

Oblivious to the war fever sweeping Asunción, and with Paraguayan invasion forces sweeping northward into Brazil, Minister Washburn now took his six-month leave to go home to marry Sallie. Stating that he didn't think the Brazilians would be ready to fight for another ten to twelve months, he left the capital on January 16, 1865. This was the day after López sent his force into the disputed area of Missiones Province to the south. Washburn must have sailed right past the smoking ruin of Paysandu, which stubborn Blanco defenders had only surrendered to the Brazilians two weeks earlier. He was back in the United States when López, for reasons still the subject of debate among historians, embarked on still another invasion, this one south along the river directly into the Argentine province of Corrientes.

The dictator perhaps hoped to spark another uprising among the caudillos against the government in Buenos Aires, but instead his move had the disastrous effect of forcing all of Paraguay's opponents together: Argentina in order to protect its northern provinces, Brazil in order to avenge the Mato

Grosso invasion, and the new Colorado government in Uruguay in order to avoid being trampled by its neighbors. They called themselves the Triple Alliance, and they were happy to take on tiny Paraguay. For the next six years, marked by bloody battles, long delays, blundering leadership on all sides, terrible problems of supply, and rampant disease, the various armies and navies would fight with nearly insane ferocity. In the end, all would suffer thousands of casualties, and Paraguay would nearly disappear as a country.

At first López was better prepared than his adversaries and the war went well for Paraguay. With an army of 30,000 against a disorganized opposition, López triumphed over both the Brazilian forces in the north and the Argentine forces in the south. But as his three opponents began to coordinate and strengthen their forces, the tide turned.

In the south, the Paraguayan navy—including the newly acquired *Marques de Olinda*—was destroyed by Brazilian steamers at the Battle of Riachuelo in June of 1865. That sealed off supplies from the outside world. In desperate fighting, part of the Paraguayan land force took a body blow at Yatai two months later, which was followed by the surrender of the rest of its invading force after a six-week siege of the Uruguayan town of Uruguaiana. Altogether, López lost nearly 9,000 men in these actions—a third of his armies, plus the best part of his navy.

As the remnants of the invaders pulled back across the Paraña into Paraguay, the oncoming allies concentrated on outflanking the Paraguayan fortress at Humaitá. Paraguayan strategy was now transformed from invading the enemy to defending the homeland against the enemy. In this, they would be fanatical.

In May 1866, the greatest battle that South America had ever seen was fought among the swamps and lagoons at Tuyuti, south of Humaitá. It involved 50,000 men—215 battalions of infantry, cavalry, and artillery. López ordered the cream of his army into repeated charges at the fixed allied position. It was a massacre, and the general lost three-quarters of his remaining army. The allies won the field and came on toward Humaitá.

Miraculously, López was able to regroup survivors and new recruits along a new defensive line at Curupaity. There, in September, the reconstituted Paraguayan force administered such a bloody defeat on their opponents that it was fourteen months before the allies attempted any further advance.

Anti-conscription revolts broke out in Argentina, and Brazil's Marquis of Caxias took over supreme allied command. As disease and starvation began to haunt the Paraguayan side, Brazil came to dominate the allied campaign, and a more professional class of officers evolved. At the battlements at Humaitá, amid the fleas and vermin, with 15,000 yards of trenches, and 300 guns, behind a triple chain boom across the river, Lopez's barefoot defenders endured nearly continuous bombardments from the Brazilian Navy for over a year.

Far away from all of this, in a glittering ceremony in New York, Charles married Sallie in May 1865. She was twenty-one; he was forty-two. The happy couple returned to South America, apparently in blissful ignorance of what was already the bloodiest war in South American history. Their bliss quickly turned to frustration, then squalor, then disaster.

The trouble started with the U.S. Navy refusing to take them back up to Asunción. A shooting war was now underway between the four countries along the Paraña River, the navy argued. Thousands had already been killed, and the path northward was blocked by hostile fortifications, mines, opposing naval vessels, chain barriers, and two campaigning armies. None of the contesting countries would grant the necessary permission for a foreign military vessel to pass through. Since

Mr. and Mrs. Charles A. Washburn, newly married
COURTESY WASHBURN LIBRARY

the river was the only route to Asunción, Charles was blocked. In his letters to Seward, to stiff-backed American admiral S. W. Godon, and to military and civilian leaders in all three of the allied countries, Charles pleaded for help to return to his post. He was ignored. The combatants distrusted America in general and Charles in particular. The allies had no intention of adding to López's legitimacy by allowing him to receive an American emissary. On top of that, the American navy, already gun-shy about Paraguay, determined to put down the upstart amateur diplomat, whose total annual budget did not equal what it cost to keep just one of their ships afloat. In subsequent testimony before Congress, Admiral Godon blandly opined that there was not one American interest that needed representation in Paraguay, and Navy Secretary Welles backed him up.

Months dragged by, Charles desperately dashing from Buenos Aires to Montevideo and finally to Argentine military headquarters of the frontline town of Corrientes, where he spent five long months amidst the mud and flies. The newspapers got hold of the story, and there was even a public subscription campaign in Buenos Aires to buy the navy coal enough to get Charles up the river. His floods of letters in all directions added to the irritation of all concerned. To the personal animosity of Godon, Charles now added the enmity of both the Brazilian commander and the Argentine president.

Finally, back in Washington, Seward at last persuaded Secretary Welles to order Admiral Godon to take Charles to Asunción. Six months later, the admiral got around to it. In one of the more unwise moves in the history of American diplomacy, as the guns briefly fell quiet on November 5, 1866, Charles and Sallie and their baggage were brought up through the opposing armies and navies on the USS *Shamokin*. Even then, passage was only permitted by the Brazilians after the American commander ordered his decks cleared for action to call their bluff.[3]

The Washburns' ignorance of what was going on around them continued. Sallie had a good time on the trip up the river. As the party appeared to be coming to an end, she wrote in her journal only that she "felt very tristy" at having to leave the officers of the *Shamokin*, who were also disappointed, as "they all expected a good time in Paraguay."[4]

The allies had just suffered a terrible defeat—over 9,000

dead—at Curupaity. Their Argentine commander was being replaced by a Brazilian. Although their land forces were regrouping, allied shelling of Humaitá was a daily occurrence. A Brazilian ironclad named *Rio de Janiero* had been blown up with all hands by a pair of mines just a few weeks earlier. Until the American vessel appeared around the bend below the batteries, the Paraguayans there had had no contact with the outside world for more than a year.

There was no sign, however, that the Washburns noticed any of the carnage or destruction as they came ashore below Humaitá, where they were transferred to a carriage and driven past the temporarily silent gun batteries to Paraguayan headquarters at Paso Pucú. López was unable to see them due to illness, but the dictator's faithful paramour, Elisa Lynch, exchanged visits with them.

Mrs. Lynch is a striking figure in the drama of Paraguay. A correspondent for a Buenos Aires newspaper described her riding by one day "gracefully and easily, firmly seated and handling her spirited horse with all the coolness of a woman who had overcome fear."[5] Elisa Lynch had five children by the dictator, was a force behind every effort to bring culture to the country, and never faltered in her support for her lover. She stayed with him to the end—even to burying her oldest son with her own bare hands. Charles alternated between disdain and tolerance of her, but Sallie enjoyed her company.

Humaitá was isolated by swamps and marshes to both the north and east. The single supply road was suitable only for oxcarts, for it was flooded for most of the year. So, in transferring to another steamer for the run up to Asunción, the Washburns again somehow never saw or smelled the mud and trenches and the half-starved, diseased, and barefoot troops. They never heard the derisive sounds of the *turututu* horns that the Paraguayans used to infuriate their Brazilian tormentors after each bombardment.

Perhaps whatever visions Charles had painted for his new bride of an easy life in the exotic and languid tropics lasted all the way to Asunción—although she did report that on the steamer she had to sleep in a bed full of roaches. In any case, blinded by an apparent vision of himself as sacrosanct, Charles had now led them deep inside an alien territory, where he had neither a friend nor a protector any closer than Washington, D.C., a hemisphere away.

Charles's six-month leave had lasted a full eighteen months, and the situation at the legation at Asunción had stagnated in his absence. From the time of his return, things deteriorated further. As Sallie struggled in the alternating heat and rain to clean up the place, Charles dealt with many applications for assistance from other foreign representatives caught in the capital. He hired several fugitive American adventurers—including one directly from jail to be a cook. In one case, a man coming in from the country arrived so ill that he died the next day and Charles had to pay for his coffin. Sallie noted the event, but seemed unaware that this may have been the dreaded cholera that was sweeping the country. They passed the days in desultory fashion, playing whist and euchre. Both took Spanish lessons. Sallie got pregnant and in October 1867, delivered a healthy daughter they named Hester.

As the pressure of the allies mounted, and supply shortages became critical, López became more paranoid about the foreigners in his midst. Peace talks, including a trip by Charles through the lines to make an unauthorized mediation offer to the new Brazilian commander in chief, got nowhere: The Brazilians were adamant that López must go, and this was the one thing the Paraguayans could not and would not do. Charles returned to Asunción having only aroused suspicion among the Paraguayans that he was conspiring with the enemy.

In 1868 López became convinced of a conspiracy against him and appointed military commissions to root out the perpetrators. Hundreds of suspects from among Asunción's elite, and even members of López's own family, were jailed. Over forty wanted people, including Germans, British, and Americans, as well as Paraguayans, begged for asylum for themselves and their possessions at the American mission. Charles graciously, but unwisely, complied, and dozens of expatriate trouble-makers moved in.

There is no evidence that Charles conspired with anybody, but he made some very bad decisions. His hospitality stretched the limits of diplomatic propriety, especially when he began to realize that his new guests were carrying papers that might be treasonous. Giving shelter to suspected spies, traitors, and deserters could be interpreted as illegal collusion on his own part. When hostile guards were posted around the American compound, it became as much a prison as a haven.

His unwanted guests also brought their pets with them. At one point these included nine parrots. When Charles happened to hear one of the birds scream out "Viva Pedro Segundo" (the emperor of Brazil) one day, he ordered the bird's neck wrung, but it was too late. Word of the treasonous utterance reached the presidential palace almost immediately. Charles wearily wrote Elihu that "this country is terribly exhausted, but shows no sign of giving in—the men are nearly all used up," and that he was using legation funds to provide financial support to destitute friends and colleagues. He closed by using the words "this dreary prison" to describe his situation.[6]

Brazilian naval vessels overcame their timidity and took advantage of high water to get past the obstacles at Humaitá in February 1868, and actually managed to lob a few shells into Asunción. Although Charles noted that the only casualties were "a couple of dogs in the marketplace," President López ordered all residents of the capital city to move inland. Charles refused, declaring theatrically that "If the allies or anybody else choose to blow up the house, they must blow me with it, for I shall not leave my post." His real reason for defying the president may have been fear of what would be discovered in the legation if it was abandoned.[7] At any rate, his refusal to move completed the break between him and the Paraguayan government.

Other foreign representatives were jailed, and Washburn's own staff was accused of treason. At least one of these men, an ex-Confederate adventurer named James Manlove, who had supposedly ridden with Nathan Bedford Forrest, was arrested and executed. Washburn claimed that, between May and December of 1868, four hundred people, including ninety-five foreigners, were either executed or died in prison. Those incarcerated included López's own mother, two of his brothers, and two of his sisters. In addition, cholera and famine stalked the land. It became harder for Sallie to find whist partners. Beyond the walls of the legation, and apart from the steady attrition of López's army at the battlefront, the entire population of the country was being decimated.

Surrounded, outnumbered, and now realizing that they were far from any outside aid, the minister and his bride at last began to fear for their own lives. Charles decided to resign. The fortress at Humaitá surrendered in July. During July and August Charles wrote a dozen long and windy letters—the last one was twenty-seven pages long—in an attempt to exonerate himself from President López's accusations. Full of inconsistencies, these communications did not add to his diplomatic luster.

Finally, under pressure from American emissaries in other countries, primarily fellow former newspaper editor James Watson Webb in Brazil, the navy at last came to the rescue. Under a tough-talking captain named Kirkland, the USS *Wasp* ran past the Paraguayan batteries at Angostura and arrived at Villeta, below Asunción, in September 1868. Kirkland marched into López's headquarters, warned the general that Washburn had powerful friends all over the U.S. government, and that the Americans had six ironclad monitors standing by to blow up Asunción and have the Paraguayan president's head if anything should happen to their representative. He then proceeded to Charles's embattled mission to pick up the shaken minister, his broken wife, and his baby daughter, together with several loaded trunks whose contents were never fully explained. Two assistants named Masterman and Bliss were left to an uncertain fate in a Paraguayan jail.

Masterman and Bliss became the final cause célèbre of Charles's diplomatic career. Despite Charles's subsequent efforts to get them released, he was roundly criticized in the press for leaving them behind. On the *Wasp*'s next trip, which brought in Washburn's replacement, General Martin T. McMahon, Masterman and Bliss were finally taken off—although not before they were forced to write elaborate legends about Charles's supposed conspiracies against López. However, they both remained friendly with Charles, and Bliss even visited The Norlands in later years.

The minister's rescue and replacement was gunboat diplomacy at its most blatant. One can only imagine what the sight of Kirkland's vessel arrogantly steaming past the blood and gore of four nations engaged in deadly combat did for American foreign policy in South America for the next few decades.

When he got to Buenos Aires, Charles was astounded to learn that López was regarded as a hero by the outside world— a plucky underdog against the forces of monarchy, slavery, and despotism among his much larger opponents. Even among the allies, Charles had trouble getting people to listen to him, although he continued to spray self-justification in all directions. One man who interviewed him at this time was the British adventurer Sir Richard Burton, a consul for the British in Brazil during the war. About Charles, Burton observed that "many of his assertions were those of a man who was hardly responsible for his actions."[8] Later, the navy questioned whether Charles had even been in danger, as he was still allowed to go out for his morning ride every day, where someone could have easily murdered him if they'd really wanted to.

Charles's actions after leaving Asunción were hardly the actions of a seasoned diplomat. He wrote a last letter to López that contained all kinds of personal accusations. When he heard about this letter, the British commander of the nearest riverside battery said that he would have opened fire on the disappearing American vessel if he had known about it in time.

Charles also left a remarkable letter for his successor, McMahon, which included the sentence "I am taking it for granted that you will not have any communication with him [López]"—hardly realistic instructions to an incoming diplomat.[9]

In addition, Washburn continued to battle with the U.S. Navy that had just rescued him. He wrote of conspiracies against him among the navy, the representatives of Argentina, Brazil, and Uruguay, the López government, and even the man who succeeded him, Martin McMahon. In an interview when he got back to New York, he called López "cowardly, cruel, and bloody"—words that might have been justified, but were hardly politic.

His public career was not quite over. But in the course of the next several months Charles himself put an end to it. To pursue his complaints about lack of cooperation from the navy, specifically Admiral Godon and his successor, Admiral Charles A. Davis, Charles insisted on a hearing before the House Foreign Relations Committee of the U.S. Congress. The end result of this, in 1871, was a mild congressional criticism of the two officers for their "disrespect." A motion to censure the two was defeated. No matter how terrible the experience had been for him, as paranoid as López may have been, and as bull-headed as the navy may have been, Charles could not arouse much sympathy for himself among the congressmen. No doubt they, like the navy, were wondering what Americans were doing in Paraguay to begin with.

Charles went back to San Francisco, where Leland Stanford arranged a fête for him—but no further employment. Back at Livermore, in between fruitless expeditions to Washington, Charles, writing in the family journal, accurately compared himself to Don Quixote, "an avenger of wrongs and a vindicator of the right. 'Tis easier to keep quiet and let fraud and oppression triumph.... Why will there be fools who will butt their heads against stone walls[?]"[10] Charles may have seen himself as Don Quixote, but in his effort to exonerate himself, he was probably lucky to avoid his own censure.

In the meantime, back in Paraguay, the allied army gradually destroyed the Paraguayan army in a series of battles during December, then captured Asunción in January 1869. Lopez still refused to surrender and took advantage of allied delays to build yet another army—this one mostly of boys, women, and old men armed with ancient flintlock muskets. It took the allies, primarily Brazilian, a year to flush out and destroy his last forces, during which time at least 5,000 more Paraguayans died. Finally, deep in the hills in the northeast part of the country, at a place called Cerro Corá, they surprised the last Paraguayan camp. On March 1, 1870, supposedly crying out, "Muerto con mi patria" (I die with my country), López fell from a combination of Brazilian bullets and lances on the muddy bank of the Aquidabán River.

His last words were accurate. Behind him, he indeed left a

Juan Manuel Blanes, the Uruguayan painter, summarized the tragedy of the Paraguayan War in 1879 with his painting La Paraguaya.
COURTESY OF ANDREA CUARTEROLO AND THE
NATIONAL MUSEUM OF VISUAL ARTS, MONTEVIDEO

dead country. Around the burned-out hulk of the presidential palace in Asunción, the streets were empty except for a few gaunt and barefoot women. The treasury and archives of the country were gone. In the countryside, the herds were gone and the farms untended. An 1870 census revealed that the total population of Paraguay was less than half what it had been ten years earlier. Only about 28,000 old men and boys were left from what had been a male population of a quarter million. Among the victors, Brazil had lost 50,000 men, and Uruguay and Argentina over 30,000 more. In the final settlement, Paraguay lost 55,000 square miles of territory and suffered Argentine and Brazilian occupation until 1876. Massive war debts, never paid, were finally pardoned in 1943, after causing severe hardship for all the combatants.

Despite the losses—which proportionately must be the most severe for any country in modern history—López is still regarded by many of his countrymen as Paraguay's greatest national hero, a Paraguayan David to the allies' Goliath. His statue, in classic equestrian pose, was completed in 1988 and emblazoned "El Napoleon de Paraguay." It is a tourist landmark in Asunción today. In a land thirsty for heroes, the statue is a powerful symbol of national identity, if not historical accuracy.

* * *

As Charles alternately expostulated, pled, and complained, his brother Elihu was progressing toward a much different level of diplomatic achievement.

Democratic governments are famous for bringing plain people to prominence. Both Washburne and Lincoln were prime examples of this. Through the trust born of his commonality with Lincoln, plain Elihu Washburne's contributions were significant. He early recognized that a distinctly unheroic-looking Grant was in fact the most competent fighter in the Union Army, and he repeatedly intervened to save and promote his protégé. He was steadfast in his support for Lincoln himself, and through his blunt honesty he earned the president's trust. His battles against corruption, his support of Lincoln's policies, and his personal courage made his influence substantial. Certainly his power in getting appointments was impressive. In 1865 there were no less than nine generals in the Union Army from his hometown of Galena alone.[11]

Elihu was just as tough-minded as his brothers, and just as devoted to principle, but he did a better job of picking friends and avoiding arguments he could not win. He also made sure that he had a strong case before he took on the forces of self-interest. Plain-spoken as he was, before his public service was over, he had earned the gratitude and respect of the most sophisticated heads of state in Europe.

Washburne's blunt honesty during the Civil War years undoubtedly made enemies among the self-interested: Frémont's contractor friends in St. Louis, the cotton speculators and military contractors in Cairo and Memphis, the regular army officers resentful of politically appointed officers, the jealous military and political competitors of Ulysses Grant, and the radical extremists in Congress, just to name a few. However, lawyers and politicians develop tough skins, and Lincoln's trust in Washburne never wavered. In view of the Union they saved together, it was a trust well placed.

At the start of the postwar Congress, Elihu Washburne, though often ill and exhausted, threw his energies into a new cause. With the great war won, he was determined to reduce the size of the federal government. He was immovably opposed to all demands for government funds by interests eager to take advantage of its new size and power—from the postwar navy unwilling to downsize, to the railroads fighting for federal land grants, to Seward's purchase of Alaska. Dubbed "Watchdog of the Treasury," he also battled to pay down the enormous war debt that the country had accumulated. His performance as chairman of the House Appropriations Committee resulted in government expenditures being slashed by a full one-third between 1866 and 1869. His budget for 1870 proposed a cut of a further twenty percent, including one-seventh in the budget of the navy, which must have yet again aroused the ire of Secretary Welles against all Washburns. Elihu never ceased his battles against waste and corruption wherever he found them. He won reelection from Illinois in 1866, as did his brother Cadwallader from his old Wisconsin district. On the side, Elihu continued to advise and protect Grant—still general of the armies and now the nation's number one hero.

Shortly after being reelected, Elihu suffered a complete collapse of his health. He resigned his important seat on the House Reconstruction Committee, and left for a six-month trip to various baths in Europe for recuperation. In his absence, the Radical Republican tide rose against President Johnson. Elihu himself became less conservative and more radical, his transition due largely to his inquiry into the Memphis riots of 1866, as well as to President Johnson's growing intransigence.

His committee's visit to Memphis produced a detailed report of murders and burnings (Elihu's handwritten summary was thirty-six pages long), and his conclusion was that the South would only change its ways under continuing Northern military pressure. When Elihu returned from Europe in August, he at first opposed the idea of impeachment, but the president's firing of Secretary of War Stanton turned him in favor of it.

Exhaustion and precarious health may have been responsible for two bizarre outbursts he made in the House of Representatives. A furious Washburne spoke on February 22, 1868, urging the House to recommend an impeachment trial before the Senate. He called the president "mendacious and malignant...surrounded by red-handed rebels, advised and counseled by the worst of men that ever crawled, like filthy reptiles, at the footstool of power," and he called the president responsible for a whole galaxy of evils in the South, including "murder, rapine, incendiarism, and crimes."[12]

The motion in favor of impeachment passed the House in February, with both Elihu and Cadwallader voting in favor. Elihu, as chair of the Committee of the Whole, attended every day of the subsequent Senate trial. When the Senate vote fell one vote short of the two-thirds required, feeling "humiliated and disgusted," Elihu was the one who had to announce the acquittal verdict to the House in May.[13]

During the impeachment proceedings, a second contretemps arose in the House involving a weary and short-tempered Elihu. Goaded by Elihu's opposition to a railroad land grant in which he had an interest, newly elected Representative Ignatius Donnelly of Minnesota rose to deliver a personal and outrageous diatribe against all the Washburns, especially Elihu. It was a good show, and the members loved it. To the delight of his audience, Donnelly observed that "every male member of that family seemed to have been born with the letters 'M.C.' franked across his broadest part." Elihu let the harangue continue until Donnelly was finished, and then answered with a blistering personal attack of his own. His language was so sulfurous that the House, out of embarrassment, subsequently withdrew a tenth article of impeachment that accused President Johnson of bringing disrespect to the House by using intemperate language there.[14] The *New York Times* chastised the entire House of Representatives for the exchange, referring to Elihu's performance as "an abominable tirade." Younger brother William Drew, who was the Republican choice back in Minnesota in 1868 to replace Donnelly, declined the nomination and decided to stay above the fray. The irrepressible Donnelly subsequently lost the seat to the Democrats.[15]

Intemperate language and personal insult had never been considered a detriment in politics along the Mississippi, but it hardly contributed to the qualifications of a diplomat such as Elihu was about to become. First, however, he had to get Grant elected president.

During the summer and fall of 1868, with both men back in Galena, Washburne acted as Grant's unofficial campaign man-

*Ignatius Donnelly, the colorful politician from
Minnesota, goaded Elihu Washburne into a rage
in Congress. Later, his political career was ended
by Elihu's younger brother William.*
COURTESY MINNESOTA HISTORICAL SOCIETY

ager, advising him as to what to say and when to say it. This
was important, because Grant was quite ignorant of the tools of
political debate, let alone the features of the Republican party
platform. He seemed to regard his possible elevation to the
presidency as just another promotion to a new job that he
would do as he had every other job he had been given, if the
people wished.

On election day, in his own front parlor, Elihu had a
Western Union ticker machine installed, and that evening

The path between Washburne's home and Grant's home in Galena still exists. Grant walked down this path to learn the results of the 1868 election that made him president.
SNAPSHOT TAKEN BY PETER W. KELSEY IN 2002

Grant came down the hill from his house to monitor the results. The two men, accompanied by several friends and newspaper reporters, listened for most of the night to the chatter of the telegraph key as the results came in from each state. Adele, back in Washington for the birth of her eighth and last child, didn't have to put up with the cigar smoke or the two brass bands trampling her flower garden when Grant's victory was made known. In the wee hours of the morning the final result was clear: Washburne's protégé would now hold the highest elected office in the land. The victory was complete. Elihu himself was reelected for a ninth term, even though he had not campaigned, and was widely known to be in line for a cabinet position if Grant won. For the first time, the Republicans even carried the city of Galena.

Rarely in the history of the country has an elected president owed so much to one man. Before the election, Grant had never held elective office—had in fact hardly ever voted. Before Washburne noticed him only seven years earlier, Grant had been an unknown clerk in an obscure western town, far from public notice. He had had no influence, no friends in high places, no legacy. What reputation he had was tainted by alcohol and business failure. Then he met Elihu Washburne. He had little interest in politics, and now he was to be president of the United States. Grant owed Washburne a lot, and he was known to pay his debts.

Long prone to malaria, Washburne was barely able to attend Grant's inauguration on March 4, 1869. He was, however, healthy enough to negotiate with the president-elect over three different cabinet positions. Health considerations aside, his budget work had clearly demonstrated his qualifications for the Treasury portfolio, but Grant felt already committed to a New York businessman for that post. Grant then offered the Interior post, which Washburne declined. The third position offered was the most unlikely one, secretary of state. Even more unexpectedly, Washburne accepted that job.

Washburne's enemies were appalled. Gideon Welles erupted in his diary: "Washburne is coarse, comparatively illiterate, a demagogue without statesmanship or enlarged views, with none of the accomplishments or attributes that should belong to a Secretary of State."[16] The *New York Times* was kinder, observing that "the foreign policy of Grant, with Washburne as secretary of state, will assuredly be independent, straightforward, and thoroughly American"—whatever that meant.[17]

Washburne in fact had few qualifications to be the nation's leading diplomat, and he knew it. He had no taste for diplomatic nicety, no experience with nuance, no sympathy for inherited power, no knowledge of foreign language, and no strength for the rigors of the job. His brother Charles, with a lot more education than he had, had just made a mess of a difficult assignment in Paraguay. As late as 1928, in an official Department of State history, Joseph V. Fuller wrote about Washburne's "belligerent and headstrong advocacy of President Johnson's impeachment...that principally raised doubts as to his temperamental fitness to conduct the country's foreign relations."[18]

However, Elihu saw the importance of holding the secretary's chair briefly in order to bolster his credentials for the job he really wanted, which was in Paris. He retained the top job in the cabinet for exactly twelve days. On March 16, after helping entice New York's superbly qualified governor, Hamilton Fish, to succeed him, he resigned from the secretaryship. The very next day he accepted the post as envoy extraordinary and minister plenipotentiary to France. Elihu Washburne would now have the most desirable of all the American diplomatic jobs around the world. Just before leaving, in one of his few official acts, he ordered the closing of the American mission to Paraguay. He thus brought to an end the vexing post that had been his brother's undoing. There would be no official American representative in Paraguay for the next forty-five years.

Washburne was not the only amateur that Grant sent to European embassies that year. His Galena friend Augustus Chetlain was in Brussels, soon to be joined by banker Russell

Jones. Former Wisconsin congressman Horace Rublee was in Berne, and his Illinois colleague Norman Judd was in Berlin, as was his old Chicago friend Herman Kreismann, who had been responsible for much of Washburne's support among German-American voters over the years. Grant's former military secretary Adam Badeau was in London. Every one of these appointments was for the purpose of repaying favors rather than rewarding competence. Fortunately, most of the recipients were capable men—none more so, it turned out, than Washburne.

Washburne had been to France many times before, but never with the cachet he had now. Wealthy Americans waited on him, the emperor's court beckoned, and ministers on their way to other European posts called on him. He was the unofficial leader of a colony of Americans that numbering at least 5,000, who owned real estate in Paris valued at at least ten million dollars. More than 7,000 American visitors passed through the city each year. After two weeks of nonstop socializing, which he reported to Adele "accomplished nothing but getting [me] tired near to death," he was granted an audience with Napoleon III at the Tuilleries Palace. He later described it as "a brilliant court, glittering splendor. Princes and Dukes, Marquises, Counts and Barons, maintained their butterfly existence."[19] This was hardly the language of a man Welles had called "comparatively illiterate."

His remarks upon being presented to the emperor were graciously received by the court, although George Bancroft, the ex-college professor who was the American minister in Berlin, found things to criticize. Washburne's newly appointed boss, Secretary of State Fish, wrote him with thanks and congratulations. Elihu's own opinion about his performance was, like the man, matter-of-fact and without illusion. That evening he wrote to his oldest brother Israel back in Maine simply, "It was for me an entry upon a new career, and into a field in which I had never had any experience."[20]

When Washburne arrived at the American legation in Paris, he found it to be "a dreary middle-class apartment, up two winding staircases" at 95 Rue de Chaillot, over a grocery on one side and a laundry on the other. Little did anyone know that before long, thousands of desperate people would crowd up these modest stairs and Elihu's daughter Marie would write that the place "had a halo over it."[21]

A bright spot was supplied by Wickham Hoffman, an urbane, bilingual, and combat-seasoned ex-Union army officer, who would be Elihu's second-in-command. They would serve together for nearly six eventful years. Looking back on their experience afterwards, Hoffman reflected that the head of an embassy *ought* to be a "new" man like Washburne. "He will attach much less importance to trifles, and act more fearlessly in emergencies.... The old diplomats grumble, but it is clearly for the advantage of the country." Such was to be the case in Paris in 1870.[22] As events occurred for which there was no precedent, Washburne's role would call for imagination, initiative, and just plain good sense. It would also require more strength than subtlety. As it turned out, his performance in Paris would verge on the heroic.

Washburne's tenure started out well. Emperor Louis Napoleon, in the wake of his disastrous sympathy for the Confederacy and his equally disastrous effort to impose a monarchy in Mexico, was anxious to regain American good-will. His initial interviews with Washburne went well, and Empress Eugenie was impressed by Washburne's political skills, especially his ability to remember the names of the hundreds of Americans he presented at court.

In addition, behind his plain clothes and bluff manner, Elihu had lost none of his rugged honesty. When he first arrived in Paris, he found that investors in France were hungrily gobbling up millions of dollars' worth of bonds in an American enterprise called the Memphis, El Paso, and Pacific Railway. Its president was General John C. Frémont, the former presidential candidate whom Washburne had helped Lincoln oust from command of the western armies in 1862. Washburne asked Fish to look into the company, and the news came back that the whole operation was a fraud. Washburne promptly exposed it, with the result that its promoters, including Frémont, were indicted, tried, and condemned in absentia. As a result, Washburne gained praise from the French government and outrage from the defrauded investors.

All was not well in the Second Empire. Although the emperor had strong support from the aristocracy, there was great unrest at the poorer levels of French society. Washburne reported this, but did not feel that the situation was serious. Though there were increasing signs of tension between the Chamber of Deputies and the emperor, Washburne was invited for a six-day visit at the palace at Compiègne, outside of Paris. Amid days of dancing and hunting parties, he had a good chance to talk with the French leader, after which he reported to Fish that the emperor "was sorry that his people were not better fitted for liberal institutions."[23] On a different level, Elihu wrote to Adele that "The standing around in company is awful on my back, and it aches this morning 'fit to kill.'"[24]

Happily, Adele and the children were eventually able to join Elihu in Paris. They settled in a comfortable home in what were then the outskirts of the city, almost opposite the main entrance to the beautiful Bois de Boulogne. Their address, 75 Avenue de l'Imperatrice, would soon become famous in several countries.

In March of 1870, following the emperor's recommendations for dilution of the legislature's power, two key ministers unexpectedly quit the cabinet. Washburne reported "excitement and uneasiness in the French political world," but when the emperor received a huge vote of approval in the national election in May, it appeared that quiet was restored once more.

In June the emperor held what turned out to be the last formal dinner ever held at the Tuilleries Palace. It was in honor of the new American minister and his wife. In the glitter and gleam and pomp of a great event of state, in a great hall of one of the most magnificent buildings in France, the Livermore farm boy and his log-cabin-raised wife enjoyed the company of the emperor and empress of France. The two couples spent a pleasant evening with no hint that anything was amiss. Washburne and his family left Paris soon afterwards—Adele and the children to the seashore, and he for another curative stay at Carlsbad, Germany. As events unfolded, he would never see Napoleon III again, and, just six months later, the Tuilleries would be a burned-out shell.

Although diplomats are never supposed to be surprised, Washburne and his colleagues were rudely jolted when the news came on July 15 that France, apparently fearing loss of the provinces of Alsace and Lorraine to the expansionist Prussians under Chancellor Bismarck, had inexplicably declared war on Prussia. Leaving his family in Bavaria, Washburne immediately departed by all-night coach and train on a grueling fifty-two-hour race back to Paris. When he got there, he found most of the American community in the city clamoring to get out, as were tens of thousands of Germans. With all contact severed between France and Germany, Washburne, as representative of the largest clearly neutral power, was authorized and financed by several governments to get their noncombatants safely out of the city. With crowds of anxious suppliants jamming the street outside the legation, he worked many eighteen-hour days, topped off with all-night stints at the railroad station, to make sure the refugees got on the trains.

In the east, after a series of spectacular defeats, the French armies shockingly surrendered, and the emperor was taken prisoner. On September 4, after legislative uproar that surpassed anything he had ever experienced in Congress, Washburne watched with satisfaction as the *Corps Legislatif* declared the end of the empire and the formation of a new republic. To the immense gratitude of the French, Washburne promptly got the American government to recognize the new government.

As Charles had been in the midst of four warring nations in Paraguay, so Elihu now found himself in the middle of two warring superpowers in Paris. He did a much better job than Charles in preserving his neutrality—the basic responsibility of any diplomat anywhere.

As the Prussian army approached the city, Washburne, largely without instruction or authorization from the State Department, purchased railroad tickets for thousands more refugees—many of them helpless German domestics abandoned by their masters. By mid-September Paris itself came under siege. As the city was surrounded, most of the major powers' representatives evacuated—but not Washburne. When fortifications went up literally across the street from his residence, the American minister moved his family to lodgings in Brussels, Belgium, where his old friend Russell Jones could keep an eye on them. Washburne elected to stay on in Paris— though in a less exposed location. His oldest son, twenty-one-year-old Gratiot Washburne, stayed with him. The young man's services were greatly needed—to help with the legation's workload and to man an ambulance that brought in French wounded for the American medical team that also stayed in the besieged city.[25]

Elihu and Gratiot were both well-equipped to be neutral. Adele's French heritage had been a big reason for their wanting to be in France, and the declaration of the Republic had removed the last obstacle to Elihu's immense sympathy for the French people. On the other hand, Elihu had long owed much of his political success to strong backing among his German-American constituents back home. He was very familiar with, and sympathetic to, their liberal support of antislavery and a democratic American government. It was easy for the Washburnes to be evenhanded, and both the combatants knew it.

In October the American minister reported that meat was growing scarce and that mule meat was being rationed by the government, as it was regarded as superior to horse meat. Conditions in the working-class districts were much worse, and there was even an abortive coup d'état on October 31 that was quickly put down. In the third month of the siege, aching with fever but working long hours with a skeleton staff, Washburne wrote Chancellor Bismarck that every day he was feeding over 1,100 helpless Germans. The German chancellor made funds available to help Washburne in these labors. As the weather got colder, firewood became scarce, and soon the great trees lining the avenues all over Paris began to be cut down for fuel. Because the barricaded streets made his residence almost inaccessible, Washburne was now living with a friend and walking two miles to the legation every day. He was also acting as go-between for the French with the German Chancellor, and protecting American property from repeated French attempts to appropriate or tax it. In December he again declined Fish's authorization to leave the city.

The Americans didn't think much of the French military leadership during this trying time. Near the end of the siege, on January 28, 1871, Washburne wrote that General Louis Jules Trochu, who was in charge of the defense of the city, was "weak as the Indian's dog which had to lean against a tree to bark."[26] Two days earlier, reporting the defeat of one of the last potential rescue armies in the provinces, a more urbane Hoffman had observed that its general had abandoned his army and attempted to commit suicide: "In German service he would undoubtedly have been tried for desertion. In France everything is pardoned for the man who acts under the influence of strong emotion...."27

In January, on the 108th day of the siege, Washburne wrote Bismarck behind the Prussian lines to stop his delivery of London newspapers, because he did not want to retain any privilege not shared by everyone else in the suffering city. As he put it, "I prefer being without news to being subject to it." (This was a big sacrifice. Elihu hungered for newspapers. Over and over again in his journal and letters, he revealed his discouragement and depression due to his isolation and lack of contact with the outside world.)28 The next day, the Prussian bombardment began. It lasted twenty-two days, during which time the number of people being fed by the Americans increased to over 3,000 a day. At the end of the month, now on the verge of starvation, the city finally surrendered.

Under the terms of the surrender agreement, the Prussians got to march their troops through the Arc de Triomphe and down the Champs-Elysées, but their presence in the city was brief. They were there only three days, caused no damage, and marched out as efficiently as they had marched in. The surrender and the Prussians' parade were peaceful compared with what was about to happen. Sparked by deep discontent in the poorest quarters of the city, a full-scale rebellion against the French national government was about to begin.

On March 18, French regulars refused to fire on militia who had seized arms and ammunition and fortified themselves on a position in the Montmartre section. Two regular army generals, LeCompte and Thomas, were executed by the mutineers. As the official government fled the city for Versailles, a self-appointed Central Committee declared Paris to be the world's first government by the workers—a commune. With red flags everywhere, a discouraging paralysis by the regular government in Versailles, a seemingly new and more fanatic group in charge of the city every day, Washburne was adrift. He had come to Paris hoping for "repose and quiet," but now realized that he was right in the middle of "the most terrible events of the century." His family had rejoined him in Paris after the armistice, but one night a mob broke into and ransacked the house next door. Another night a spent shell came in an open window and landed right on Washburne's bed. Only then did Washburne move his family out, and eventually to a small house outside the city. Again he chose to stay at his post, and that night he wrote, "All is one great shipwreck in Paris"[29] A murderous anarchy descended on the city, lasting from the middle of March to the end of May. During this time of fear and lawlessness, Washburne, alternately torn by anger and discouragement, moved back and forth across the lines between Versailles, his family, and the legation. He issued safe-passage certificates to more than 4,000 additional refugees, mostly from the now lost provinces of Alsace and Lorraine. At the request of the Papal Nuncio, and after lengthy wrangling with various Commune representatives, he was also able to visit Archbishop Darboy, who was being held at Le Roquette Prison as a hostage for several prominent Communards who had been captured. However, the French government at Versailles under Adolphe Thiers took a tough stance and refused to negotiate. This left Washburne helpless.

In April a reorganized and vengeful national army undertook to crush the Commune, even if they had to destroy the whole city to do it. The Communards became equally desperate. They engaged in an orgy of arrests and executions and burned down many of the most historic buildings in the city—

*Desperate militia battled French national forces all around Elihu
Washburne as the Paris Commune slowly came apart in 1871. Anarchy
and looting greatly disturbed the American minister, who, nonetheless,
never abandoned his post.* COURTESY LIBRARY OF CONGRESS

including the former seat of government, the Hotel de Ville, as
well as the Tuilleries Palace where Washburne himself had so
recently been feted. In the confusion, no one was safe. The
destruction and terror went on and on. His neighborhood was
exposed to daily artillery fire from the government batteries at
Mont Valerien, on the opposite side of the Bois de Boulogne.
The day after he saw Darboy, his own house was hit again by
government fire, and again he had to move out. Finally, gov-

ernment troops entered Paris on May 22 and began a block-by-block annihilation of the Communards. Before the last holdouts were shot down at Pere Lachaise Cemetery, no less than 30,000 Parisians lost their lives, either in combat or by firing squad. In the final death throes of the Commune, the humble Archbishop Darboy was also executed.

Fifteen years afterwards, Washburne's memories of this terrible time still reflected his shock. Like the apostle of law and order that he was, he wrote, "What must ever excite amazement is the knowledge of the vast number of the people in Paris at this time who not only were in sympathy with the Commune, but who abetted and sustained it in its career of crime and blood. The minority, embracing the better class of Paris at this time, was completely cowed and subdued by this vast insurrectionary mass of population."[30] Faced with the world's first communist revolution, the country boy from Maine was sounding very much like the outraged member of the American bourgeoisie that he had become.

As the leading neutral representative in the city, his immediate reaction had been one of compassion for those caught in the middle of the conflict. In Paris, by the war's end, Washburne had issued safe passes, arranged rail transport, and given financial assistance to nearly 40,000 refugees from numerous countries. His performance in feeding and protecting thousands more refugees during this time (a current estimate puts the number at 20,000)[31], and his accounting for every penny spent, gained him the gratitude of both French President Thiers and German Chancellor Bismarck.

Though sick and weary, Washburne never lost his personal courage. As Hoffman put it, "If we heard of any part of Paris where shells were likely to burst and bullets to whistle, Washburne was sure to have important business in that direction."[32] Though he lost twenty pounds during the ordeal, he never asked for treatment any different from that which his neighbors were receiving.

Through his hurly-burly days on the frontier and his experiences in the Civil War, Washburne had never been a stranger to gunfire. Nevertheless, the uncertainties of his time in a lawless Paris left an indelible mark on him. As he listened to mobs sack the homes of his neighbors, he found that the loss of order was the most disturbing part of the experience. He wrote that he was shocked and disgusted by the anarchy around him. He described the Commune's last days as "a fight for power and plunder on the part of...desperate and wicked men, unlimited, unchecked, and unrestrained by any human power."33

It was an experience that the world would see again during the upheavals in Russia fifty years later. The two cataclysms were, of course, connected: Karl Marx inspired them both. The leaders of the second, however, learned from the first to be much more complete and merciless in their destruction of the established power structures.

The Washburnes stayed on in Paris for six more years after the Commune was put down. They saw the trees grow back, much of the destruction repaired, and the old atmosphere return. Elihu's malaria kept reappearing, which was one reason he declined an offer to become secretary of the Treasury in 1874. In 1875 he returned to Bavaria for the waters, and that same year provided shelter and entertainment for his brother William and his family—including a junket to Egypt to see the newly opened Suez Canal. He also saw and approved the plan and model for the Statue of Liberty, which was shipped in pieces to New York the following year.

When Washburne finally requested to be recalled in 1877, he was proud to record that he had served as minister to France for eight and a half years—longer than any of his predecessors. Russell Jones, attempting to cheer up Grant amidst the president's many problems with other appointees, put a good label on Washburne's administration of the Paris legation at the height of the Commune. "I am sure you will be gratified to know," wrote Jones, "that you have at least one Representative abroad who runs his machine on high moral principles."34

But Washburne has also been criticized for his performance as a diplomat during his time in France. Though he reported regularly, critics have pointed to his lack of interpretation and assessment of the local situation so as to "help the United States Government to understand, in a broader context, what was happening."35 As the first proletarian revolution in modern history unfolded before his eyes, what he saw was the breakdown of order but not its causes. Washburne was not alone in this. Few in positions of power, including the Iron Chancellor himself, could have predicted the violence of total revolution that descended on Paris in 1871. As Hoffman later wrote in the memoir he dedicated to Washburne, "No one could have been better fitted for the difficult task he was suddenly called upon to undertake than Mr. Washburne. He trusted to the dictates of a sound judgment, a kind heart, and a fearless temperament; and these are pretty safe guides in the long run." 36

The posture of the United States during the Franco-Prussian War was one of neutrality. For their representative on the ground, who was caught literally in the middle of the conflict, retaining impartiality could not have been easy. By nature a fighter, the rough-and-tumble country lawyer from Galena did a superb job of keeping his composure amid the violence. After it was all over, he turned down many awards in recognition of his service—including the above-mentioned offer to become secretary of the Treasury.

However, Elihu did accept, with some satisfaction, three gifts. One was a portrait of Leon Gambetta, given by the founder of the French Republic himself. The other two were portraits of Chancellor Bismark and Emperor Wilhelm of Prussia, presented by the Prussian government. No better acknowledgment of Washburne's compassionate and evenhanded performance could have been made than these honors from the two combatants themselves.

That neither Washburne nor his diplomatic colleagues saw the battle coming should not be cause for castigation. In the 140 years that have passed since the outbreak of the Franco-Prussian War, a more experienced and better-equipped American diplomatic corps has been caught many times just as Washburne was. Events at Pearl Harbor, Havana, and Teheran come to mind right away, with consequences far more damaging to America's national interests.

The diplomatic adventures of Elihu and Charles Washburn offer interesting comparisons. Both brothers represented their country as political appointees, and neither brother had much in the way of foreign experience or language fluency to call on.

Their two assignments differed markedly. Charles was sent to a remote country whose recent relations with the United States had been characterized by American arrogance and Paraguayan hypersensitivity, which graduated into resentment and then anger. In addition, there was a real question as to the wisdom of having an American presence in the country at all. Elihu was sent to a major power which was easily accessible, eager to have him, and worked hard to welcome him. He had a hundred years of good relations to build on. Elihu's French hosts were anxious to repair relations in the wake of their sympathies for the Confederacy in the late war and their failed experiment with Maximilian's monarchy in Mexico. In contrast, Charles's hosts had little in the way of good history with Americans, were resentful of American highhandedness, and were suspicious of American motives.

Both brothers were unexpectedly caught up in war and

destruction. Under pressure, both brothers exhibited a generous spirit, for which they earned the gratitude of the people they protected. Both labored hard to retain their neutrality, although Elihu's long years as an elected politician no doubt served him better—particularly in regard to the sensitivities of the various competing nations among which he was placed.

The pressure on Charles caused him to react in the same way he usually reacted to pressure—by turning inward and spraying letters of self-justification in all directions. His wife was of little help, and it is quite possible that she amplified what for a Washburn was a new experience—fear. In the end, Charles's performance earned him first official annoyance, then a public Congressional hearing, and then oblivion.

The pressure on Elihu was more familiar to him—yet no less fearsome. Haphazard shelling, crazed mobs, and isolation from the outside world all preyed on him. Unlike Charles, however, he had plenty to do, his family was out of danger (most of the time), and he knew that many people were counting on him. As always, he reacted to confrontations stoutly, and with common sense as well as personal courage. In the end, Elihu's performance in Paris almost earned him a presidential nomination.

1. Letter from Martin T. McMahon to the New York *Evening Post*, January 13, 1871.
2. From Howell manuscript fragment (Washburn Library), 69.
3. Gilbert Phelps, *The Tragedy of Paraguay* (London: 1975), 184.
4. Sallie's diary, entry for November 5, 1866 (Washburn Library).
5. Phelps, 57.
6. CAW to EBW, January 15, 1868 (Washburn Library).
7. Phelps, 50, 184, 200–01.
8. Harris Gaylord Warren, *Paraguay: An Informal History* (Norman, OK:1949) 247–48.
9. C. A. Washburn Papers (Washburn Library).
10 Washburn Family Journal, entry for November 17, 1869 (Washburn Library).

11. The nine were: Augustus Chetlain, John Duer, Ulysses Grant, Jasper Maltby, Ely Parker, John Rawlins, William Rowley, John Corson Smith, and John Eugene Smith.

12. EBW: "Impeachment Speech" before the House, Feburary 22, 1868.

13. Hans Trefousse, *Andrew Johnson, A Biography* (New York: 1989), 330.

14. Martin Ridge, *Ignatius Donnelly: The Portrait of a Politician* (Chicago: 1962), 113.

15. The entire exchange was reported in the *New York Times* on May 3, 1868. (See Mark Waashburne, vol. 3, 224.

16. Gideon Welles, *Diary*, III, 543

17. *New York Times*, March 6, 1869.

18. Joseph V. Fuller, *The Amercian Secretaries of State*, vol. 7 (New York: 1928), 120.

19. EBW to Adele, May 16, 1869 (Washburn Library); Washburne, Elihu, *Recollections of a Minister to France*, I: 2,3.

20. EBW to IW Jr., May 23, 1869 (Washburn Library).

21. Marie Washburne Fowler, *Reminiscences—My Mother and I* (privately published, 1927), 33.

22. Wickham Hoffman, *Camp, Court, and Siege* (New York, 1877) 155.

23. EBW to Fish, November 17, 1869 (from Washburne) 439.

24. EBW to Adele, November 13, 1869 (Washburn Library).

25. Gratiot was later awarded the Cross of the Legion of Honor by the French government for his services.

26. EBW, *Recollections*, entry for January 28, 1871, I, 328–29.

27. Hoffman, 232–33.

28. From Francis X Gannon, "A Study of Elihu Benjamin Washburne: American Minister to France During the Franco-Prussian War and the Commune," unpublished PhD thesis, Georgetown University, 1950, 168.

29. EBW, *Recollections*, II, 100.

30. *Recollections*, II, 238.

31. Alistair Horne, *The Fall of Paris: The Siege and the Commune, 1870–71* (London, 1965, 7.

32. Hoffman, 268.

33. EBW, *Recollections*, vol. 2, 192.

34. Jones to Grant, February 26, 1871, *The Papers of Ulysses S. Grant*, XXI, 173.

35. Sister Patricia Dougherty, *American Diplomats and the Franco Prussian War* (Washington, D.C.: Institute for the Study of Diplomacy, Georgetown University, 1980), 35.

36. Hoffman, 154

EIGHT

Lumber, Lignite, and Feeding theWorld

WHEN THE CIVIL WAR ENDED, America became a different country. The great issue that had torn Americans apart for seventy years was suddenly gone. There was no compromise, no half measure, no gradual emancipation. Slavery was just gone. With its disappearance, the great crusade to remove it was also gone. The Union had been saved, and the American people were able to move on to new priorities and more mundane concerns.

In politics, high principles were replaced by lower expectations. The government, having been preserved and reauthorized, was now expected to get out of the way. The nation's preoccupation went from moral to practical. The armies and navies were cut back. Budgets were cut. Foreign affairs, never a high priority anyway, disappeared from the public consciousness. The ruins of the old world were replaced by hopes for the new. Government appointments were once again made for reasons of political expediency rather than for competence. Political empires grew, as did malfeasance in public office, while most of the voters turned their attention elsewhere: to the pursuit of economic opportunity.

The Washburns moved with the times. As foreign affairs became almost invisible, Charles Washburn and Paraguay disappeared from public view, and Elihu returned from his tumultuous experience in France to a much quieter life at home. The country's attention moved to expansion and to new chances to make money. All of the Washburns jumped at the new opportunities, and two of them enjoyed spectacular success.

Their most successful enterprises involved building things. Apart from the wealth they created, these Washburn enterprises were impressive for the alterations they left in the landscape. The brothers redirected rivers and punched railroads across untracked prairies and over the adamantine ledges and bottomless swamps of the northern forest. They built extravagant castles and humming factory complexes, as well as steamships and state-of the-art scientific facilities. In addition to their political, military, and diplomatic adventures, the Washburns are notable for the monuments they left behind.

They themselves measured their success in commercial terms. There is a family legend about a poll that all the brothers took one year to see who they themselves thought had been the most successful. The result of the first ballot was supposedly a seven-way tie. Nobody was happy with this result, so a second ballot was taken. This time, it was Cadwallader who emerged as the choice of his siblings as the most successful. Given the size of the monument that he ordered for his grave in La Crosse—a forty-five-foot obelisk that stills towers over everything else at Oak Grove Cemetery—we can guess that Cadwallader thought so, too. All of his brothers engaged in various business enterprises, but Cad's efforts started the most humbly, achieved the greatest size, and lasted the longest.

When C. C. Washburn rode into La Crosse in 1859, there was little to indicate the humble origins of the man or the poverty with which he had arrived in the west twenty years earlier. Indeed, Washburn was one of the best-known figures in western Wisconsin. He had for fifteen years been a respected lawyer, land agent, and banker in Mineral Point. He had taken advantage of the boom in western lands to build his fortune, and now he was heavily involved in the lumber business—a major player in the great woods along the Black, the Chippewa, and the St. Croix rivers. He and his investors owned or controlled thousands of acres of prime timberland, and he had literally millions of feet of lumber floating in booms at sawmills from Iowa to Missouri. On top of all this, up beyond St. Paul in Minnesota he was undertaking to build a dam and canal on the western side of St. Anthony Falls. The Mississippi River was where the action was, and businessman Washburn was moving into La Crosse to get closer to that action.

To look at, Washburn gave the impression of power and confidence. He was a square-built five feet, eight inches tall. He spoke softly and looked you straight in the eye. His speech was plain, and he didn't laugh much. He was impatient and a little aloof. He had few close friends, but gave off an aura of quiet command. People felt comfortable under his steady hand. He had a reputation for hard work, absolute integrity, and restless energy. When he came to La Crosse, he was forty-one years old.

Based on his appearance, there was no way the townspeople could know that their new neighbor was in fact exhausted by worry and deeply discouraged. The bottom had dropped out of the lumber market in 1856, leaving Washburn with over six and a half million feet of unsold lumber. His lumberyards were nearly idle for lack of customers. Creditors were pressing him on all sides. Up in Minnesota, his energetic youngest brother William had lined up several important tenants for the dam they were building there, but if Cadwallader was ever to see income, he had to find funds to keep this project going. His brother Sam had given up a career at sea to help him build and manage a lumber camp up on the Chippewa. The previous winter Cad had been unable to send even a single crew into the woods to cut trees, and a bored Sam was causing him great frustration. His enterprises in Mineral Point were petering out with the lead mines, and he'd had to shut down his banking operations there. Southern Wisconsin was filling up with permanent settlers, and land speculation was dying down—his land agency with it. His fifteen-year partnership with Cyrus Woodman was over, although not their friendship. His eastern investors were themselves pressed to the limit by the economic depression that had crushed the country since 1857. Perhaps only Washburn's status as a congressman was keeping them at bay.

At home, the doctors had given up hope that his wife Jeanette, now in her sixth year in a hospital for the insane in New York, would ever be able to resume her role as homemaker and mother for their two daughters. Washburn had sent the girls to be raised like orphans by their grandparents back in Maine. He brought his frustrations and worries into LaCrosse alone.

And this was not all. Back in Madison, the state legislature handed Cad a humiliating political setback. Although the Republicans won the White House in 1860, Cad had been rejected by the legislature in Madison for a seat in the U.S. Senate. Only the Civil War saved him from political ignominy, as well as from his creditors.

Now it was May 1865, and the cataclysm of the war was over. The former major general put his stars away and returned to La Crosse. There and then, at last, things began looking up. The price of lumber rebounded. It would continue high for the next five years. Washburn's empire was saved—and saved to flourish. Many of the payments for the holdings he had sold were in kind—rafts of logs and yards of cut lumber at 1864 prices. His sales at 1865 prices were more than enough to pay off his creditors.

Of course, far from being satisfied to pay off debts, Washburn promptly moved to create new ones. His calls to associates in the East never ceased. His visions grew larger. He used his experience clearing the Yazoo Pass in 1863 to start major improvements on the Black River to facilitate the transit of logs, such as dikes to redirect the current, cribs to hold logs in case of jams, and dams to hold back water to extend the log-driving season. By redirecting the Black's main channel across the northern edge of the city of La Crosse itself, Washburn enabled the eventual establishment of more than twenty sawmills there. The biggest one, of course, was to be his.

He still owned over 200,000,000 board feet of standing pine on the Black River, and in 1871 he joined with four other Maine Yankees to form the La Crosse Lumber Company and build a huge new sawmill on the banks of the redirected river. When completed, the mill's saws were powered by ten boilers, and it employed 165 men. By 1875 he had bought out his partners, and by 1880 the mill was producing 20,000,000 board feet a year, plus the largest shingle output in the upper Mississippi River Valley. Washburn also owned a lumberyard to which he was floating Black River logs as far south as Louisiana, Missouri, only seventy miles north of St. Louis. The great forests seemed inexhaustible. Despite the fact that there were more than thirty mills now in full operation at La Crosse, it would be another twenty years before the great trees were gone. When Cad Washburn died in 1882, the Black River pinery was still at its height, and his estate included close to 30,000 acres there.

Of greater impact than all this activity in Wisconsin, however, was the restless attention Washburn focused on Minnesota. Leaving the day-to-day management of his lumber enterprises to others, he saw an enormous new opportunity in the country to the north.

It has been often said that the line between genius and madness is a thin one. Similar is the difference between vision and hallucination. As we look back at Cadwallader Washburn from the perspective of a century and a half, what jumps out about him is his capacity to see things that other men couldn't. No better example in his lifetime can be found than the moment when he first saw the west shore of the Mississippi River at St. Anthony Falls, Minnesota.

Back in 1856, Washburn's cousin, Dorilus Morrison, who had already acquired timberland for Washburn along Minnesota's Rum River, desired to build a sawmill downstream from these woodlands at a place on the Mississippi River called St. Anthony. There were falls here—the river dropped about forty-six feet in a quarter of a mile—and Morrison figured to power his mill with water diverted from these falls. Although there was some development on the east side at the village of St. Anthony, the west side was still available.

Washburn visited the site. He looked over at the west side of the roaring water. Except for an occasional house or Indian tepee, the land there was empty. Cad saw it, and had a bigger vision. He saw the vast plains to the west full of new settlers— an army of settlers, tending wheat fields all the way to the Rocky Mountains. He saw this sea of wheat crisscrossed by a network of roads and railroads bringing the settlers into the country and taking the wheat back out of it—right to these very falls. He saw the dam he would build channeling a constant flow of water through the canal he would also build. He saw that flow of water directed through sluices to the wheel pits that would power a series of giant mills—mills that he would build to grind the wheat and mill the flour to make the bread to feed the world.

Thus was born the Minneapolis Mill Company. With several partners, Cadwallader purchased eighty-nine acres, includ-

This rare photo of the falls at St. Anthony in 1851 shows what C. C. Washburn saw, and what he helped turn into the city of Minneapolis.
COURTESY MINNESOTA HISTORICAL SOCIETY

ing the rights to the water on the west side of the falls. The company's plan was to provide water power and the sites to use that power. Washburn was an original incorporator, along with nine other expatriate New Englanders, including Morrison. In the wake of the bank panic of 1857, financial pressures on the investors were very great. One of these men, Robert Smith of Alton, Illinois, later wrote Cad that "I never want to live to see another time such as we have had in the dam and canal affair."[1] Two years later, Smith was out of the business.

It was 1863 before the price of lumber began to rebound and Cad could keep his head above water. From his military headquarters in Mississippi, he wrote Elihu in a triumphant tone that "I feel I am now being in a small degree repaid for the trials I have withstood, resisting the prediction of friends and

One hundred years later, the same area looked like this.
COURTESY GENERAL MILLS CORPORATION

foes that I should go down without leaving a bubble to mark the spot."[2] Not for the last time, a cataclysm had passed, and the Washburn brothers were among the few still standing.

In 1865 Cadwallader became president of the company. By 1869 he had bought out Smith and all the other investors except for his youngest brother William and his cousin Morrison. Total capitalization was now $160,000.

The original plan had been to build a dam that would provide a platform for several sawmills. The company would then build a canal, with headraces and wheel pits to provide reliable water power to enable tenants to operate a wide range of factories there. Back in 1857, Cad had appointed his young brother William Drew Washburn, just three years out of Bowdoin College, to be agent for the company, responsible for carrying out the construction and finding some tenants. William did the job, and the city of Minneapolis was born.

The dam was completed in 1859, and by 1860 had four small sawmills on it. William, who completed the Palisade flour mill in 1866, paid no rent, nor did Cad, who completed his Washburn "B" flour mill on the canal the same year. By the mid-1870s, with the help of the Corps of Engineers, a series of low dams, a dike, and an apron were completed, so as to arrest the natural receding of the falls in the soft limestone over which they flowed.

Cadwallader Washburn kept a low profile in Minnesota due to his continuing interest in Wisconsin politics. He easily won election back to his old seat in Congress in 1866 and again in 1868. This service required him to be in Washington four months a year but left him plenty of time to pursue his affairs in La Crosse and Minneapolis. Although associated with the radical faction pressing for the impeachment of President Johnson, he made no major speeches. He worked hard for post offices, post roads, and a district court for his district, and for navigation improvements on the Mississippi River. He was unsuccessful in his opposition to the purchase of Alaska and in his support for a federalized telegraph system. In 1871, almost as a reward for his years of service, he was nominated and elected governor of Wisconsin. Interestingly, he beat James R. Doolittle, a skilled public speaker, not with rhetoric, but with the logic and irrefutable facts that he brought to their debates. With this election, Cad became the second Washburn brother to be governor of a state.

Washburn served for a single two-year term in the governor's chair in Wisconsin. His physical office was a good bit grander than his brother's had been in Augusta, because during his term a fine new state capitol building was completed. Like Israel's governorship in Maine, Cad's term featured many instances of stubborn honesty—albeit politically incorrect. Although he himself was building railroads to feed his mills in Minnesota, he pushed for government regulation of the railroads. He opposed a bill to help Milwaukee tycoon Alexander Mitchell build a bridge for his Chicago, Milwaukee, and St. Paul Railroad across the Mississippi River at La Crosse. This enraged Mitchell but gained favor with the Grangers, a reform group among farmers who depended on reasonable freight rates to get their products to market. Plain-spoken Washburn then alienated his beer-loving German constituents in Milwaukee by favoring restrictions on the sale of liquor in the state, and he weakened his support among farmers by confessing before the State Agricultural Society that, although raised on a farm, he had little but painful memories of it.

His opponents renamed themselves the Reform party, nominated the head of the Grangers as their candidate, and then, using Mitchell's money, upset Washburn in his bid to be reelected governor in 1873. His honesty and his fair-play administration won him respect but not political capital, especially in the eastern part of the state. Three times, in 1861, 1869, and 1875, Cadwallader Washburn was defeated by the legislature for a seat in the U.S. Senate. As one of his eulogists later stated, "His nature was rather unbending, and he could not draw around him those warm friendships that are essentially necessary to political success."3 In retrospect, Cad Washburn was a much better businessman than he was a politician.

Washburn never gave up his affection for Wisconsin or his residence at La Crosse on South Ferry Street. It was a crazy house in design, but occupied a lovely grove overlooking the river. He probably wasn't there enough to notice whether its design worked or didn't work, but his daughters, on their occasional visits, did notice.

Cad was given an honorary degree by the state university in 1873, and later, out of gratitude for his gift of a state-of-the-art observatory there, he was made a life regent. For a man with only the most minimal formal education himself, this was tribute indeed.

His interest in new technology blossomed in Minneapolis. Although he was no more involved with daily operations at the flour mills than in any of his other enterprises, he became a key figure in the evolution of modern milling. This was partly because of the capital he was able to provide, but also because of his willingness to try new things and his great luck in finding good people to implement his plans. As his managers improved and expanded production, he was able to process a broad range of wheats from greater and greater distances. At the same time, his flour reached the highest levels of purity and uniformity, and his agents began to expand his markets across the country.

The decade between 1870 and 1880 saw a revolution in the milling industry, with Washburn's people and Washburn's investors at the head of every development. First there was George H. Christian, recommended by William to manage the "B" mill, a six-story stone building housing twelve pairs of millstones, completed on the canal in 1866. Because of its unprecedented cost of $100,000 and its capacity to produce quantities of flour far in excess of visible demand, it was quickly dubbed "Washburn's Folly." Within a decade, however, it would prove immensely profitable.

Christian brought in Edmund LaCroix, who developed a "purifier" machine that separated the husk of the wheat berry from the rest of the ground material. This "new process" development produced a uniformly high-quality "patent flour" out of the spring wheat that had previously been hard to sell. Demand for the product began to grow. A man named George Smith developed a traveling brush that eliminated clogging in the flour purifiers and greatly increased production.

In 1873 there were a dozen mills grinding flour on the west side canal and paying rent to the Minneapolis Mill Company. The "B" mill was producing 600 barrels of top-quality flour every day, and Cad expected to make a profit of two dollars on every barrel. He began construction of a much larger mill, which he called the "A" mill—but more trouble was ahead.

The bank panic and Washburn's unexpected loss of the Wisconsin governorship in November dampened the fall of 1873 for him. That winter, as money became tight and interest rates soared, his brother William Drew, fearfully overextended through his own headlong construction of sawmills, flour mills, and railroads, was faced with bankruptcy. Despite the heavy expenses for the "A" mill, Cadwallader stepped in to guarantee William's debts, which amounted to several hundred thousand dollars. To do it, he had to use all his resources, including aid from his brother Elihu, who took a mortgage on the new mill, as well as a mortgage on the house in Washington that Cad had just built for his younger daughter Fanny.

Although William's tolerance for debt seems not to have been affected by the harrowing experiences of 1873 and 1874, his brother Cadwallader became thoroughly determined never to go through such an ordeal again. As he wrote Elihu, "I have conceived such a horror of being in debt that a little indebtedness worries me greatly. I am resolved to clear myself at the earliest moment."4

The early 1870s were also a time when Cadwallader made a brave attempt to restore the domestic life that he had lost with his wife's hospitalization in 1852. But it was really too late. In 1869 at La Crosse, his oldest daughter Nettie had married Albert Warren Kelsey, a young man she had met while at school in Massachusetts. Largely financed by his contractor

Cadwallader's effort to reunite his family centered around his purchase of the Edgewood mansion in Madison, shown here in 1876. In the wake of his defeat for a U.S. Senate seat, his daughters and their families moved elsewhere, and he gave the property to the Sisters of Sinsinawa, who made it into today's Edgewood College.
COURTESY WISCONSIN HISTORICAL SOCIETY

father, "Warren" had operated an unsuccessful brickyard in St. Louis. Cad invited the Kelseys, who by that time had one child and were expecting another, to come live with him in an enormous mansion he called Edgewood, which he had purchased in Madison.

Then, in 1872, in a big ceremony at Madison, Governor Washburn oversaw the wedding of his youngest daughter Fanny to Charles Payson, a translator for the State Department whom she had met in Washington. The governor gave her a set of diamonds and a check for $10,000. For a while the Paysons, too, were added to the household.

Everything came apart, however. Cadwallader was upset in his bid to be reelected governor by the leader of the Wisconsin Grange organization, a farmer named William R. Taylor. The Paysons headed back to Washington, where Cad had built them a new house at the corner of 15th and K streets as another wedding present. Then, in 1875, Cad was defeated once more for a seat in the U.S. Senate, this time by the forces of Matthew Carpenter.

Smarting from this humiliation, with his political life seemingly at an end, he must have been hard to live with that year. He had been alone too long not to be master of his own castle. There were some tempests with Nettie—probably over Warren. For Nettie, it was a struggle between the man who had shown her love, and the man who had shown her only authority since the day she was born. She had a will equal to her father's, and in the end she departed with her husband and her children, first back to St. Louis, and then to a new start in Philadelphia. If Cad wanted to see his grandchildren, from then on he would do it as a visitor, not as head of the household. Graciously, he accepted the break and set up a trust to assure Nettie of a comfortable income, even enlisting Cyrus Woodman as trustee.

Thus Cad's political and domestic lives were ended at the same time, and with them went any reason for him to remain in Madison. He gave Edgewood to the Dominican Sisters of Sinsinawa, and it became the campus for present-day Edgewood College.

C. C. Washburn's time in the state capital had finished badly, but better times were ahead. In the next three years, the *Northwestern Miller* trade journal reported that the "B" Mill generated a profit of $650,000. The new "A" mill, with a

Interior of the Washburn "A" Mill, taken about 1875, showing the barrels in which the flour was shipped. Three years after this picture was taken, this entire building blew up, killing eighteen men.
COURTESY MINNESOTA HISTORICAL SOCIETY

capacity to produce 2,600 barrels of flour a day, was completed for an amazing $250,000.

Once again, Cadwallader left day-to-day operation to others. Christian retired, and a company run by his brothers acted as manager of the mills. There were problems until 1877, when Washburn once again found first-class management talent. This time it was John Crosby, an experienced manager from

Bangor, Maine, together with Charles Martin, his long-time personal secretary, and a promising marketing man named William H. Dunwoody. The new Washburn Crosby Company continued as an annually renewed partnership until Washburn's death in 1882.

Dunwoody made the first big contribution. In 1877 he made a trip to call on flour buyers in Liverpool, London, and Glasgow. His reception was not friendly. He had to battle through walls of disbelief, distrust, and fear, but he persevered. Acceptance came in 1878, when foreign orders to Washburn Crosby topped 100,000 barrels. By 1885 they topped two million, and they doubled again to four million barrels by 1895. Dunwoody's cold calling turned out to be a spectacular success.

However, the new team quickly had its baptism by fire. On the evening of May 2, 1878, with an explosion that broke windows seven miles away, the "A" mill blew up and, along with five other mills, was totally destroyed. Although he grieved for the eighteen workmen who were killed in the blast, Washburn maintained an image of calm. He was in Madison when he got the news. After a no-doubt sleepless night, he kept an appointment the next morning with the University of Wisconsin to finalize his gift of the new observatory. Cad's only stipulation regarding the telescope was that it be "bigger than Harvard's." (It was—by one-half an inch.5) Only after the Madison meeting did he proceed to the scene of the disaster in Minneapolis. There, among the still-smoking ruins, he made arrangements for the families of the men who had died in the explosion, then paced out a massive addition to the "B" mill and authorized a new "A" mill as well. Undeterred by the devastation all around him, he was calmly planning to double his production.

The explosion also brought management changes to the company. Always organized as an annually renewed partnership, at Crosby's insistence it was renewed in 1878 without

*The total destruction of nine mills in 1878 only made Cadwallader
Washburn more determined. He rebuilt with twice his earlier capacity.*
COURTESY MINNESOTA HISTORICAL SOCIETY

brother William. In addition, because of friction between the
Christians and Cad's nephew Frederick Stephenson, they were
all omitted as well. As he had shown with his brother Sam at
Waubeek, Cad's priority was always to back good managers
over family members.

For the next eighteen months Washburn waged a huge battle with the insurance companies to pay the coverages promised in their policies. His fight was on behalf of the entire
milling industry. His opponents—a solid wall of eighty-two
insurance companies—fought to avoid paying such claims on
the grounds that their liability was for fire, not explosion.
Finally Cad broke through their obstruction and eventually
collected every cent of what was owed—although at consider-

able cost to his own health. For his own mills, he brought in two more superstars, a Scottish engineer named William Dixon Gray and a Frenchman from the flour-milling business in Europe named William de la Barre, to oversee the new construction.

The new buildings were to contain several revolutionary changes, including a machine for catching the explosive flour dust, and new roller assemblies to replace the millstones that had been used to grind flour since ancient times. Cylindrical rollers made of chilled cast iron held the promise of safer and still higher volumes of production. Urged on by Gray, Washburn agreed to experiment with the new technology, but only on the condition that he wouldn't have to pay for it if it didn't work. It did work, and Washburn gladly purchased twenty-two pairs of the new rollers when the "C" mill and others were built.

There were other innovations, too. As new rail lines were extended out into the wheat country and grain elevators went up at every loading point, in Minneapolis an entire network of railroad tracks was elevated to parallel "mill row" and serve each mill for fastest possible unloading and loading. Special accommodations were even made for unloading and loading railroad freight cars *inside* the mills, including water-powered winches.

Thanks to these and other improvements, by 1881 the Washburn Crosby firm was producing over 6,000 barrels of flour a day. Thanks to Dunwoody, a market for all this production was found first in New England, and then in Europe. In five years' time, 20 percent of all exported American flour was coming from Minneapolis.

In addition, the company began to show a genius for marketing. It won gold, silver, and bronze medals at an international millers' convention in Cincinnati in 1880, and as a

Cadwallader's original vision had included railroads across wheatfields westward to the Rocky Mountains. This picture, taken in western Minnesota in 1868, shows that vision becoming a reality.
Courtesy Minnesota Historical Society

result named its flagship product Gold Medal Flour. This was the first of many marketing triumphs—from Betty Crocker to singing radio commercials—that have characterized General Mills to the present day.

Washburn's health failed him in 1881, but not before he had to build a railroad in order to save his business. Railroad interests in Milwaukee and Chicago had long been hostile to the millers of Minneapolis, including both Cad and William. As the "Chicago Pool" gobbled up other railroads across Wisconsin and Minnesota, they threatened to gain a strangle-hold on all the routes by which the brothers could get their wheat in and their flour out. Both the millers and the farmers could be held hostage to whatever rates the railroad companies wanted to charge. As early as 1871, the Washburns formed a

*Twenty-two years later, this 1890 picture of "mill row" in Minneapolis
shows the complete integration of the railroads with all the mills.*
Courtesy Minnesota Historical Society

consortium of investors determined to build a railroad outward
from Minneapolis in two directions: north to Duluth, the seasonal outlet to the east via the Great Lakes, and south to shipping points past the Des Moines Rapids above St. Louis.

Cad himself had little interest in the railroad business, but
he raised millions and, with William as president, began construction of the Minneapolis and St. Louis Railroad line. His
main purpose was to demonstrate to the Chicagoans that he
was serious about going around them. Also, for the millers, it
was the fastest route south. By 1877 fully one-half of all the
flour manufactured in Minneapolis was being shipped south to
St. Louis on the M&SL Railroad. In 1879 both sides finally
decided to negotiate, and Minneapolis forces at last secured the
long-term shipping rate security they needed. With that goal

attained, Cadwallader was happy to leave railroading to his brother William.

* * *

As Cadwallader used his vision and tenacity to build for the long haul, his younger brother William, "Young Rapid," left a dazzling trail of shorter-term enterprises. He was the most spectacular of the Washburn entrepreneurs, partly because of the sheer number and variety of his undertakings, and partly because of the rapidity with which they all disappeared from his estate. William Drew Washburn—almost a generation younger than his oldest brother Israel, tore across the Minnesota sky like a comet—and disappeared almost as fast as he had appeared. By the time he reached his twenty-first year, he was already the most impressive—in both appearance and education—of all of the brothers and sisters. Slim, dark-haired, six feet tall, and always well dressed, he had a polish shared by none of his siblings. Indeed, they had done their best to make it so.

Thanks to them, William benefited from private schooling and social experience, which complemented the work ethic, honesty, and religious faith that all the Washburns received on their little farm in Livermore. His formal schooling culminated with his graduation from Bowdoin College in 1854. He was only the second of the seven brothers to receive a college degree. His oldest brother Israel, by then a second-term congressman, provided him with summer jobs clerking in Washington at the Treasury Department and then in Congress. In Washington he shared lodgings with his congressmen brothers. After this heady experience, Israel took William under his wing to study for the law in Orono and then under Judge John A. Peters (later chief justice of the Maine Supreme Judicial Court) in Bangor. He was admitted to the Maine bar there in 1857.

Israel and his wife also saw that William was introduced into Bangor society. During one outing, he met the beautiful Elizabeth Muzzy. About him, she later wrote that she "quietly decided that I had never seen anyone so perfectly stunning."[6]

With his handsome looks and genteel education, William was the virtual princeling of the family. Nevertheless, he now made a career decision that showed he was not afraid of risk. Rather than join the Establishment in the east—for which he was richly qualified—he decided to take his chances in the rugged west. He picked Minneapolis, in the frontier territory of Minnesota, where his brother Cadwallader was brewing big plans for taming the Mississippi River. At the time, the place consisted of a small community scattered across the west bank of St. Anthony Falls, ten miles to the west of the territorial capital at St. Paul.

William's first two moves in Minneapolis reflected his top priorities. First, he hung out his lawyer's shingle, advertising his services related to the same land dealings that had provided early careers for his congressman brothers, Israel, Elihu, and Cadwallader. Second, he took rooms with several other young expatriate New Englanders. They called themselves the Passadumkeag Club, and within ten years they would be the most influential men in town. Thus, from almost his first day there, William charted a course that combined the risks of high-stakes speculation with the security of an inner circle of movers and shakers. For the next fifty years he would always have a foot in both camps—the risk-takers and the Establishment.

His brother Cadwallader gave him a fast immersion into the world of risk. Despite the fact that an economic depression had darkened the country, the older brother had gathered a group of investors and formed a company that obtained land along the shore and the rights to develop water power on the west side of the falls. Cadwallader was the driving force as well a chief investor behind the company. But because Cad was tied up with his lumber enterprises in Wisconsin, his political career in Washington, and his creditors all over the East, he needed an agent he could trust to see that the work at the falls got done. He picked young William and brought him into the new company. Directly or indirectly, William would be involved with the power company for most of the next four decades.

It made no difference that the young man knew nothing about dams or sawmills. Cadwallader got him the money, and Young Rapid tore into the job. Within a year, a dam had been built, a sawmill set up on it, and canal construction was underway.

William was good at building things. Within nine years, there would be a total of nine sawmills operating on the property—and William himself would own one of them, together with upstream timberlands to feed it.

From the beginning, young William was eager to see Minneapolis keep up with its neighbor city of St. Paul. He became treasurer, then corresponding secretary, of the first business group in town, the Union Commercial Association. He headed the town's first Universalist Society. He helped establish an athenaeum in town, which housed the town's first library. He was even elected to the territorial legislature, but before he could take his seat, Minnesota became a state and William's new seat was redistricted out of existence.

The young man now decided to bring an end to his bachelorhood. He went back to Bangor to woo and win Elizabeth Muzzy, and to persuade her to join him for a new life on the frontier. He was apparently a good salesman, and the couple was married in Bangor on April 19, 1859. Lizzie survived the rugged trip west, including evaluation by the four Washburn siblings in Galena. She also endured several months' stay at the Nicollet Hotel—the only boardinghouse then in the primitive town. She got used to the mud and dust, and grew to appreciate the respect that her husband was earning in the community. Within six months, the couple was able to rent a small house (after cleaning chicken feathers out of it), and Lizzie wrote with pride about making her husband a pair of blue denim overalls.

As the mill company continued to eat up cash, some of the partners were unable to meet their assessments. Debts, including unpaid taxes, began to mount. Juggling obligations, Agent Washburn was still able to attract three additional sawmills to the dam, and in 1859 brought the first flour mill—the Cataract Mill—to the canal. Construction expenses far outpaced income, however, and it would be many years before the Minneapolis Mill Company's enormous investment would see a profit. As it happened, most of the other partners had to sell out, and Cadwallader, William, and their cousin Dorilus Morrison wound up sole owners.

William was not as vulnerable to the depressed state of the lumber business as were the other two, but still Cadwallader thought that the tough times might do him good. He wrote Sid about William, "He professes great distress of mind that he has not been able to meet this obligation, all of which I should believe, were he less reckless and extravagant. If he can be harassed awhile, it may do him some good."[7]

It didn't. By 1866, with lumber prices high again, William had a note outstanding to Elihu of $3,000 for the construction of his Lincoln sawmill. A river of short-term paper was also flowing between him and his banker brother Sid back in Hallowell, and there were obligations to Boston banks. Finally, in 1874, it all caught up with him. On the verge of bankruptcy, William bared himself to his creditors. He suspended his business and turned everything over to pay his debts. Cadwallader, stretched thin himself, stood stoutly by in support. (William wrote Elihu that "Cad stood by me like a hero.")[8] When the dust finally settled, $600,000 in debts were paid off, and William still had some impressive assets left over: his home, his property and two mills at Anoka, 11,000 acres of pinelands in Minnesota and Wisconsin, 8,000,000 feet of cut lumber, and from $300,000 and $400,000 of "miscellaneous."[9]

In the wake of this embarrassment, it was no surprise the following June, perhaps with Cad's approval, that Elihu, then minister to France, invited William and his family to get out of Minneapolis and come visit him in Paris. With Lizzie and the children settled with Adele and her family in Paris, the two brothers went off to visit the newly opened Suez Canal and hobnob with Ferdinand de Lesseps, the man who had built it. This might have had the result of cooling William off, or of heating him up again, since de Lesseps was a world-class risk-taker in his own right.

* * *

So far in this narrative of big dreams and unflinching determination, we have not spent much time with the second Washburn son. Easygoing Algernon Sidney Washburn was the most gregarious of the brood. He loved to laugh, and his more serious siblings loved him for it. In addition, he was unfailingly there for them—an early source of funding when they needed it most. Not as ambitious or visionary as his brothers, he was a rock of support that linked them to their native state.

For Sid back in Maine, his generosity toward his brothers turned into a considerable business. His early loans to Cad and Elihu were short-term notes, and every one was repaid promptly—with interest. As the loans continued and grew in size, so did the interest. It went from a few dollars every few months to a steady stream sufficient enough for Sid to live on.

Back in 1852 Cadwallader had approached Sid with the scheme that would change his life. The brothers and their investors had begun to consider the advantages of owning their own bank. They could provide the initial backing with promissory notes. Like any bank, they could earn income through the interest they charged on money they loaned out, and they could be the biggest recipients of their own loans. In the era before there was a national currency or instant communication, they could also loan cash in the form of bank notes they printed themselves, which would save them the need for capital until the notes were presented back for redemption. This might be months later, if their bank's home base was far enough away from where the notes were being circulated.

The ideal venue would be in a small town in a small eastern state. No federal approval was necessary. State regulators were amenable if the community was, and both were sympathetic to commercial enterprises. Despite the checkered history of business schemes in the west, investment there was still the best hope for putting eastern dollars to work. What was needed to get started was experience with western lands and a trusted local connection. Cad had plenty of experience and no shortage of investment ideas. Sid, he decided, would provide the local trust.

Banks in nineteenth-century America were essentially local institutions, and out-of-town ownership was generally not welcome. To be accepted in a community, the bank needed to be owned and operated by people who were known in that community. Cad and his investors were thwarted by this parochialism in several efforts to buy banks in northern New England between 1850 and 1852. Finally, they learned that a charter was about to become available in a community that knew them all very well—Hallowell, Maine. Cad swung into action. He persuaded one of the most successful men in the town, Artemas Leonard (the same man who had originally sold Israel Sr. his farm in Livermore) to sponsor the operation and to be its figurehead president. Then, together with his brother Elihu, he approached Sid.

Would their easy-to-like brother, who was already well known in the town, be willing to forsake his mercantile career in Boston, return to Hallowell, and take charge of the operation of the new bank as its cashier? Sid, tired of dealing with delinquent customers in Boston, as ever, was amenable.

With his brothers carefully out of sight in the background, other well-known local people were signed up as investors. Sid came to town and charmed prominent locals by rolling tenpins with them on the village green. Potential opponents were brought into the fold with promises of loans, and in 1852 the Bank of Hallowell was incorporated with A. S. Washburn listed as cashier and owner of 15,000 shares of stock. On June 22 Sid wrote Elihu that the bank's notes were going "like hotcakes."

Sid's main job was printing bills and shipping them west for circulation by his brothers and their associates up and down the Mississippi. He was also in charge of the bank's specie, and he redeemed the notes when they eventually found their way "home." He also presented a friendly and reassuring face around the town. That he did this well was evidenced by the state banking commissioners in 1854, who reported that the Bank of Hallowell was "owned mostly by men of wealth and of good business capacity" and that "we regard this bank as sound and good."[10]

For three years the bank paid a dividend, and Sidney became a fixture of the town. On January 11, 1854, at the age of thirty-nine, he brought his long bachelorhood to an end and married Sarah Moore of Bangor. The following year, the first of their three children was born. The Washburns were soon established in a lovely home on Middle Street, which Sid's siblings soon christened "Blythe House," due to the happy times they had during visits there. It was a cherished refuge for them all.

Cad's enterprises in the west, and now his debts in the east, were dependent on a steady flow of cash from his lumber operations in Wisconsin. When the bottom dropped out of the lumber market in 1856, Cad found himself desperately overextended. His status as a congressman helped stave off most of his creditors, but his eagle-eyed Yankee bank partners were more demanding, as were the state banking commissioners. Late that year, they initiated an injunction to shut down the Hallowell bank's operations. They listed sixteen reasons, the biggest of which was insufficient capital to cover obligations—especially the over $40,000 in uncovered notes that the bank had in circulation. Although Sid got the injunction postponed, and then modified, Cad's interest in the Bank of Hallowell began to cool.

Fewer agencies in the west would now take their notes, and competitors in Boston and Chicago presented an increasing threat to show up without warning with large amounts of notes to be redeemed. As their specie was threatened, so was the trust with which the brothers had established the bank. Cad's new source of cash was proving far more time-consuming and worrisome than he had anticipated.

It was also providing fodder for his political opponents. Cad had won a seat in Congress in 1854, but only after overcoming a false last-minute rumor that his bank had failed. Congressman Elihu also had to go to great lengths to protect his political flanks from similar charges in that campaign. In 1855 Cad decided to shut the bank down. In line with state laws, they stayed open two more years but issued no further notes, and finally closed their doors, just ahead of the Panic of 1857, and just ahead of the receivers appointed by the bank commissioners in Maine.

It is hard today to estimate who won and who lost with the closure of the Bank of Hallowell. The 1858 commissioners' report listed assets of $42,000 for the bank, mostly in loans outside the state. Since the borrowers who got to use the money were the stockholders who owned the bank, their net losses were probably small. Seventeen stockholders were listed, with less than ten percent of the listed stock held within the state of Maine. Elihu (Illinois) and Cadwallader (Wisconsin) owned almost 40,000 of the 80,000 shares outstanding, brother-in-law Charles Stephenson (Illinois) owned 10,000, and Sid himself was listed as owning over 5,000. Much of this stock may never have been paid for, so its ownership represented no loss. As for the thousands of Hallowell "shin plasters" in circulation, it can be supposed that, after two years, most of those that were never presented for redemption were squirreled away in mattresses, lost or forgotten. A few, bearing Sid's and Artemus Leonard's signatures, can be found in antique stores today.

Cad later admitted that no enterprise he had ever tried had caused him as much mortification and regret as the Bank of Hallowell, but despite the experience, he was reelected to Congress four more times. Elihu was reelected seven more times and became an important ally of both Abraham Lincoln

COURTESY FRANK TRASK

and Ulysses Grant. Their crusty cousin Dorilus Morrison, who had also invested in the Bank of Hallowell and used its notes to pay his lumber crews in Minnesota, later referred to the bank as "a disreputable, shyster machine." However, he invested again with Sid five years later. In fact, the stubbornness with which Cad honored his Hallowell notes may have contributed to the strengthening of his reputation in those circles of investors he would later need most to help him build his flour mills in Minneapolis.

The closure of the Bank of Hallowell took place with little effect on the town's placidity. No fact argues more strongly for this than Sid's own continuing career there afterward. Far from being a pariah, he happily stayed in the town, his reputation apparently none the worse for wear. In 1859 he was appointed secretary and clerk of the Hallowell and Chelsea Bridge Company, a group of local merchants who built a toll bridge across the Kennebec River, so that farmers in the country on the opposite side could more easily get their produce into town. He also served as clerk of the Gas Light Company, another new business enterprise aimed at contributing to the public good in Hallowell.

He was even made a justice of the peace, and he was no doubt present at the state capitol just up the road from Hallowell in Augusta to see his older brother Israel sworn in as governor of Maine in January 1860. A loyal worker for the Republican cause, Sid was one of the six Washburn brothers who journeyed to Washington to see Lincoln inaugurated two months later.

Other than these events, however, Sid kept a low public profile. His income came from continued private loan activities, plus occasional sales of lumber from his Wisconsin lands. He oversaw major repairs to the farmhouse in Livermore and collected from his brothers to help pay for them.

Algernon Sidney Washburn
Courtesy Washburn Library

The war brought many changes, especially in the increased strength of the central government. High on the list of these changes was the rebirth of a central bank, the creation of a federal banking system, and the launching of a single national currency. In anticipation of these changes, in February 1862 Sid joined a group of local citizens to organize the First National Bank of Hallowell. As in his previous enterprise, he was to be cashier. Again Cad, Sid, younger brother William, and even cousin Dorilus bought stock in the new institution, despite any lingering bad taste in their mouths from their Bank of Hallowell experience. They were cautious, however. Elihu wrote Sid in 1864, "You can not be too careful in your management of your concern.... Unless it be entirely different from your old concern, it will go to the devil in no time...."[11]

Young brother William was beginning to have major need for capital. In 1864 he wrote to Sid for a loan of "two to three thousand dollars. Can you let me have it? I have $15,000 to $20,000 in logs lying back."[12] The informal phrasing of this request makes it sound as if it was being made outside Sid's new bank. As their fortunes ebbed and flowed, all the brothers seem to have preferred the flexibility and confidentiality of paying for money as an article of trust between brothers, rather than as part of a reportable business. Sid's new bank could have used this business.

What the bank did get from William was a very unhappy stockholder. After Sid blasted William for not paying his loans as they matured, William complained to Sid about the bank loaning at twelve percent but declaring a dividend of only seven percent. Later, William wrote Sid, "I wish you would sell my stock [at] the first opportunity."[13]

Sadly, documentation on the First National Bank of Hallowell is scarce. We know that it was chartered on March 11, 1864, along with two other national banks in Hallowell. We also know that it was liquidated on April 19, 1869. It issued a total of $54,350 in federally backed notes, so it must have had at least $75,000 invested into it. But there is no official record as to who the stockholders were or why the bank was shut down.

What we do know is that in 1866 the new bank lost Sid's attention. The cause was no one's fault. Life that year dealt easygoing Sid an almost unendurable tragedy.

In February, Sarah, after a very difficult pregnancy, died in childbirth. The baby, another boy, lived less than a week longer. As if that weren't enough, Sid's oldest boy James, age ten, died in June, just three months after that. The cause was listed as diabetes. In four months' time, the happy house on Middle Street had gone from five people expecting to be six, to three people with no expectations. Sid and his two motherless sons were alone.

When the bank quietly closed in 1869, the stock certificates from various family members were surrendered with no complaints. When Elihu sent Sid some money from France in 1870 to deposit into savings accounts for his four children, he instructed Sid to set up the accounts in a savings bank in Augusta.

Letters to Sid from his brother William show a continuing stream of short-term loans. In 1869 William had $7,000 outstanding from Sid, and by 1873 William was rolling over two $2,500 notes every month and paying his brother from $40 to $85 in interest each time. The Panic of 1873 resulted in an enormous cash crunch for William, and both Sid and Cad had to bail him out. The appeals of his two entrepreneur brothers to Sid give an idea about the scale of his private lending activities: "I must have $10,000 or bust"; "I need money badly, very badly"; "This money I must have"; and "I must have $10,000 in 30 days. Must have." By the following spring the crisis was past, and Cad wrote Sid that he expected to get "caught up by August 14th." However, Cad was still making payments to Sid five years later. Between his two anxious western brothers, the Hallowell banker was realizing a comfortable living by making quiet loans outside any official channels.[14]

Following a vacation trip to Minneapolis in 1870, Sid also began acting as an informal flour broker for his brothers. He reported in September 1874 that their "new process" flour was selling well at the Hallowell grocery store, and a week later William was writing that he was shipping a carload more of it.

Sid also continued to realize income from the sale of logs off

Sid and his two surviving sons, John and Robert, known as "the mackerel brigade." COURTESY OF WASHBURN LIBRARY

his Wisconsin lands, and from the sale of the lands themselves. As his two sons each prepared for Bowdoin College at Westbrook Seminary (where Uncle Israel had long been a trustee), Sid maintained his bachelor quarters at Blythe House in Hallowell, much to the concern of his sisters-in-law. (Elizabeth, William's wife, reported after an 1873 visit that the food there was unfit to eat.) Sid's justice of the peace duties continued in Hallowell through 1874, and his oldest son John, who would be the most successful of the entire next generation of the family, entered Bowdoin in 1876. (See Appendix A.)

* * *

A less successful entrepreneurial experience was in store for
navy veteran Sam after he was discharged in October 1865—
though it started with a success. During the war, Cad had
wanted to buy back Sam's share of Waubeek, but Sam held out
for a price of $4,000. Cad grudgingly offered $3,000, and ful-
minated to Elihu that, with this kind of money Sam would
surely resign from the navy and would be a failure at any other
business he tried. A month later, Cad finally caved in, agreeing
to meet Sam's price of $4,000 with payments of $500 semian-
nually. The general commented to Elihu, "I shall be glad to be
clear of him [Sam] in a business way on any terms. The most
unfortunate act of my life was to entrust him with my business.
If he gets this money which I propose to pay him, I am almost
certain that he will resign. If you can prevent it, do it. He is
wholly incompetent to make a dollar if left to himself and will
soon get rid of what he has."[15]

On his discharge papers, Sam listed his address as Durand,
Pepin County, Wisconsin—the nearest post office to Waubeek.
It was there that the two stubborn Washburn brothers at last
completed their deal. Cad got Sam out of Waubeek, and Sam
got income enough to try his own hand at business. He thought
he knew something about the lumber business, so he decided
to take advantage of the floods of new settlers who were
streaming into the farm country of southern Minnesota by
establishing a lumber business there. He picked the settlement
of Owatonna, in good farm country about fifty miles south and
west of the Chippewa River.

It was a good choice. When he and Lorette and Bennie got
there, the place had a population of 700. By 1871 it had tripled.
Unfortunately, so had the competition. By 1868, there were
three lumber dealers in town, and by 1870 there were five. The
business required hard physical work and close attention to

accounts. Sam's wounded leg made physical work almost impossible, and he began to have trouble collecting the money his customers owed him. Although he advertised free delivery in the *Owatonna Journal*, there was just too much supply and not enough demand. Cad's dour predictions began to come true.

Sam was well liked around the town. He was nominated to fill a vacancy on the board of aldermen, and in 1867 he was elected mayor. In 1868 he was elected to the local school board and made an officer of the Masonic Lodge, but everything fell apart for him in 1869. In February Lorette died as a result of giving birth to the second of two babies since 1866. Both of these babies also died. Like his brother Sid with his two sons, Sam and seven-year-old Bennie were suddenly alone. In addition, Cadwallader's payments for Waubeek came to an end. Sam hung on for another year, probably financed by Sid back in Maine, to whom he wrote in April of 1870, "Times are awful and no money in sight."[16] He chaired the annual meeting of Republicans in Owatonna in 1871, but in July there was a notice that all the unpaid debts of the lumberyard had gone to collection, and Sam and Bennie headed back to Livermore. Behind them, the furniture was auctioned off for $700 in October, and the house was sold in February.

* * *

As Sam quietly crashed in Owatonna, William, like Icarus, was flying higher and higher in Minneapolis. Following the war, he had continued to represent Cad's interests in Minneapolis, as well as developing new ones of his own. Far from being content with the Minneapolis Mill Company, Young Rapid attracted enough investment support to tear into other ventures. He now had flour mills of his own and became all too aware of the millers' increasing dependence on rail transportation.

In 1869 William wrote several urgent letters to Cadwallader about the threats of a man named Merrill, agent for the

Milwaukee Railroad, who he called "a scoundrel" and "a he-devil." Merrill was conspiring to put his main line into rival St. Paul, relegate the mills at Minneapolis to a spare track, and exert total control over the rates charged to transport their flour. One dark night, Milwaukee crews even removed one spur line that was vital for the Minneapolis millers. As William wrote, "we have got to have other railroad connections or we are gone up."17

As it turned out, building railroads was something William could do very well. He was happy to become director of the construction company that began building the new line north to Duluth and south toward St. Louis. With partner Henry Titus Welles, William boasted that they built their line without the aid of a single federal land grant. Over swamp and tundra and prairie, through financial bust and boom, he overcame every obstacle to connect with the Rock Island Line at Albert Lea, Minnesota, in 1877, thus creating the shortest route to St. Louis from Minneapolis.18

It is significant that William Drew Washburn, elected to the Minnesota State Legislature in 1871, like his brother as governor in Wisconsin two years later, supported legislation in favor of some degree of state authority over railroads. Both brothers, despite their personal stake in the railroad business, were concerned about their vulnerability to big-city railroad monopolists. They supported the radical idea that some government control over the railroads was in their own best interests, as well as in the interest of the public at large. They were squarely on the side of the farmers who supplied them their raw materials. To them, unlike most of the famous railroad barons of the day, railroads were always an adjunct to the main business of milling and never an object of profit in themselves.

William's interest in the civic affairs of the community was not always received well. In 1872 he offered a choice piece of land to the city for a new city hall and courthouse, but was rebuffed by a city council suspicious of his motives. On the other hand, that same year he became an incorporator of a new street railway company for the city, and came within a single vote of winning the Republican nomination for governor.

William's business enterprises multiplied—perhaps too fast. He chose Anoka, twenty miles upstream and closer to his forestlands than Minneapolis, for a gigantic new sawmill, and he formed the W. D. Washburn Company to run it. When completed, this operation, which included planing mills and dry houses, produced twenty-five million board feet of lumber per year. (It inspired Cadwallader to build an equally enormous sawmill at his home city of La Crosse.) William also opened another flouring mill in Minneapolis, the Palisade Mill.

William reached a pinnacle of recognition in the business community when he was elected president of the newly evolved Minneapolis Board of Trade. He arranged a notable event for this group in 1873 by inviting his oldest brother Israel, then collector of customs in Portland, Maine, to come west with his wife Maud to visit their son, and to give a speech to the Board of Trade. This Israel did. He used the occasion to make a radical proposal to the assembled businessmen of Minneapolis. He suggested that there was another way of bypassing the grasp of the railroad barons in Milwaukee and Chicago—a much faster route east than via St. Louis. He pointed to Michigan's remote Upper Penninsula, and to the exciting new railroad connections being built in Canada. The Grand Trunk Railroad was now running smoothly between Montreal and Portland's enormous ice-free harbor, and large grain elevators were in place at the waterfront there. By building a new road across northern Michigan, to connect with the Canadian Pacific at Sault Ste. Marie, the Minnesotans could gain direct access to friendly East Coast export facilities at

Portland—avoiding completely the danger of arbitrary rate hikes or deliberate delays in unfriendly Milwaukee and Chicago. This was a great dream, and William listened carefully.

Sadly for them all, Israel's wife Maud became ill and died at William's home later that summer. This was the prelude for a cascade of other troubles in 1873. On October 1, the crash of Jay Cooke's bank in Philadelphia precipitated a national economic crisis to which the overheated economy of the upper Mississippi River Valley was especially vulnerable. Cooke's fall carried with it the Northern Pacific Railroad, which controlled the finances of the Minneapolis and St. Louis. The line reverted to local control, and William was caught badly overextended. Though he didn't know how much money he owed, he remained upbeat as always. He promised his brother Sid in August a wheat crop that "shall astonish the natives," but in September reported that "this infernal row" might result in "a temporary stagnation of our business," despite good orders from the east and overseas. He also hoped that "our Eastern friends will be in a position to give us a good boost." By January, he was blithely reporting that "we are all foxy and well."[19]

Cadwallader was not so blithe. At the beginning of the crisis, one of William's notes that had gone through Sid apparently went to court for collection. When he heard about it, Cad reacted with outrage at both Sid and William. He was angry that William had gotten himself so overextended, and he was even more upset that Sid had allowed William's troubles to be exposed to public view. "I am vexed beyond experience and mad as a March hare," he wrote Sid.[20] Nevertheless, although it stretched him badly, Cad stepped in. He covered the note in question and pledged his own credit toward William's other obligations. William's milling business was suspended "for a few months" while Cad paid off the most pressing debts. Brother Elihu, now in France, had to throw in some money to keep

Cadwallader himself afloat. It was a scary time for them all, but somehow the brothers made it through. William, the prodigal son, was operating under some powerful protection. As Mother Patty had observed years earlier, her boys "lifted each other up."

William's seemingly carefree attitude toward debt marked another example of the differences between the older and younger members of this remarkable generation of Maine farm boys. Debt for Israel and Elihu and Cadwallader during their formative years had meant fear, dislocation, abandonment, and brutal hard work, to say nothing of disgrace and humiliation. None of the younger children had to endure what their older siblings had had to go through. Cadwallader emerged from the 1873 crisis greatly sobered, and determined never to be so exposed again. William, on the other hand, did not seem to be so affected by the crisis. He had been bailed out by his big brother again, and his other big brother Elihu was about to spirit him out of the country entirely to allow things to cool off a bit in Minneapolis. But Young Rapid never lost his appetite for taking chances. When his older brothers were no longer there to protect him, William's enormous optimism would bring him to ruin.

Following the crisis of 1873, William had to reorganize the W. D. Washburn Company as the Washburn Mill Company. He had to pledge all of his assets to his creditors, but after they had liquidated more than $600,000 worth, in October 1874 he still felt easy enough to come east for a reunion of Bowdoin classmates. To his brother Sid, still fretting over past-due obligations in Maine, William wrote, "Keep cool."[21] He even had Sid selling flour for him in Maine.

Upon his return to Minneapolis after his trip to France and Egypt in 1875, an unchastened William Drew ran faster than ever. He had already built and owned, fully or in part, four different businesses. Besides the water-power company, these

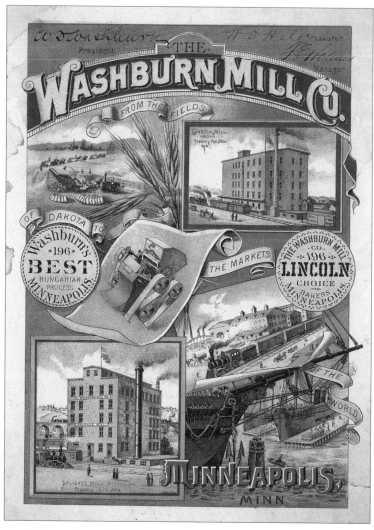

"From the Fields of Dakota to the Markets of the World,"
a promotional poster for William's flour mill, which he later
merged with the Pillsbury mills.
COURTESY MINNESOTA HISTORICAL SOCIETY

included his sawmills and flour mills, and, of course, the Minneapolis and St. Louis Railroad.

As Cadwallader succeeded in selling his interest in the M&SL at good terms, his younger brother clung to the dream of bypassing the Chicago railroads. when the Minneapolis and St. Louis was completed to the coal fields south of Fort Dodge, Iowa, in 1877, William resigned its presidency in order to take on another railroad challenge. Always remembering Israel's speech to the Board of Trade in 1873, and still apprehensive about the millers' vulnerability to the railroad moguls in Chicago and Milwaukee, William undertook to build the line that Israel had suggested. William found eleven partners to build a railroad eastward to Canada and westward to the Dakotas. In 1883 the Minneapolis and Sault Ste. Marie Railroad was born.

The railroad line across Upper Michigan was William's greatest accomplishment. Called "perhaps the cleanest railroad project of its size in the country," the route was built without stock manipulations, federal land grants, or any significant subsidies. For six years William drove construction at a furious pace across some of the most challenging wilderness in the country—300 miles of alternating Pre-cambrian schist, bottomless swamps, and trackless forest of the Upper Michigan peninsula.

Daniel Willard, later President of the Baltimore and Ohio Railroad, remembered at the beginning of this project, "We had ten miles of railroad, a second-hand engine, and a flat car. The old gentleman, who was President and financier of the road, used to sit on a soap box on the flat car, while I, the first brakeman, screwed down the brakes. I rode with him many times over the Soo Line, when he was running the locomotive."[22] On occasions like this Young Rapid must have lived up to his nickname.

Rough country for railroad building in Upper Michigan. This rock cut near L'Anse Township illustrates the challenges that had to be overcome in building the 300-mile route from Minneapolis to Sault Ste. Marie.
COURTESY ARCHIVES OF MICHIGAN

William's ambitious line was also extended from Minneapolis five hundred miles westward across the wheat fields to Montana. In 1888, the year William became the only Washburn brother elected to the U.S. Senate, the Soo Line, nicknamed "the Miller's Road," fulfilled Cadwallader's vision of bringing wheat from the Rockies to the world. That first year, the Soo Line carried over a million barrels of flour to eastern markets. The port of Portland, Maine, sprouted two enormous sets of grain elevators, and up to 400 vessels at a time could be seen at anchor in Portland's copious harbor. William's only regret was that his big brother Israel, who had died in 1883, was not there to see the realization of his original vision.[23]

There seemed to be nothing William wouldn't try. In 1881 he took on the famous mogul of St. Paul, James J. Hill. The venue was the fashionable watering hole of Lake Minnetonka, to the west of Minneapolis. William built the nation's first electrified steamboat there, the *City of Genius*, to compete with Hill's boat in serving the resorts along the lakeshore that each man's railroads had developed. Prominent rusticators of the day long remembered the fiery races across the lake, the two side-wheelers belching smoke and churning the placid evening waters, three decks crowded with cheering passengers on each vessel.

Over the next three decades William would build six more businesses. From northern Michigan to the plains of Montana, there would be three more railroads, uncounted grain elevators, the big sawmill plus a flour mill at Anoka, and the largest lignite coal mine in the world in North Dakota. He would also engineer two massive consolidations.

The first of these latter was the Pillsbury-Washburn Flour Milling Company, Ltd., which included his two flour mills, the water-power company, and the entire Pillsbury milling operation on the east bank of the river. The Pillsburys had long been Washburn rivals in the flour business, and both had enjoyed phenomenal growth. In 1882, the year that Cad died, Minneapolis was providing an estimated twenty-five loaves of bread a year for every person in the nation.[24] Such growth attracted the attention of investors from overseas, and in 1889 a team from England appeared in Minneapolis eager to get a share in the impressive returns being generated by the millers there. Their pockets were deep, and they offered a good price. The Pillsburys, Charles A. and John S., were tired and ready to pass their responsibilities on to others. William Washburn was riding high. His new railroad had been completed to Sault Ste.

Marie the previous year, and he had just been elected to the U.S. Senate. His new mansion was the talk of Minneapolis. Unlike Cad, he did not seem to possess the ability to concentrate his enormous energies in any one enterprise for long. Once each new enterprise was built, his attention seemed to wander, and he was happy to sell out.

So a deal was done with the British. The new company, capitalized for the equivalent of almost eight million U.S. dollars, retained the Pillsburys and William on its American Management Committee. Washburn was paid $1,525,000 in cash, debentures, and stock.[25] Their five flouring mills (representing about half the flour production in Minneapolis), 150 grain elevators across Minnesota and the Dakotas, and the rights to water power on both sides of the river, were now in the control of 300 investors in London. Vast amounts of British capital were soon poured into various improvements, and three years later Pillsbury-Washburn was the largest flour-milling company in the world, with a capacity of producing 14,800 barrels of flour every day—almost half again as much as Cad's Washburn Crosby Company.

Washburn Crosby held out against the foreign-owned behemoth. Cad's managers stoutly and successfully fended off all buyout offers, even overcoming the opposition of some of Cad's family. The name Washburn on each of the two biggest flour millers in town apparently had no damaging effect on sales. Washburn Crosby retained its independence and local ownership, going on to become General Mills in 1928. The ultimate triumph came for them seventy-three years later, in 2001, when the company purchased Pillsbury for an amount that would have dazzled even William—more than $10 billion.

William's second consolidation was the creation of the Soo Line Railroad, nick-named "the Miller's Road."

Cash was short in 1888, and the best source for much-

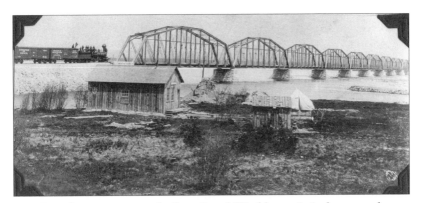

*First flour train over the Soo: Israel Washburn, Jr.'s dream and,
after eight years of effort, William Drew Washburn's greatest triumph.
With this train, poised to cross the new bridge to Canada, the first
all-season route for the Minneapolis millers to markets on the
East Coast and beyond was secure at last.*
COURTESY OF GORDON T. DAUN COLLECTION,
BAYLISS PUBLIC LIBRARY, SAULT STE. MARIE, MICHIGAN

needed funding was in Canada. Assembled at the insistence of
Canadian investors, the Soo system was a combination of the
four lines William had built, extending from Sault Ste. Marie
across the pine forests of northern Michigan, and west to the
plains of Alberta and Montana, and south to Iowa. The new
system continued to free both farmers and millers alike from
the threat of usurious rates at the rail hubs of Chicago and
Milwaukee. Once the construction and consolidation were
complete in 1889, as usual William moved on, but retained his
board membership. He had new responsibilities that went with
his new seat in the Senate.

Over the years, William would become owner or major
stockholder in many smaller businesses around Minneapolis:
the first electric company, the first streetcar company, a
foundry, a farm equipment factory and a woolen mill in
Minneapolis, a bank and an opera house in Anoka, a silver

mining company, as well as the aforementioned first electrified steamboat in the country on Lake Minnetonka.

William and Cadwallader had both emerged from the 1873 crisis bloodied but unbowed. The years that followed brought new triumphs to both of them, and to brother Elihu, as well. Israel's last years would be quieter, but full of honors. Sid's and Charles's last years would be still quieter, and Sam's and his sisters' would be the quietest of all. It would be crown prince William who would rise the highest and fall the farthest. His final story is shrouded in mystery, but, like the fabled green flash of sunsets in the Caribbean, it adds a spectacular element to the sunset of this remarkable generation.

1. Robert Smith to CCW, September 20, 1858 (EBW Papers, LC).

2. CCW to EBW, July 12, 1863 (EBW Papers, LC).

3. From *Memorial Addresses on the Life and Character of C. C. Washburn*, delivered before the Wisconsin Historical Society, July 25, 1882, and printed by the society, 1883, 18.

4. CCW to EBW, Feburary 8, 1875 (EBW Papers, LC)

5. Robert C. Bless, *The History of Washburn Observatory*, (Madison, WI: 1978), 1.

6. From "Early Memories of Elizabeth Muzzy Washburn," a paper by her daughter Mary Washburn Baldwin (Washburn Library), 37.

7. CCW to ASW, October 15, 1859, from ASW Papers.

8. WDW to EBW, December 6, 1874 (Washburn Library).

9. Article in *Minneapolis Miller* dated October 27, 1874, WDW collection (Washburn Library).

10. *Maine State Bank Commisioner's Annual Report*, (Augusta, Maine, 1853), 8.

11. EBW to ASW, April 11, 1864 (Washburn Papers, Duke University Library).

12. WDW to ASW, Aug 27, 1864 (Duke).

13. WDW to ASW, Oct 23, 1864 (Duke).

14. From misc. letters (Washburn Library).

15. CCW to EBW, September 11 and 14 and October 11, 1863 (LC)

16. SBW to ASW, April 9, 1870 (Washburn Library).

17. WDW to CCW, May 6 and 10, 1869 (CCW Papers, Minnesota Historical Society).

18. From the biography of WDW by Robert M. Frame III in *Railroads in the*

Nineteenth Century, 425–28.

19. WDW to ASW, August 27, October 3 and 5, 1873, and January 14, 1874 (ASW Papers, Minnesota Historical Society).

20. CCW to ASW, June 29, 1873 (Duke).

21. WDW to ASW August 4, 1874 (Duke).

22. Stanley Washburn, Sr., manuscript of autobiography (Washburn Library), 7.

23. See John A. Gjevre, *The Saga of the Soo,* privately published by the author, 1973.

24. William J. Powell, *Pillsbury's Best* (Minneapolis: 1985), 9.

25. Powell 46.

———•••———

NINE

Gilded Age Finale

THE LAST YEARS OF EACH of the Washburn siblings, and the fortunes of their children, were as varied as were the rest of their lives. All were driven by their common integrity. Some were more stiff-backed than others. Some finished their lives quietly, well away from the center of the stage. Others were larger than life to the end. Their exceptional range of activity and fortune continued to the end of their lives.

They were more separated chronologically at their deaths than they had been at their births. They had been born within twenty years of one another, but their deaths spanned a period of almost sixty years—from post–Civil War to post–World War I. Their deeds reflected their times, and, for the youngest, their times were very different.

As we have seen, Mary Buffum was the first to go. She died at her home on the edge of Lyons, Iowa, in 1867, as did the twins to whom she had just given birth. She was buried with her twins at Oakland Cemetery in Clinton, Iowa, of which Lyons is now a part. Always a practical man, Gustavus Buffum came back to Orono, Maine, to find a replacement for Mary. This he soon did, in the person of Roxanna Kent Chase, who immediately returned with him to Lyons to help with his remaining three children. In 1873 Cad decided to move his lumberyard farther south, closer to St. Louis. With Buffam's help he chose Louisiana, Missouri, seventy miles north of St. Louis, at a point where railroads extended both west across Missouri and east into central Illinois, and a railroad bridge had just been completed across the river. When Cad died in 1882, Gustavus and his two sons continued to manage the yard in Louisiana. In 1888, as part of the final settlement of Cad's estate, his executors sold the La Crosse Lumber operation in Missouri to the Buffums. Gustavus continued his evenhanded management there, brought his two sons into the business with him, and became a solid enough citizen that the state governor even made him an honorary colonel.

As with the mills in Minneapolis, Cad's choice of managers for his lumber business in Louisiana turned out well. Long after the giant mill in La Crosse had run out of trees and shut down, under the Buffums' management the Missouri operation had spread across Missouri and Illinois. After Gustavus died in 1899, the company lived on under his sons and grandsons. The La Crosse Lumber Company flourishes in multiple locations across Illinois and Missouri to this day, and two Buffum descendants still serve on its board.

After the death of sister Mary in Lyons, brother Sid was the next Washburn sibling to go. He never got over the disaster of losing his wife and half of his children in 1866. In the ten years that followed, he and the surviving boys spent much of the time at the farm in Livermore. They played an important role acting as overseers during the construction projects that took place there. These started when Boyscroft burned while being renovated in 1867, and the brothers immediately decided to replace it with a much better accommodation for their elderly father.

All the brothers dug deep, especially Elihu, William, Israel Jr., and Cad, and the result was a fine mansion. Sid and Israel kept an eye on construction, and Sid paid the bills. Visiting by turns, they raced to beat the oncoming winter. Israel noted in October that there were twenty-four carpenters, five masons, and five others hard at work, and that the cost would be more than he and Sid had estimated, but less than the western brothers predicted. The total cost on December 31 was listed as $4,500—probably more money than had ever before been spent on a house in Livermore.

Over the years Sid's brothers had criticized him for his relaxed manner and casual way of accepting responsibility. Although he did enjoy a solitary cigar in the evening and a glass of claret with his dinner, he was not adverse to hard work. He was more skilled than any of their other helpers in the brutal field work of using the "break-up plough" in the spring. When new workmen arrived to put the finishing touches on the new house in April 1868, Sid made a terse entry in the journal that didn't sound at all like the old Sid: "Posts for alley, timber, and boards—all these things ought to have been in readiness a month ago. A sharp stick is wanted every day, every hour, every minute, and somebody to handle it."[1]

The new place provided a retreat for the whole family. A prized feature was an adjoining carriage house and bowling alley that provided a venue for many spirited competitions. The mansion also featured a magnificent porch that extended all around the place on three sides and during the summer evenings provided many a platform for philosophic discussion late into the night. Along with enthusiastic games of euchre, animated conversation, and readings (at which Sid was especially skilled), to say nothing of visits to and from neighbors, time passed pleasantly there for everyone. The place also provided a much-needed refuge for two of the brothers whose recent lives had not been kind.

Also in 1868, younger brother Charles returned to Livermore from his desperate experience as the American representative in Paraguay. With him came the troublesome Sallie, now expecting their second child, and their three-year-old daughter Hester. Charles had no plans—other than to avenge himself on all those who'd done him wrong in Paraguay. During one howling winter storm he coined a name for the place, The Norlands, from the poem "Ballad of Oriana" by Alfred Lord Tennyson. The name stuck, and remains today. Charles and his wife would stay there for over a year, a period which included the birth of their second child, Thurlow. They left in 1870, but came back intermittently over the next several years. Each time, Charles left a florid trail in the family journal.

Another brother, far more taciturn, also sought lengthy refuge at the place. Samuel, broken in body and soul from his wounds in the war, his business failure in Minnesota, and the loss of his wife and two children there, limped into Livermore in 1870 with his one surviving child, Bennie. For the next several years his presence at The Norlands was constant, but almost invisible. He didn't talk much, and the children thought he was shy. It was more likely that he preferred to avoid being swallowed up by his distinguished siblings, who loved conversation and big ideas, and all of whom had plenty of personal stories about the rich and powerful.

Like many other former sailors, Captain Sam enjoyed working the land. He was happy to help with the farm work as much as he could, and to care for their aged father, who was now nearly blind. He also made occasional ships-log-like entries in the family journal, and he drove the buggy for his siblings and their families as they came and went. This latter was a much-needed task, for at times the mansion held as many as twenty visitors. And yet, as his relatives reunited and reminisced in crinolines and broadcloth on the great veranda, Sam preferred to be out by himself hoeing potatoes in the fields.

In 1872 the family began a two-year remodeling job on the

church. When complete, the brothers had a big dedication ceremony for it. The famous Edwin Chapin came up from New York to preach, drawing a crowd of 1,500 people for a building that was designed to seat 150. The crowd was so big that Governor Nelson Dingley, who arrived late, had to be hoisted in through a window.

The last work at The Norlands, a Gothic stone library, was completed in 1885. It was dedicated in another big ceremony that included both Elihu and Hannibal Hamlin, who both delivered lengthy orations glorifying virtually everybody in the town. Of the whole Washburn compound in Livermore today, nothing contrasts as much with its agricultural surroundings as does this stark and serious little building and the important artifacts it contains.

Sid and his boys were at The Norlands for most of the summer of 1876. He recorded his father's death there at the age of almost ninety-two, on September 1. After the funeral, Captain Sam took Sid back to Hallowell, and it was almost a year before the smiling banker made another visit to the old place.

The gloomy year of 1876 ended badly for many of the Washburn siblings. Health problems began to crop up for Sid. Although his brothers worried about him, he recovered enough to participate in a three-month trip to Europe with Israel and his new bride, even though he was ill for much of the trip. This was also the year that Cadwallader, having lost his last chance for a Senate election in Wisconsin, also lost his last chance for a normal family life. The departure of his daughters brought to an end his tenure in Madison. The famously hung national election in November finally resulted in the end of Israel's long tenure at the Customs House in Portland. He learned about his termination the day after President Rutherford B. Hayes was inaugurated in March 1877. As an ailing Lot Morrill took Israel's place, a satisfied James G. Blaine sat securely in

Morrill's former seat in the U.S. Senate. Hayes's arrival also brought brother Elihu's resignation from his equally impressive tenure in Paris. Out in Minneapolis, brother William spent most of the year trying to pull his tattered fortunes together. Charles was in Hartford, Connecticut, where Cad reported that he was still trying to find "the missing ingredient."

In Livermore, brother Sam's job of nursing his father was now ended. Although his new wife, Addie Reade of Lewiston, had presented him with two daughters, one of them had died in his arms in 1875. On top of the constant pain from his war injury, tension between Addie and Charles's unhappy wife Sallie had soured the atmosphere at Livermore for him. In 1876 Sam quietly pulled up stakes with Addie and their surviving daughter and moved to Portland. There, with Israel's help, in 1881 he had major surgery on his leg and successfully applied for a disability pension from the government.

Israel recorded that Sid had an intestinal attack during a visit to Livermore in September 1877 that was serious enough to call a doctor from Hallowell. Israel blamed Sid for overeating, and gave Sam much credit for his skills in nursing his brother. Things got worse, however. On September 29, 1879, with Sam at his side, the always cheerful and generous Sid died at Hallowell. His two boys, John and Robert, were both students at Bowdoin at the time. Sam wrote in a sadly poetic and non-maritime epitaph to Sid in the family journal: "His life seemed to be all sunshine.... 'Tis sad at Blyth[e] House. The light of the house has gone out for ever."[2]

* * *

What Sid, with his early and ever-growing financial support, had helped to start in the west now thundered there night and day. Washburn sawmills screamed at La Crosse, Waubeek, Minneapolis, and Anoka. Washburn waterwheels and grinding rollers rumbled along the river at Minneapolis and Anoka, and long Washburn trains filled with either harvested grain or barrels of Gold Medal Flour rattled across the landscape from the Dakotas to Maine and from Duluth to St. Louis.

Rarely was Cadwallader Washburn in one place for long. He was constantly traveling to Boston or New York to deal with investors, to Madison and Washington on political business, to Maine to visit his brothers, to Europe grand-touring with his daughters' families and exploring new milling technology, or up and down the Mississippi to visit his holdings and confer with his managers. Exhausted by his long battle with the insurance companies in connection with the great mill explosion of 1878, his robust health began to break down at last. He suffered a stroke in 1881 that greatly curtailed his involvement with the mills. Following a last trip to Europe, the most successful, and probably the loneliest, Washburn died while trying to find a cure at Eureka Springs, Arkansas, in 1882. He was sixty-four years old.

Cad's funeral was the most spectacular of several spectacular Washburn funerals. After a memorial service in Chicago, his remains were transported by train to La Crosse for one of the biggest ceremonies the city had ever seen. Met at the depot by a crowd estimated at 2,000 people, and accompanied by several units of military honor guards, he was taken to the rotunda of the courthouse, where he lay in state and under guard all that night and the next morning while thousands passed by to view the catafalque, which was nearly buried in flowers. Contributors ranged from the Chicago Union Veterans to the Minneapolis Millers to the Dominican Sisters of Sinsinawa. Special trains brought nearly 10,000 friends and colleagues in from Minneapolis, Madison, and Milwaukee. His cortege to the Oak Grove Cemetery, which the local paper called "one of the most imposing ever seen in the northwest," was estimated to be a mile in length and took an hour to pass. All business in the city was suspended, as were the great mills in Minneapolis. His seven living brothers and sisters were there as well as his daughter Fanny and her husband, and four of the Buffums. (His other daughter, Jeanette, was in Europe with her family.) The cortege included the state's governor, chief justice, and five past governors, plus his old adversary Alexander Mitchell, who provided the trains. Over three hundred mourners also came from Minnesota, including the governor, the mayor of Minneapolis, and thirteen aldermen.

A quieter and more poetic epitaph written by Sam appeared back in the family journal at Livermore. "Thou kindest and best of brothers, hail and farewell," he wrote.[3] For all the frustration and worry that Cad had had about Sam, the feeling was not mutual. Sam may not have wanted to work for Cad again, but he knew his brother had been good to him.

Cadwallader Washburn was never a conspicuous spender. He was never in one place long enough to justify an imposing residence, and other than a devoted manservant named Freeman, his personal trappings were few. However, he knew what he had accomplished in his lifetime, and he saw that it got properly acknowledged after his death. Cad's will required his executors to erect a spectacular monument. A special railroad spur was built to bring in the twenty-ton base stone, and then the forty-ton obelisk that went on top of it. In all, it took a crew from Westerly, Rhode Island, three weeks and four special railroad cars to erect. When finished three years after the funeral, that spire towered fifty-two feet above the ground. It was the tallest monument in the state and still dominates Oak Grove Cemetery to this day.[4]

Since Washburn had personally controlled almost every activity of his life, it was no surprise that his affairs fell into some confusion without him. It took his executors seven years to settle his estate—during which time it grew to substantial

C. C. Washburn's monument in La Crosse is still one of the largest in the American Midwest. The inscription reads "An Eminent Citizen, A Noble Statesman, A Patriotic Soldier. He won success in all lines of labor by energy, sagacity, untiring perseverance, and unswerving honesty, a liberal patron of science and education, a generous philanthropist. He will live in the annals of Wisconsin, his adopted, and of Minnesota, his neighbor state."
PHOTO COURTESY OF PETER W. KELSEY

value. The process ultimately included decisions by the supreme courts of both Wisconsin and Minnesota to settle challenges by his daughter Nettie, and a publicly published explanation of his will by Washburn's old friend Cyrus

Woodman, who had drafted it. Properties from Missouri to Minnesota, from abandoned lead mines to grain elevators, from railroad bonds to pine woods to the great flouring mills themselves, were eventually disposed of, and scores of beneficiaries enjoyed the proceeds.

He not only provided comfortably for all of his siblings and children, but also for his long-institutionalized wife, who lived until 1909. In addition, he gave to the city of Minneapolis an enormous school and farm for orphaned children. As the Washburn Child Guidance Center, it still flourishes there today. Also, the city of La Crosse got a gleaming new library— years before Andrew Carnegie popularized the act of giving libraries. As with his commercial enterprises, these not-for-profit institutions have grown and thrived in the 130 years since Cadwallader Washburn died. They reflect both the importance of the needs their donor wished to fill, and the ability of the managers his executors picked to run them.

Without question, the biggest memorials left by Cadwallader Washburn were his commercial enterprises. His executors, led by his old banker friend, Gisbert Van Steenwyck, sold most of the La Crosse Lumber Company to Gustavus Buffum, whose descendants, as previously noted above, have made it a successful company across Missouri and southern Illinois to this day. In Minneapolis, after a perilous struggle, Cad's hard-working managers saved his flour mills from being bought by British speculators. With a lifesaving infusion of cash from Dunwoody, they then succeeded in purchasing control of the mills from the estate. His daughters were most generously provided for, and neither Charles Payson nor Albert Warren Kelsey ever had to work again.

Washburn and his successors built well, and his investors were repaid many times over for their faith in him. Surviving wars, economic depressions, and huge changes in their markets,

*Cadwallader Washburn, his daughters Nettie and Fanny,
and grandson Albert Kelsey, shortly before they all left Madison.*
COURTESY EDGEWOOD COLLEGE

the C. C. Washburn Flouring Mills became the cornerstone for General Mills, which now sells more than $10 billion in diversified food products every year and has never failed to pay a dividend.

The great trees are gone from Wisconsin now—though a few great carcasses sunk in the Chippewa mud remain to remind us. Similarly, there is no sign of the thundering sawmills or the great log rafts. Even the huge buildings of the Minneapolis mill district stand ghostly empty, or under the wrecker's ball, as diversification and gentrification take their course. They are all history, but today there is a magnificent museum in the very shell of Washburn's "A" mill to remind us of the vision and determination of the entrepreneurs like the Washburns who built the city.

Cadwallader Colden Washburn, whose first move on the Mississippi was to spend his last four dollars on a pair of shoes so he could teach school, and whose speculations caused so much anxiety during his lifetime, would no doubt be pleased—but not surprised. When we look at the confidence and power that emanate from the portrait taken with his daughters in Madison around 1875, we can sense somehow that if he were still with us today, he might have moved on to other things—and he would still be very much in charge of all of them.

* * *

Israel Jr. was next sibling to pass on. He enjoyed seven good years after the unexpected end of his collectorship in Portland in 1877. Among other honors, he helped build a hospital and a library in Portland, served on the boards of the Maine Historical Society and Westbrook Seminary, and was a pillar of the Congress Square Universalist Church, which included many years teaching Sunday school. He even helped write a hymn book. Since his election to preside over the national Universalist conference in Boston in 1862, and the publication of his many articles in the *Universalist Quarterly* magazine, Israel had been a national leader in the Universalist Church.

His longest service was as a founding trustee of Tufts College in Massachusetts, which he had helped set up as a training institution for Universalist ministers. As one of only three non-clerical trustees, he served on the board for thirty years. He was even offered the presidency of Tufts, but he declined because he preferred to stay in Maine with his family.

Israel also took on several commercial connections. He served on the boards of two railroads and as president of a third, and he was involved in expansion and construction at all three. In 1878 he even had a railroad locomotive named after him. He purchased half a township of timberland in Aroostook County for some steady income from stumpage fees, and he kept a careful eye on all the construction that was carried out at The Norlands. Like his brothers, he lectured widely around Maine and New England. He spoke on subjects like Scottish ballads and Scottish poets, rules for achieving success, and education—subjects relating to his interests, rather than to his own career. He was an early member of the Fraternity Club in Portland and developed one lecture there about the evils of too much power in the central government—a phenomenon which his own efforts during the war had done much to bring about.

When his beloved Maud died, Israel grieved for two years but then remarried. His new bride, Robina Brown, was almost three decades younger than he was. They were married at Livermore in 1876, probably in the Norlands church which he had helped rebuild, and they had a jam-packed honeymoon trip of several months in Europe with Sidney accompanying them. They met brothers Elihu and William in Paris, where Robina was subjected to plenty of "old Livermore jokes."5 Back in Portland, Israel also undertook several impressive writing efforts and continued a wonderful personal journal filled with pointed memories of everyone from Ralph Waldo Emerson to Daniel Webster.

In these most private pages, he was particularly pointed with regard to his old nemesis James G. Blaine, but with never a reference to his own disappointments at Blaine's hand. Underlying the vast differences between the two men, his list of Blaine's weaknesses reflected his own strengths. He criticized Blaine's lack of depth. "Mr. Blaine is not and cannot be a statesman.... He has no insight...he cannot grasp cause and consequence...he is always mistaking appearance for reality." These were the words of the Washburns' deepest thinker and most astute lawyer.

He criticized Blaine's lack of principles, and went on to confess, "If I have erred in my duty to the state and to the Republican party, it has been in not exposing the method and character of this man. But the many agreeable qualities and social fascinations of the individual and, more, my own disinclination to get into a fuss, have deterred me."[6] The writer of these lines was indeed high of principle, gentle in nature, and a fervid team player, reluctant to stir up trouble for the party he had helped create.

It was too bad for the Republicans that Israel did not speak out. The year after Israel died, the party gave its presidential nomination to Blaine, and the scandal-tainted "Plumed Knight" lost to the Democrats—the first time the party had lost control of the White House in a quarter of a century.

Israel's last years were notable for two superb efforts—one spoken and the other written. Always a speaker in great demand, he chose the occasion of the dedication of a soldiers memorial in the tiny town of Cherryfield, Maine, to deliver one of his best speeches, on July 4, 1873. Under the whispering pines of the little country graveyard, surrounded by miles of wilderness, he spoke presciently of the dangers of "centralization" in government (a prominent Republican theme even now), and of his very Washburn-like and very Universalist faith in the people. "They are slow, patient, and long-suffering, but in this country have always been found sure and reliable in the end," he concluded.7

Israel had long been simmering about the Webster-Ashburton Treaty of 1842, and in 1881 he completed a long paper for the Maine Historical Society on that subject. In it, he set the record straight about the full size of the sacrifice Maine had had to make in that agreement. The paper combined careful legal argument with exhaustive historical fact from a man who had been there—the writer himself. As a thorough dissection of the entire Northeast Boundary controversy—all fifty years of it—the paper is of historic value to this day. In view of the reticence of anyone on either side of the present border to stir up unpleasantness, the paper is also a grand example of Washburn political incorrectness. No matter that his readers may not have wanted to hear old controversies resurrected; he used this paper to make a permanent record of the early sacrifices that his state made in the interest of the country as a whole.

With his new wife Robina and two of his four children in the comfortable house he built in Portland in 1868, Israel enjoyed a large circle of friends and a secure reputation as Maine's War Governor. But his eyesight deteriorated and his health began to get worse in 1882. He died while undergoing treatment for Bright's disease in Philadelphia in 1883. As an indication of the high regard in which he was held in Maine, he was given two impressive memorial services, one in his home city of Portland and, after a special train was engaged, a second at the Mount Hope Cemetery in Bangor, where he was buried in the Webster family plot. Each ceremony drew a crowd of several hundred and included business leaders and notables from every branch of government and the justice system. William and Sam were also there, as was sister Martha. Though not as grand as the ceremonies for Cadwallader in La Crosse the year before, the eulogies were just as indicative of the respect and love this Washburn had enjoyed among his fellow citizens.

* * *

As the presidential election of 1860 was significant for the war it started, so the election of 1876 was significant for the things it brought to an end, including Grant's second term as president. The election was extremely close, resulted in a tie vote in the electoral college, and was not finally settled by the Congress until the day before President Rutherford B. Hayes was inaugurated. Within days of its resolution, the last federal troops were removed from the South, and the great social experiment of Reconstruction came to an end. The South would remain Democratic and "unreconstructed" for the next hundred years.

Grant's second term had ended in a cloud of controversy and failed appointments, and the general left the country on a lengthy world tour to enjoy clearer air. Ironically, he arrived in France in a midst of the first election confrontation between conservatives and republicans since the Commune. Ambassador Elihu Washburne, still there due to delays in his replacement's arrival, had to wave his old friend off to avoid ruffling sensitive feathers among the French. By this point in time, Elihu's political antennae were much more attuned to the politics of France than they had been in 1870.

Elihu did not leave Europe until September 1877. When he got home, he decided to sell the considerable forestland acreage in Wisconsin that he had been holding for thirty years. The lumber business was booming, and he was able to realize a profit of about forty times what he had originally paid. He used this to purchase an Italianate mansion on North La Salle Street in Chicago, and settled in to enjoy a well-earned retirement. The new place made a handsome setting for the coming-out party he threw there for his oldest daughter Susie in 1880. As he wrote a friend before he left France, his new home would be a perfect place for "such old fogy country people" as his wife and himself.[8]

Elihu was now sixty-one years of age. Thanks to his experiences in France, he had a story to tell which a great many Americans wanted to hear. From Toronto to San Francisco, in multiple articles, essays, and lectures, he poured out his account of the birth of the Third Republic, the Siege of Paris, the Commune, his efforts on behalf of Archbishop Darboy, and America's aid to Germany in 1870–71. He joined the Chicago Historical Society,[9] and later consolidated his memories into the two-volume *Recollections of a Minister to France*, which was published shortly after his death. This work has remained a standard reference for the period ever since.

His political reputation was still robust. He was an impressive figure, five feet, ten inches tall, and he inspired one Washington observer to write, "No one has filled a room as Washburne does since the days of Daniel Webster."[10] His name was several times prominently mentioned for both a Senate seat and the Illinois governor's chair, although nothing came of it. Powerful forces from the southern part of the state, led by John Logan, succeeded in heading off these nominations.

Washburne's political career, and his relationship with Ulysses Grant, were not quite finished. Grant returned early from his world tour, during which he had corresponded regularly with Washburne. Grant, always the national hero rather than the ambitious office-seeker, had liked being president. He was no public speaker, had no magic message, and had never had to campaign for the job. He seemed to feel as if the coun-

try owed him another term. Now, under the pressure of
depleted finances, he was open to the idea of serving again, if
the people called. In this ambition he received the strongest
encouragement from three powerful political figures: Senator
Roscoe Conkling of New York, Senator Don Cameron of
Pennsylvania, and Senator John Logan of Illinois. Each controlled formidable political machines which in turn controlled
the three pivotal states. Each had benefited in various ways
from the previous Grant presidency, and each was eager to see
it renewed. They began to promote him for an unprecedented
third term.

Grant never recognized the hurt that his friends had done
to his previous administrations, but others in the party certainly did. There was powerful opposition among the Republicans to giving Grant a third term. Israel's nemesis, Senator
James G. Blaine, was in this group, but only because he was
now ambitious for the presidency himself. Among other names
mentioned as alternative candidates to Grant in 1880 was the
name of Elihu Benjamin Washburne.

Elihu's star was high. Despite war and rebellion, he had
stuck to his post in Paris. His actions had gained much praise
among Germans and Catholics in America, and he had been
telling his story in lectures all over the country. He had been
well clear of the scandals of Grant's second term. His honesty
and reputation were beyond reproach. If the Grant bandwagon
ran into trouble, Grant had only to give the word of his
endorsement and Elihu would get the nomination.

His bandwagon did get into trouble, but Grant never saw it.
The endorsement of Washburne was never given. The manip-
ulations of John Logan were instrumental here. Logan was con-
cerned about losing his own influence among Illinois
Republicans. He used his power in the state legislature to derail
Elihu's candidacy for the U.S. Senate, and then persuaded

Grant that his friend Washburne lacked sufficient support to carry his own state of Illinois as a presidential nominee.

Blaine's, Grant's, and Washburne's names were all proposed at the Republican nominating convention in Chicago. Although he felt that Grant had no chance, Elihu deferred to his old friend. He did nothing to indicate he was interested in the nomination. Despite this, more than thirty convention delegates stuck with Washburne for thirty-three exhausting ballots. In the end, after five weary days, all were disappointed. Dark horse James A. Garfield won the nomination, and the 1880 election as well. Elihu's name was also proposed for vice president, but Chester A. Arthur won that slot. In view of the murder of Garfield the following year, Elihu thus lost two chances to be president of the country.

Political power after the Civil War rested on the ability to make and remove appointments, thus rewarding loyalty and punishing disloyalty. This kind of power game was of no interest to any of the political Washburns. To a man, they had entered politics to fight for principles. Power went with public office, and they undoubtedly enjoyed it, but power for its own sake had little appeal for them. So it was that the great operators of the day—Blaine, Conkling, Cameron, and Logan—distrusted the Washburns. The Washburns could not be controlled, and, as these superb political power brokers saw it, a man you couldn't control was a man you couldn't trust. Far better for you if the man you couldn't control could be removed from the game board entirely.

Starting in 1876, one by one all the political Washburns were removed from the board. Elihu was last to go. After the 1880 convention, Logan, still determined to minimize Elihu's influence among Illinois Republicans, persuaded the frustrated Grant that Washburne had betrayed him. Elihu himself was also frustrated. Grant, the man who owed him so much, as in

*Portrait of elder statesman Elihu Benjamin Washburne
by G. P. A. Healey.*
COURTESY OF T. D. WASHBURNE

1876 had again not spoken for him when it was clear that his own chance was gone. The upshot was that the two men did not speak to each other again; their eventful friendship was over.[11] Washburne made a special trip to New York in 1885 when Grant was dying, but the general would not see him.

Elihu's last years were filled with writing, both about his own and his wife's families, about Illinois history, and about his own experiences. After other travels, and the deaths of his brothers Sidney, Cadwallader, and Israel, he sold his home in

Galena. He came east to help dedicate the Washburn Library at Livermore in 1885.

Then, in 1887, back in Chicago, he was devastated by the sudden and unexpected death of his wife Adele. He followed her seven months later, the victim of a heart attack. As with his brothers Cad and Israel, Elihu's passing was marked by two memorial services—one in Chicago and the other in Galena—and was attended by major figures from politics, the law, the military, and the German-American community. In Galena, the funeral procession to Greenwood Cemetery was said to have been the longest in the town's history. The obelisk erected over his grave was quite similar to his brother Cadwallader's in La Crosse, though not as large. No doubt the brothers would have had a good laugh about that.

Elihu died a wealthy man, with about $850,000 worth of assets. He had interest in no less than forty-six parcels of real estate, mostly in and around Galena, and he had done well with an early investment in Chicago street railways.

Like his brothers, he was a country lad who made himself a competent lawyer and an even more competent politician. He had the courage to embrace a principle that was opposed by both major parties in the 1850s, and to lead the way to victory by building a whole new party. Through good luck and good judgment, he recognized early the talents of Abraham Lincoln and Ulysses S. Grant. By his unwavering support and promotion of both of them, plus hard work and personal integrity, he was able to make major contributions to both the preservation and the fiscal health of the Union. In the distinguished pantheon of his Washburn siblings, Israel Jr. might have been the most articulate, and Cadwallader the most successful, but Elihu deserves the title of most influential.

* * *

Two more Washburn siblings would die in the three years after Elihu. The first was that self-proclaimed wanderer, Charles Ames Washburn. Following his Paraguayan adventure and the time spent recuperating in Livermore afterwards, he followed a meandering course. He may have been hounded by his wife or by his dreams or by his failures, but he was unsuccessful in putting down roots anywhere. He went back to San Francisco, where he was honored by the Republican party. They gave him a big banquet and briefly considered him as a candidate for the governorship, but nothing came of it. He returned to Livermore, where his second child was born in 1868.

Sallie grew as restless as he was. She didn't like Livermore or Cape May or Bethlehem or Oakland, California, where Leland Stanford gave Charles a job in a bank. He got laid off at the first economic downturn, and after three years they were back at Livermore—where Sallie quarreled with Sam's new wife Addie, which led to trouble between Charles and Sam. Part of Sallie's problem may have been the steadily deteriorating state of Charles's finances. However, she did nothing to help.

Charles had taken to tinkering, and he had come up with an early version of the typewriter, which he called a "typeograph." Brother Cadwallader asked about it, but Sallie pooh-poohed the invention, snorting that there were plenty of women stenographers who didn't need any machines to help them. According to daughter Hester, this caused Cad to shy away from the project. About her mother after this incident Hester wrote, "Poor foolish woman. That remark cost her a fortune."[12] So Sallie cried and bit her fingers as her diamond earrings and brooch were pawned, and stayed pawned.

They were back in Reading, Pennsylvania, Sallie's hometown, when their third child was born in 1870. They were in

Hartford, Connecticut, in 1875 when Cadwallader visited them and humorously reported that Charles thought he had found "the missing ingredient."

Charles continued to write. He completed his two volumes on Paraguay and published two novels. He worked on his type-writing machine and also invented a turnstile. After years of campaigning with the patent office and battling with lawyers, he got his typeograph machine patented and sold it to the Underwood Company for the lordly sum of $500. He invested in a scheme to build a canal across Florida, but the canal never got built. The family finally settled in Morristown, New Jersey.

There was economic hardship. Charles was unable to afford the price of a ticket to attend the funerals of either his brother Cadwallader or his brother Elihu. Cadwallader left money to provide for Charles and his family, but Charles spent the remaining years of his life at loose ends, dreaming of great things and suffering the endless litany of his wife's complaints. One day, in New York City to attend a meeting of promoters of an early version of the phonograph in which he had bought stock, Charles collapsed while riding on a horsecar in Manhattan. He died with Sallie at his side at St. Vincent's Hospital in January 1889. He was sixty-six years of age. He was buried with little notice at the cemetery behind The Norlands on Waters Hill in Livermore. There were none of the memori-als for him that had followed the deaths of his older brothers.

What was Charles's problem? He was not a bad person. He was not unintelligent—unwise perhaps, but not stupid. Why did he seem to arouse so much antipathy wherever he went? As Theodore Webb, who has written and researched much on all the Washburns, observed, his very righteousness may have done him in. As Webb put it, Charles could not be trusted by the politicians in California, not because he was untrustworthy, but because he was unpredictable. He was seen as putting on airs of superiority, and he was unable to transcend the personal in his communication with others. This brought on isolation, the death knell for any politician.

All his life, he took refuge from life in his writing. His song was long and varied, and eloquently delivered. Unfortunately, as the years went by, it was sung to an increasingly empty house. This most original of the Washburns may also have been the family's least effective.

* * *

Charles's brother Sam was also having health problems. He had hurt a knee in 1877, which put him on crutches and exacerbated the deterioration started by his war wound. The pain was constant and gradually increased until he required surgery in 1881. The operation cured the pain, but resulted in the permanent loss of use of his left leg. Shortly afterwards, his second wife Addie, aided by Israel Jr., began the correspondence to apply for a government pension for Sam. Only now was there any recording on paper by Sam of the grievous hurt he had suffered back in 1862. Life at Norlands was now too difficult for him, and the little family bought a house on seven acres and moved to the Deering section of Portland in 1883, just a couple of miles from brother Israel.

Sometime in 1883, Sam's health being further deteriorated and brother Israel having died, the family sold the Deering house and moved out to western New York State. Sam was admitted to a sanitarium in Avon Springs, not far from Lorette's original hometown of LeRoy. He died there three years later, on March 4, 1890, at the age of sixty-six. His son Bennie, who worked at Cad's "A" Mill in Minneapolis, was at his bedside. The death certificate listed the cause as "exhaustion from long continued suffering in consequence of wounds and injuries received on board U.S.S. Gunboat Galena." This was apparently enough to get Addie a widow's pension.

Compared with his brothers, plain Sam Washburn was just that: uncomplicated and straightforward. His brothers may have outclassed him in energy and in wit, but he was as tough or tougher than they were, he was as dependable as they were, and he shared the uncompromising honesty of the entire family. Like them, he gave up years of his life in the service of his country. He loved a good fight, and he was the only brother who actually shed his blood for the Northern cause—but he thought this so unimportant that he never mentioned a word about it in writing until forced to for his family's sake almost twenty years afterward.

He was a stubborn individual like his brother Cad, and—also like his brother Cad—he found it easiest to work with a group only if he was in charge of it. Like all his brothers, he enjoyed politics, but he never aspired to take a prominent role in it. In his later life, when circumstances forced him into proximity with his overachieving brothers, he stayed in the background. As always, he enjoyed their company, but he never competed with them. He was happy to be the one who drove the buggy.

* * *

In the year 1890 the political and commercial adventures of the Washburn siblings were still not over. Seven of the ten siblings were now dead, but more Washburn comet trails were still to be etched across the nation's skies. Sam died the year after youngest brother William reached still another height. As Sam breathed his last in the sanitarium in Avon Springs, William was winding up his first year in the U.S. Senate and beginning to lay plans to entertain the Republican high and mighty at his new eighty-room mansion in Minneapolis during their 1892 convention there. It was a convention that would briefly consider him for its nomination for vice president.

William's three older brothers had all served in the House

Hon. W. D. WASHBURN,
President.

The Prince Charming: William Drew Washburn,
newly elected U.S. senator from Minnesota, as seen in 1880.
COURTESY MINNESOTA HISTORICAL SOCIETY

as representatives from three different states, and two of them
had served as governors of their states. Brother Elihu, upon his
return from France, had climbed high enough to be a serious
contender for a presidential nomination. But none of these
political achievers had ever won a seat in the U.S. Senate.
William Drew Washburn—youngest brother, Prince Charming
of the family, and dashing representative of Minneapolis's most
gilded age—gained even this prize. However, his road to the
U.S. Senate would not be all peaches and cream.

In 1878 William and Lizzie had had a year of both tragedy and joy. Their oldest son, Frank, drowned during a family vacation in Maine, but six months later Lizzie presented the family with another son, Stanley. In the fall, William was once more nominated for Congress in the Third District by the Minnesota Republicans. His opponent was none other than the irrepressible Ignatius Donnelly again. This time, unlike 1868, William stayed in the fight. In a famous campaign still known as the "Brass Kettle Campaign," and despite the same Granger reform movement that had defeated Cadwallader in Wisconsin three years earlier, William successfully defended his progressive credentials, proved that his railroad's rates were kinder to the farmers than any other line, and won the election.[13]

As Congress opened in 1878, William took his seat as the fourth Washburn brother to be elected to the U.S. Congress from four different states. Over the next six years, thanks to his successful campaigning for federal funds to build a series of dams and reservoirs that evened out the seasonal flow of the Mississippi River, he was reelected twice. He would serve in the House until 1885, when he declined to run for a fourth term.

After his return to private life in 1885, William stayed in the public eye. Minneapolis now had its first daily newspaper, *The Journal,* and William was a majority stockholder. He continued to be a pillar of the chamber of commerce in Minneapolis, and organized and served as president of a major industrial exposition for the city in 1886.

In the legislature, there was much animosity toward the incumbent U.S. Senator, Dwight M. Sabin, perhaps due to antagonisms left over from Sabin's controversial election earlier. In March 1889, as Sabin's term came to an end, William Drew Washburn—handsome, wealthy, and with six years of experience in Congress behind him—was the Republicans' choice for the seat. He was elected easily.

His career in the Senate was remembered for the lavish entertaining that he and Lizzie carried on in Washington, and for his strong and repeated opposition to the trade in wheat and cotton futures, which he explained was nothing more than "gambling, pure, simple, and absolutely cold-blooded."14 His bill to curb the trade in options passed the Senate but was buried in committee in the House. This was the work of the dictatorial Thomas Bracken Reed, the famous Mainer who governed the House of Representatives from the Speaker's chair. Correspondence at the Washburn Library includes the following words about Reed: "Mr. Reed is ugly and perverse. I cannot account for his conduct on any ground except that of original sin."15

In 1891 William persuaded Congress to authorize a ship to transport more than $100,000 worth of wheat—donated by the millers of Minneapolis—to relieve the famine that had overcome large areas of southern Russia. This earned him the gratitude of the Russian czar when William visited there a few years later. William thus joined Elihu as the second of the Livermore brothers to be thanked for his services by a crowned head of Europe.

William's moral ground was not as high as that of his two brothers, however. His vote in the U.S. Senate to kill the Force Bill of 1890 provided more dramatic evidence of the space which separated him from his older siblings. This bill would have provided federal protection to Negroes voting in federal elections in the South. It was favored by both William's party and its president, Benjamin Harrison. William explained that he didn't want to bring on a renewal of sectional antipathies— a concern that hadn't bothered any of his older brothers thirty years earlier. The Force Bill died as a result of William's vote, and seventy-five years would pass before there was another attempt to impose voting rights on the South.

Historians have noted the *defeats* of both William and Cadwallader Washburn in their efforts to get reelected more than their original victories. William's Minnesota defeat for re-election to the Senate in 1895 was hauntingly similar to Cadwallader's defeat for reelection as governor in Wisconsin in 1873. Like Cadwallader, William, as the incumbent, started in a favored position. Like Cadwallader, William was upset by a popular farmer (Governor Knute Nelson, who would hold the seat for twenty-nine years). Also like Cadwallader, William's opponents were financed by a rival railroad baron (James J. Hill, angry at William for building his westward railroad line right next to two of Hill's own lines). In addition, like Cadwallader, William lost key voter support by stubbornly holding to a position based on moral principle. (Cadwallader had aroused fears among his beer-loving German constituents over his support for controlling the sale of alcohol in Wisconsin. William earned the enmity of the Chicago Futures Exchange over his opposition to gambling on the future prices of wheat.) Like Israel with Blaine, Elihu with President Johnson, and Cadwallader with the Germans in Milwaukee, William took a moral high position, stuck to it perhaps too stiffly, and lost public support as a result.

With William's failure to get reelected in 1895, the Washburn era of national service finally came to an end. Between the four brothers, from Israel to William, by 1895, their string in national office had extended a total of thirty-nine out of forty-four consecutive years. William's senatorial defeat may have brought to an end his political career, but not his business career.

His railroad activities west of Minneapolis and into the Dakotas opened up still another opportunity for enterprise at the turn of the century. Twenty-four miles north of where his main line reached the Missouri River at Bismarck, North

Dakota, and mostly located fifty feet under the barren plain, there were extensive deposits of soft coal. William's construction crews had discovered them while digging a cut for a branch line they were building up from Bismarck. In 1899, when he was sixty-eight years old, William Washburn and two other Minneapolis investors purchased 113,000 empty acres there. In the center of the tract he established the town of Wilton and finished construction of the rail line to connect the site with the main line at Bismarck. When the line was complete, he incorporated the Washburn Lignite Coal Company in Wilton in 1902. After mining operations were well underway, he sold the railroad—by that time including grain elevators, two hotels, and two steamboats—to the Soo Line, which had assisted the enterprise from the beginning.

His paternalistic management of the mines was remembered for the provision of hot showers for the crews, a free turkey for all hands at Christmastime, and his occasional grand visits to the town in his private railroad car. By the time of William's death thirteen years later, the Wilton mine, with 400 employees, was considered the largest underground lignite coal mine in the world.

Today the mines are long gone, but a unique railroad depot building remains in Wilton. In the middle of that endless plain, this unusual building contains an upstairs apartment built for William, with a roof reminiscent of a Chinese pagoda. It is said to have been inspired by the pagodas Lizzie Washburn saw in China during her trip to that country, when William was exploring still another railroad venture there in 1896. (If his key contact person hadn't fallen out of favor with the Chinese Emperor at a critical moment, William would have built a railroad from Hankow to Beijing in 1897. The scheme had all the grandiosity that William loved, and it gave him another opportunity to mount a grand expedition. The entourage he

The Soo Line depot at Wilton, North Dakota, as seen in 1914.
The pagoda-like top floor of the building on the right contained
an apartment for William Drew Washburn.
COURTESY NORTH DAKOTA STATE HISTORICAL SOCIETY

led to China even included his niece from Maine, Israel's daughter Maud.)

William should also be remembered for his long-time work for the Universalist Church. He helped build a new and larger house of worship in Minneapolis, the Church of the Redeemer, where he was a regular attendee for fifty years. He received national recognition when he was asked to be president of the 1881 national Universalist convention in Buffalo. Even more significantly, he served two years, from 1901 to 1903, as president of the National Convention of the Universalist Church—the equivalent of national leader of the organization. His brother Israel had held the same position nineteen years earlier.

It was a time when William would need spiritual strength. His banker brother Sid, who had financed him for so long, died in 1879. Lizzie lost another child, Alice, and brother

Cadwallader—under whose implicit protection he had been operating since leaving Maine—had a stroke that incapacitated him.

Ironically, Cadwallader's death in 1882 had beneficial effects for William. Cad's will provided William with another bounce-back opportunity. William was named in the will as a representative of Cad's estate, and so found himself back in the management of the Washburn Crosby Company during the five years it took to settle ownership of the company.

William's intermittent associations with Cad's flouring enterprises tell a lot about the different temperaments and priorities of the two men. Cad took the long view in everything he built, whereas William was more mercurial.

Cad built for the future, and nothing was more important to him than establishing strong day-to-day management so that he could be free to solicit financial backing, research new technologies, and build an international marketing organization. His success was evident in the phenomenal growth of Washburn Crosby during the five years it took to settle his estate.

William followed the excitement, wherever it was. He came off as brash, opinionated, and arrogant. He was not a detail man, and he clashed with those who were. This led to inevitable collisions with the new men Cadwallader brought in.

Back in 1877, Cadwallader had brought John Crosby into his company as a partner on the same basis as William. The two men clashed almost immediately. After the terrible explosion of 1878 and the massive rebuilding that followed it, William was not included in the partnership agreement of 1879. Cadwallader, as he had at done Waubeek against Sam, backed the outsider against his brother. So William moved out. He was stubborn, excitable, and often deaf to the ideas of others—not an easy combination for colleagues to work with.

Now Cadwallader was gone, and William, representing the estate, was back on the management team. With buyout offers coming from all sides, the company growing in every direction, and Cad's heirs eager to sell, it must have been a difficult time for John Crosby. Somehow, though, he managed to get along with William, fend off both the British *and* William next door at Pillsbury-Washburn, and finesse the Philadelphia bankers representing Cad's heirs. It may have cost him his life, for he died in 1887.

Now there was another collision involving William, this time with James S. Bell, who was brought in to succeed John Crosby. Bell, a quiet Quaker with an excellent track record in the flour business in Philadelphia, turned out to be the best manager of all. As Cad's estate was settled and control of the company was won back into local hands, William was removed from the company a second and final time in 1889. A key player in the evolution was William H. Dunwoody, the marketing genius, who stepped in to help rescue the company, but only on the condition that William leave it. Bell was building an organization, and William was never an organization man.

Sid's oldest son, John Washburn, had come west in 1880 to get into the flour business himself. After a few years, when John was considering going out on his own, William advised him not to, and urged him to join "our own concern."[16] When the firm incorporated in 1887, John was still under thirty. To keep a Washburn involved in the firm he was admitted as one of five principals of the new corporation. John would show real genius in the art of purchasing wheat and would rise to become Washburn Crosby's president and board chairman.

Shrugging off his ouster from the mill, in 1883 William decided to build a proper monument to himself. To the consternation of his Pillsbury, Dunwoody, Bell, and Morrison neighbors, he purchased twenty prime acres right across the

The fabulous mansion that William built at Fair Oaks, in 1886—
an exuberant example of Gilded Age extravagance.
The kindness of the Minneapolis city fathers allowed him
to stay in his home until his death in 1912.
COURTESY MINNESOTA HISTORICAL SOCIETY

street from them in Minneapolis and proceeded to sink more than $500,000 into a huge new eighty-room mansion there. He called the place Fair Oaks, and surrounded it with spectacular gardens designed by Frederick Law Olmstead. It was said to require a staff of forty servants to keep it up and a ton of coal a week to keep warm in the winter—which might help explain why William got so interested in mining coal in North Dakota. The Washburns became famous for the huge New Year's parties they gave each year at Fair Oaks.

When the 1892 Republican national convention came to Minneapolis, William and Lizzie welcomed party bigwigs, including several presidents, behind the massive mahogany doors and under the sparkling chandeliers of their castle. Such hospitality may have been the reason that William was proposed by the Minnesota delegation that year as a favorite-son candidate for the vice presidential nomination. (Although he was beaten out by newspaperman Whitelaw Reid, this made him the second Washburn brother, after Elihu, to be a candidate for vice president.) Unfortunately, the incumbent Republicans lost the election to Democrat Grover Cleveland in that fall's election, and the party never came back to Minneapolis.

Besides his contributions in business and the church, William would chair the committee that built a new city hall and courthouse for Minneapolis (the same project he had been rebuffed about in 1872), and for over thirty years he would direct the Washburn Memorial Orphan Asylum, an institution made possible by a bequest of his brother Cadwallader.

William gained a lot of weight, and started annual trips to Germany to take advantage of the waters at Carlsbad. He would outlive all but one of his ten brothers and sisters. Of his six surviving children, he would see four reach national prominence on their own. And yet, William would die in the shadow of scandal, with his wealth gone and little to show for his enormous drive and energy.

Wheat, like lumber, could fluctuate greatly in price. Like any commodity, its supply was subject to the vagaries of the weather across the plains, as well as to the general health of the country's economy. When supply was tight, grain prices could also be driven up by speculators. Of all their costs of doing business, what the millers had to pay for their raw material was the biggest—and also the most unpredictable. As Minneapolis flour achieved worldwide market acceptance, the millers' need for grain skyrocketed to numbers in excess of a million bushels every day. With all their other costs relatively predictable, and shareholder interest and dividends to be paid, it became imperative for the millers somehow to protect themselves against spikes in the prices they had to pay for grain.

One solution was to build an extensive network of silos along their railroad lines. This provided buying sites closer to the farmers, and also a network of storage points where they could hold inventory in order to balance out the average costs of what they paid. As a result, wherever the landscape of the high plains was laced with steel rails, so also it was spiked with grain elevators and sidings every few miles.

The other answer to the dilemma was to create a futures market. Just as they *bought* the wheat for the flour they expected to sell at some date in the future, they also entered into a futures contract to *sell* an equivalent amount of wheat on that same future date. Any gain or loss in the price of the wheat in inventory would be offset by an opposite gain or loss in the futures contract. The mill thus hedged its inventory and achieved a more predictable profit.

However, as William himself had said in the Senate thirteen years earlier, there was only a thin line separating hedging with futures contracts and outright gambling with them. A hedging contract was always backed up with actual inventory. A gambling contract was not supported by any actual inventory, but was a financial obligation nonetheless. Regardless of what happened to market prices, when the contract came due, you had to pay.

Banks could get caught in this. If they loaned the cash to buy a contract, and to pay for it when it came due, they could be the losers if it turned out there was no collateral for them to fall back on.

These contracts cost money, and most mills did not hedge all the wheat in their inventories. On the other hand, their inventories at the end of the year had to be carried on the books at the market price on that date. If the price had fallen, then the loss had to be charged against earnings. The Panic of

1893 led to a depression which dropped the price mills could get for a barrel of flour from $4.12 in 1892 to $2.83 in 1896. Farmers and millers suffered alike. At the same time, overhead costs increased as electricity began to replace water power, and new milling facilities were constructed at Buffalo to better meet the demand for flour in East Coast markets.

Profits had been steadily squeezed during the decade before William Drew Washburn was elected chairman of the American Management Committee of Pillsbury-Washburn in 1901. More and more, the performance of the whole company depended on the price it paid for its grain—a cost that, in the wake of reports of crop damage in 1907, was forced upwards as much as forty percent by speculators. Continuing pressures such as these on profits must have made the temptation to speculate very great, and William had been a gambler all his life.

Overall, British investors in Pillsbury-Washburn never did see the profits they had expected, but no one anticipated the bombshell they received in 1908. Without warning, on August 8, 1908, Pillsbury-Washburn Flour Mills Company, Ltd., the largest flour milling concern in the world, went into receivership. The company was reported to have $5,000,000 in unsecured debt and had neither cash nor available credit with which to pay. The debt included over a million dollars in notes issued in the company's name but not recorded on its books. These liabilities, mostly related to unauthorized speculations in grain, had apparently been concealed for some time.

Henry L. Little, the firm's president, took the blame and resigned, as did his treasurer. However, many felt the real blame lay elsewhere. By September 8, the *New York Times* was reporting that British investors were blaming the losses on "some of the managers" of the company, and attention eventually shifted to the firm's American management committee.[17] Washburn Crosby's William H. Dunwoody wrote that "Henry

Little and his associates followed out the plan that was in use by their predecessor, by looking to speculation in wheat to make a considerable part of their profits.... Somehow they were able to conceal their losses from the auditors, who went through the accounts once a year...I think the whole of their organization was demoralized by the speculative disposition of their predecessor."[18] That predecessor could have been William Drew Washburn.

The assets and cash flow of Pillsbury-Washburn were sound, however, and the reorganization plan that saved it from bankruptcy involved a purchase of those assets for $2,250,000—mostly Pillsbury family money. The company was reborn under the new name of Pillsbury Flour Mills Company. After what was described as a "tempestuous" meeting in London in 1910, British shareholders grudgingly accepted the plan. This agreement closed off discussion about possible criminal proceedings and restitution suits. After only eighteen months in receivership, the Pillsburys got their company back for a bigger and better future.

William had served as a director and head of the American management committee on the Pillsbury-Washburn board until 1907, when he retired at the age of seventy-six. He had just been recognized by Bowdoin College with an honorary doctorate of law, and was enjoying a life full of opulence, travel, and his usual casual attitude about expenses.

To this day, there is no direct evidence connecting William to the wreck of Pillsbury-Washburn. The absence of financial information is in itself surprising. However, the circumstantial evidence of a connection is compelling. To begin with, the timing fits. Contracts to purchase wheat at a given price can be extended well into the future. Lenient creditors can be strung out with future promises of repayment. In fact, almost two million dollars of the debt was shown to have been incurred in

1905.[19] Obligations due in 1908 could have easily been incurred—and hidden—while William was chairman of the American management committee.

William outlived Pillsbury-Washburn by five years—more than enough time for aggrieved stockholders to come after his personal assets. While the Pillsburys managed to reconstitute their company after only eighteen months of receivership and no criminal charges were ever filed, five years was time enough for William to get quietly stripped of his assets by creditors—as had already happened to him once, in 1874.

He was definitely under the shadow. Frank Spencer was an adamant member of the British board of directors who wanted restitution for their losses. In 1910, William de la Barre, the engineer who ran the always-profitable power operations of the company, wrote Spencer of the futility of pursuing criminal action against the former management. He listed five potential targets, including one he named by the initials W.D.W., of whom he wrote sarcastically, he "has one foot in the grave and has no guilt."[20]

De la Barre's advice to Spencer reflected the nature of the relationship between the milling industry and the Minneapolis community: The mills *were* the community. Virtually everyone in town either worked in the business or depended on it in some way. Their interests were the same. Bad news from one had a bad effect on all. Therefore, the small circle of men who ran the town cleaned up the mess quietly; the outsiders were advised to take their lumps and move on. There was to be no record—other than the silence that rang loudly around town after William's death in 1912.

The most visible evidence of his responsibility in the debacle was, of course, the disappearance of his name from the organization. Although William was right there in Minneapolis during its eighteen months of receivership, he played no part in the efforts to reconstitute it, and his name was dropped from the new organization without comment.

Beyond this, however, is the shocking disappearance of William's income and estate afterwards. Apparently, during 1909 and 1910, there was a confidential investigation conducted by Pillsbury-Washburn's New York attorneys. In 1910, it was announced that William was giving his palace at Fair Oaks to the city of Minneapolis to be used as an art museum after he and Lizzie died. It is likely that his generosity was prompted by insufficient income to pay the taxes or the upkeep on the place. Indeed, after Lizzie died, the city could no more afford to operate it than he could. They tore it down in 1924, and the land was turned into present-day Fair Oaks Park.

In 1912 William fell suddenly ill in Europe and barely made it home to Fair Oaks. The *Tribune* made a front-page epic of the race to get him home,[21] and he died on July 24, 1912. The real shock came with the news of his estate.

In a news item that appeared in the *Washington Post* on August 3, 1912, William's executor listed his estate at a total of just $105,000. Of that, he reported $100,000 as personal property and only $5,000 as real estate.[22] The probate record in the Hennepin County Court bears out the report. William's probated estate contains no sign of any of his myriad enterprises. Nor is there any sign of further assets in Lizzie's estate, probated after her death in 1916.

He had a record of selling out, or getting bought out, of things he had started. Still, the absence of any trace in his estate of any of these assets states loudly that there was some kind of huge interruption in his fortune behind the scenes.

In the probate report, there was listed not one share of stock in the three railroads he had built, or in the largest flour milling combine in the world—which he had assembled and for which he had been paid $1.5 million twenty-two years earlier. There was no stock or bonds from the water-power company or the world's largest lignite coal mine or the sawmills or the newspaper or the foundry or the streetcar company or the electric utility or the harvester factory or the farms in Dakota or the mansions in Minneapolis and Washington or the steamboats or the grain elevators or the bank and the opera house in Anoka or the summer houses in Maine or of all the thousands of acres of rich timberlands he had owned across Minnesota and Wisconsin. For all his long life of furious energy and restless eye, at the end there was very little to show.

William had a long history of taking chances and living beyond his means. He liked to live well and drive fast. As early as 1859, his extravagant lifestyle and carelessness about debt had bothered Cadwallader enough to mention it in a letter to Sid (see previous chapter). Since then, there had been no visible change in his pattern, despite the events of 1873 that had so terrified his brother.

Memories of William in Livermore, as elsewhere, confirm his extravagance. He never made much of an effort to mix with the locals when he was there, which was annually for many, many summers. The family journals, which are full of entries by his siblings, do not contain a single entry by William. Local legends about him include tales of near collisions on neighborhood roads, vehement family debates around the dinner table, and quantities of William's cigar butts strewn around the mansion's great porch.

It is interesting to compare William, in death as in life, with his brother Cadwallader. William, with his happy marriage and large family, left a long, long record of community service to his city, his church, and his state. His hand could be found in virtually every element of the city's cultural and business life: churches, libraries, schools, museums, municipal buildings, trade organizations, political parties, railroads, flour mills, sawmills, power plants—even its streetcars. Cadwallader, on the other hand, other than with his businesses, made no local impact during his lifetime. He was not a regular church-goer, his home in La Crosse was modest, and he was rarely there. He was not part of any social establishment, and, being to all intents and purposes a bachelor, he did no entertaining.

Nevertheless, it was Cadwallader who made the most sig-nificant bequests: Edgewood College and Washburn Observatory in Madison, the Washburn Library in La Crosse, and the orphan asylum, now the Washburn Child Guidance Center, in Minneapolis. It was Cadwallader who received the biggest monument and, apparently, the highest posthumous regard. The memorial to Cadwallader published by the Wisconsin Historical Society in 1882 was forty-two pages long. By contrast, the written memorial for William by the Minnesota Historical Society in 1915 amounted to a single page. After his death, his son was rumored to have destroyed all his papers and financial records.

Both brothers were generous regarding the preservation and enlargement of the family property back in Maine, now called the Washburn-Norlands Living History Center. William, living longer, was able to do more. He helped in the construction of the library, paid to replace the steeple on the church, and even supplied a bell. He helped acquire additional land and make many improvements to the mansion itself, and built riding paths through the surrounding woods. He acquired three summer houses in the neighborhood for his children.

William Drew Washburn, the last of the famous brothers, shared the important strengths and weaknesses of his siblings. Although nurtured and protected during his early years, he carved out his own path. He shared every bit of his family's Yankee Protestant rectitude, their certainty in the correctness of their chosen courses, their fascination with politics, and above all, their prodigious energy and unquenchable optimism. He also, apparently, had no fear—the nerve, or foolishness, of a riverboat gambler. It is a supreme irony that William may have been brought down by the very wheat speculating activity that, as a United States senator, he had fought against.

William stands alone among the Washburns in the sheer number of enterprises he started and the partners he attracted, and in the impact he was able to make on his community. His Anoka partner, W. D. Hale, spoke generously of William, his "easy and agreeable manner" and "unfailing courtesy." In an observation that has been made by contemporaries about every Washburn sibling, Hale noted that William's "most noticeable characteristic is that of optimism." [23]

It could very well be that William Drew Washburn, in his progress from family crown prince to pioneer entrepreneur, was a little too optimistic. Like Icarus of Greek mythology, in the end he flew too close to the sun.

1. Washburn Ffamily Journal entry for May 7, 1868 (Washburn Library).

2. Washburn Family Journal, entries for September 29 and 30, 1879 (Washburn Library).

3. Washburn Family Journal, entry for May 15, 1882 (Washburn Library)

4. From the La Crosse *Republican Leader* for May 19, 1882, and October 17, 1885 (La Crosse County Historical Society).

5. Theodore E. Nichols, *A Victorian Honeymoon*, privately printed, Cloverdale, CA: 7.

6. IW personal journal, entry for March 7, 1881 (Washburn Library)

7. IW, *Dedication of the Soldiers Monument at Cherryfield, Maine*, privately printed, Portland, 1874.

8. EBW to a man named Skinner in Chicago, March 21, 1874 (EBW Papers, LC).

9. Israel, Elihu, and Cadwallader were all prominent in their respective state historical societies.

10. Julia Washburn, quoted by Gaillard Hunt in *Israel, Elihu, and Cadwallader Washburn, A Study in American Biography* (New York: 1925), 195.

11. See Roland M. Frye, "The Relationship Between Elihu B. Washburne and

Ulysses S. Grant," an unpublished 1972 thesis for Princeton University, for an excellent analysis of this break.

12. Hester Howell journal fragment (Washburn Library), 302.

13. Donnelly didn't go down easily. After the election he mounted a challenge to the vote count that was itself exposed as fraudulent, complete with forgeries by Donnelly's own attorney.

14. From an unpublished paper, "The Life of William Drew Washburn," by Gaillard Hunt, written circa 1922 (Washburn Library).

15. Letter to WDW from CK__, June 7, 1898 (WDW Papers, Washburn Library).

16. WDW to JW April 26, 1884 (Duke).

17. See *New York Times* articles Aug 9 and 10 and Sept 8, 1908.

18. Powell, 80.

19. Powell, 83.

20. Powell, 93.

21. Issue of July 30, 1912.

22. See *Washington Post*, August 3, 1912.

23. Quoted in WDW's obituary, *Minneapolis Morning Tribune*, July 30, 1912.

———•••———

TEN

On Giants
Seen from a Distance

THE FURTHER AWAY WE GET from anything big, the smaller it becomes. In history, the more time that passes after a person or an event happens, the more objective we can be about it. This is especially true with family history. Sources of information about families get more objective, the further removed both the writer and the reader are from the subject of their study.

Most American families are now, at a minimum, five generations removed from the Civil War. The first of the ten Washburns who are the subject of this book was born nearly two hundred years ago, and the last died nearly a hundred years ago. This is enough time to get past several stages of objectivity—from very little to quite a lot. It is also enough time to get past the self-serving memories of the participants themselves. It is time enough to get by the efforts of their children and contemporaries to clean up the glitches and nourish the myths. It is well past the time where anything unpleasant reflects badly on either the teller or the listener. It is time enough for the mythology to fade and historical fact to emerge.

Compared with other American families of the nineteenth century, the Washburns are unique for the volume of records they left behind. They even built a library to hold their papers, as well as to provide books for their hometown of Livermore. Their record is far from complete, however. There is suspicion that certain information about William was expunged from the record. Material on the women is minimal at best. Brother Samuel left a twelve-year period of his career at sea without a record. In addition, in the tradition of a sea captain who wants nothing unhappy to appear in the log that he keeps for his ships' owners, Captain Sam omitted anything unpleasant in what records we do have from him. He tells us nothing about his mishaps with his brothers, his mishaps with the U.S. Navy, or the wartime injury he received and suffered from for the rest of his life. Brother Sid left no record at all about the second bank in Hallowell that he helped to establish, and that lasted only five years. Apparently, neither these people nor their descendants felt that their papers were worth saving. We can only speculate about what was there.

With or without alterations, there is ample evidence that their contemporaries regarded certain members of the Washburn clan as larger than life. In a forty-page collection of eulogies following Cadwallader's death, the Wisconsin Historical Society went on record calling him "our Hercules" and "a pioneer hero."[1]

He wasn't the only sibling thus honored. Eighteen years after the death of the oldest brother, Israel Washburn, Jr., a feature article in the *Portland Sunday Telegram* referred to him as "the little giant."[2]

* * *

What did these "giants" think of each other? Although always circumspect about putting anything less than laudatory in public speech or writing about their siblings, over their lifetimes the ten Washburns did allow several hints to be recorded as to their real feelings about one another.

Israel and Cadwallader were without blemish in the eyes of

their siblings. With regard to Israel, this may have been the natural lot of the oldest—the role model for the rest. It may also have been out of gratitude for his unfailing years of support—as host, patron, tutor, and door-opener in both Orono and Washington. Of Israel's nine siblings, no less than six directly benefited from his support. All six of his brothers followed his political lead into the Republican party, and four of them followed him into the study of law. Five of them, including Charles, answered his calls to supply funds for The Norlands.

Cadwallader's unbroken drive for financial success was the object of admiration by his siblings, but more often in their letters appear appreciations of his generosity. Indeed, all the siblings and their families benefited from bequests in his will. In addition, all were sympathetic toward him and his children because of the early misfortune of his wife's sudden incapacity. Beyond this, while he lived, we know Cad was fair in all his dealings with Elihu and generous in his support of Charles, and he never hesitated to put his own fortunes in danger in order to defend his impetuous brother William. Though sometimes bellowing protests, he provided employment for both William and Sam, and employment or investment opportunities for two of his sisters' husbands, Charles Stephenson and Gustavus Buffum.

But not all the siblings were so admired. Prominent on this list was youngest brother William. As late as 1943, Gysbert Van Steenwyck, Jr., son of one of Cadwallader Washburn's three executors and closest friends, still remembered that his father, and also James S. Bell and C. C. Hovey, two of Washburn Crosby's key executives, had "equal disregard" for William Drew Washburn.[3] The list of people who couldn't work with William also included George Christian, Cad's first good mill manager, and John Crosby, Cadwallader's most important partner. Both these men got so mad at William that they told Cad that he would have choose between them—and in both cases Cad chose outsiders over his brother.

The same thing happened between Cadwallader and his brother Sam. Marooned and lonely in the lumber camp they had built together at Waubeek, Sam caused his brother plenty of headaches and heartaches over operations there. Caught between the falling price of lumber and the pressure of his debts and other obligations to eastern investors, Cad pressed Sam to improve production at Waubeek. When this got no result, Cad brought in other people to manage the operation—including Sam's own brother-in-law, Gus Buffum. Apparently Sam tried to undercut the new men with the workers, which enraged Cadwallader even more. At one point, he screamed to Sid that "I have sacrificed enough for the sake of giving incompetent relations something to do. They can run me in debt, and that is about all the good they do me."[4]

When the war broke out, Cad begged Elihu, who also had a stake in the camp, to get Sam a place in the navy so he could be removed from Waubeek. Later, when Sam was feeling disillusioned in the navy and threatening to quit, Cad again begged Elihu to do anything he could to keep Sam where he was, predicting that Sam would be a failure in any business he tried. His prediction later proved correct, as Sam apparently went through all the proceeds from his share of Waubeek in the course of his unsuccessful lumber business at Owatonna.

Captain Sam may have incurred his brother's wrath at Waubeek, and there are large gaps in the record of his years at sea, but he still appears to have been a fairly straightforward figure. He was physically tough, and his weakest times appeared to be when, like Charles, he was desperately campaigning for the permanent company of a woman. After the war, when he was beaten down in mind and body by pain, the deaths of his wife and children, and by the collapse of his business, he grew still quieter. He stayed out of the limelight—perhaps to avoid comparison with his brothers.

Elihu, especially in the tumultuous year of 1868, was also not universally admired. Though he had two great political friends in Lincoln and Grant, he also had powerful political enemies in the congress, such as Thad Stevens, John Logan, and Roscoe Conkling. When he was derided at length on the floor of the House by the impetuous Ignatius Donnelly, the entire body roared with laughter—which may have been one reason for the unseemly vituperation with which Elihu replied to the Minnesota gadfly. This could have just been a bad day for Elihu. More likely, it was the result of other pressures, plus his own poor health and exhaustion, for the record shows that he had been equally intemperate in his speech urging the impeachment of President Johnson a few days earlier. People such as self-righteous Gideon Welles and the carefully moderate professionals of the diplomatic corps remembered these outbursts and doubted Elihu because of them. Fortunately, after his performance in France, most of the doubters came around.

Charles had no such redemption. Despite his eloquence, his education, and his powerful brothers, he never did have a close friend—let alone a personal ally. Almost universally—in California, in Argentina, in Paraguay, and in Washington—he left a trail of irritated and distrustful colleagues and adversaries, and few friends. He was defended by those to whom he had been kind, but there was no one who seemed to want to repeat his or her experience with him. Only the children were easy with him, and even they were aware that he was always dreaming of some big scheme that never resulted in anything.

Like Charles, older brother Sid's last years were quiet. However, there was a difference. Sid was remembered for his laughter and the happiness of his house. He was, above all, remembered for his unquestioning support of his brothers during their early years. Sid was genuinely loved, whereas Charles was a subject of worry by his brothers in the early years, and for protection after that.

William, seen from a distance, is an enigma. Despite a spectacular list of accomplishments, he left few papers. He lived thirty years longer than his brothers, so there is nothing in his siblings' papers about him after he reached the age of forty. Records in Minneapolis, where he cut such a swath, are full of requisite praise and obligatory recognition, but very little about the person, and nothing at all about the disappointments with regard to the Pillsbury-Washburn Company. There is plenty of legend about William at Livermore: his annual arrival by private rail car with complete entourage, including servants and mountains of baggage; the three houses he provided there for his children; and his breakneck buggy rides around the neighborhood. The impression is of unquenchable enthusiasms, a life lived at top speed, the arrogance of one who regarded himself as royalty, and recklessness verging on the foolhardy.

Three references about William and his family add some color to the black broadcloth and grim demeanor of the early photographs. The first was a family legend memorialized by Professor James Gray in his 1954 book about General Mills titled *Business Without Boundary*. Gray recounted a tale he was told by a family member about discussions at the family dinner table:

> Surrounded by his four sons and two daughters, all as opinionated as himself, Washburn would dominate their discussion even as its crescendo of challenge and defiance grew higher and higher. One of the sons was deaf and dumb, a handicap which with characteristic Washburn determination he refused to acknowledge. At

the peak of a family wrangle he would demand, by sign language, to be told what the argument was about. It would then begin all over again at the tips of flying fingers. To conclude the matter, the Senator would refer the point at issue to the encyclopedia and if this authority failed to sustain his own opinion he disdainfully hurled the corpulent volume across the room.[5]

The second came from a book by William's fourth son, Edwin Chapin Washburn, who wrote several historical novels including one for boys called *The 17*, about the construction of the Minneapolis and Sault Ste. Marie railroad line. At one point in the book, the president of the company admonishes a young employee with words that sound very like a Washburn: "If you cannot become enthusiastic about the work you're doing, you'd better try some other job, for little can be accomplished without enthusiasm."[6]

Equally sympathetic to William was a paragraph penned after his death by George Brackett, a Bowdoin classmate who went west with him and was his close friend for over sixty years. It referred to that first impression of arrogance that William, like his brothers Cadwallader, Elihu, and Charles, often left with people:

One great handicap to success followed Mr. Washburn in early days. He was naturally aristocratic. When one got to know him, he was affable, approachable, amiable, and in every way a charming man. Yet Mr. Washburn had a manner about him that was not the kind of manner to make a man popular with men. It was just his natural dignity, just the natural bearing of a man well born, well educated, of high ideals, but by some it was misunderstood. Consequently he achieved his political success and his political honors only by reason of the fact that men recognized in him a splendid type of man, a high-minded man and one of great ability and so they voted for him.7

This is hardly the description of a common man. It touches on that indefinable aura that was shared by the most successful Washburns. It wasn't anything they learned at Livermore. It was an aura that came from their experiences, their victories and their defeats. It drew men to them, and made men want to follow where they led. Thousands did follow them, and the world was changed as a result.

The Washburns as a group never lost their interest in what was going on in the world around them. Ironically, the two brothers who suffered the most severe isolation from world affairs were the two who represented their country in the world beyond its shores. Both Charles, trapped in Paraguay, a country that most Americans had never heard of, and Elihu, trapped in Paris in a shooting war between the two greatest armies in Europe, became very depressed when they had no mail or newspapers to read. For both, this was a major deprivation.

The hunger for news from the outside world was also an ongoing passion when they returned to Livermore. Hester Howell, Charles's oldest daughter, writing in 1930, remembered one story about the gentlest brother, her Uncle Sidney. One day Sidney went to the South Livermore post office to pick up the mail:

The sack came up from Strickland's Ferry, and no one to receive it was there. It laid on the floor of the room used as a post office. Sidney sputtered, he knew he had letters, he was always an impatient man, he raved the man should be there to receive it at once, at once! He ram-

paged and finally he took his pen knife and opened it.
The Postmaster finished with his load of hay, drove it in
the barn, and found Sidney reading his mail. There was
a grand row! The pot called the kettle black!! As postmaster he should have been there, hay or no hay, but on
the other side Sidney had no business to cut a mail bag.
The neighborhood echoed for awhile, and then they
compromised: one would be there on time, and the
other never meddle.[8]

Impatience is a theme which crops up repeatedly with the
Washburn brothers. Cadwallader's four-year rage with the
Union Army was largely fueled by his impatience over the slow
pace with which his various campaigns were carried out, and
with the hesitancy and incompetence of his commanders. Sam
was impatient to get out of Waubeek, and William's entire
career of rushing from one enterprise to another was driven by
the same energy and impatience that earned him the nickname
Young Rapid at an early age. There was a very real fire burning
in these men.

The brothers who were most interested in the world around
them were also most concerned about history. Besides building
a library, they saved most of their correspondence, kept personal journals, and undertook major historical writing projects
as well as lectures. They were well aware of the historic significance of the events they had been a part of. Israel exulted in
the Republican sweep of Maine in 1856, and all the brothers
saw the full necessity of going to war in 1860. Israel Jr., Elihu,
and Cadwallader all staunchly supported local historical societies in the 1870s, and contributed leadership as well as financial support to these organizations. Although Elihu was
prominent in the Chicago Historical Society for the last six
years of his life, in the aftermath of the great Chicago fire he

left his voluminous collections with the Library of Congress because the society failed to build a fireproof building for them—even though Elihu was willing to pay much of the cost.

For two of the brothers, Charles and William, their interest in history was subordinate to their efforts to burnish their own personal images. For Charles this took the form of furious writing. His sensitivity about his own image and importance scuttled his political career and built an insuperable obstacle to his diplomatic effectiveness. For William, his personal image was his lavish lifestyle. As he grew older the impetuous dashes of his youth evolved into royal adventures. While his entourage amazed his neighbors in Livermore, and his castle dazzled reporters in Minneapolis, his baubles gained him little when he was matched against a popular opponent in politics (i.e., Knute Nelson for a Senate seat) or an efficient manager in business (i.e., George Christian, John Crosby, or James Bell at Washburn-Crosby). Neither Charles nor William could match the achievements of their older brothers Israel Jr. and Elihu when it came to success in a large organization.

* * *

What aspects of these ten siblings appear to be most giant-like to the historians of today? They were all smart. Their careers in the courtroom certainly aided brothers Israel Jr., Elihu, and Cadwallader in becoming canny, as well as well-read. In his work to get elected to Congress, and then to direct the birth and triumph of the Republican party, Israel Jr. approached the level of political genius. His effectiveness was evident in his results. He may have been diminutive, but his legacy was huge: a united legislature in Maine, a new political party that was to dominate the country for seventy-five years and dominate Maine for over a hundred, the saving of the Union, the long-delayed recognition of Maine's importance by the national government, and his own huge popularity among the voters of

the state. A brilliant speaker, an absolutely honest man, a foun-
tain of energy, the bespectacled Israel Jr. indeed cast a giant
shadow across the political landscape of his time.

Cadwallader's "giant-ness" lay in his vision, his capacity to
see opportunity where other men could not, and then his ability to concentrate awesome energy into achieving that vision.
To this end he harvested forests in Wisconsin, cut through
hundred-mile swamps in Mississippi, redirected rivers in
Wisconsin and Minnesota, dammed and redirected the
Mississippi River itself, crossed the prairies with rail lines and
dotted them with wheat elevators, built the biggest flour mills
and the biggest sawmills that had ever been seen (far ahead of
any visible markets for them to serve), and filled them with
new technology. In so doing, he revolutionized the flour-
milling business. He then picked superbly talented people to
carry on after him so that his enterprises would not die. He led
men, inspired bankers and investors, and revitalized at least
three huge industries (milling, railroads, and lumbering). His
last battle probably made material changes in the insurance
business which covered them. He also promoted—and
shared—new inventions such as the purifier, the dust collector,
and the steel roller mill. These advances, plus his leadership in
controlling railroad shipping costs and fighting for fair insurance settlements, benefited not just his company, but the entire
milling industry.

Cadwallader was also giant-like in his drive to make money,
and he made a very great deal of money. Always, however, for
him money was a means to an end. He concentrated his energy,
attention, and resources on a limited number of enterprises,
and then plowed every cent of return into making them bigger
and more efficient, and into bringing their products to an ever
wider market. At the same time that his flagship product was
winning the awards that inspired the name Gold Medal, for

example, his marketers were breaking into the European flour market. In 1870, trapped in the siege of Paris, Elihu reported in his journal that a warehouse full of Minnesota flour helped ward off famine in the French capital.

From an early age, Cadwallader had an air of quiet authority, and few except his brother Elihu were aware of the furnace of frustration that burned within him when his expectations were not met. But at the same time, he had a high code of honor, which would not allow him—ever—to take the easy way out. So he soldiered through his frustrations following the 1857 crisis, and he stuck it out amid the incompetence and corruption that surrounded him for most of his career in the army. He shrugged off his disappointments in Madison in 1875, and he positively charged through the wreckage of the explosion of his Minneapolis flour mills in 1878.

Cad's greatest handicap was at home. Alone among the siblings, he really didn't have a home. He may have wanted one, but when he tried to build one, it was too late. He had no wife, and he was honor-bound never to have one. He tried to compensate for this with his energy—never being in one place long enough to need a home—and with his generosity. From Minneapolis to La Crosse to Philadelphia to Washington, there were many doors always open to him, but few that he darkened for long. Loved and respected though he was, the end finally came for him in an Arkansas hotel room.

Then there was Elihu, a different kind of giant. No Washburn rose higher in politics, or had more influence, than Elihu: Party-builder on the frontier, political strategist and wire-puller, intimate of two presidents, Watchdog of the Treasury detested by an army of governmental hangers-on and favor-seekers, toughened with a stubbornness that earned admiration from the crowned heads of Europe. He was the enemy of every kind of commercial privilege and unearned government handout, and for him the most important thing in life was honesty—personal honesty.

Comfortable in retirement in Chicago, honored by his country, and full of the need to pass his principles on to future generations, in 1885 he penned a letter of advice to his second son, Hempstead. The young lawyer had just won his first elected office, that of city attorney for Chicago. Speaking as a leader who had seen a lot, and also as a loving father, Elihu, the giant of political influence, revealed himself as a giant of integrity:

> You will soon enter upon the duties of your office, and in the way you discharge them will depend all your future. It is a vital moment in your life. Let all your action be marked by unquestioned honesty and the most unsullied integrity. There is no basis of success in life but honesty, never under any circumstances are your public positions for private gain. You will be approached in every possible way and in the most insidious manner, but scorn any unworthy possibilities and regard every man who makes it as an enemy.... No public man can have a lasting or an honorable career unless he is honest, honest, honest. Let a man know in his own heart that he is honest, he can defy the whole world.... You will have vast interests to act upon, but discharge them all with the most scrupulous fidelity. Never betray a public trust, neither a private trust. Be very careful in all your accounts, and keep a true record of all your official days, so when you get through all the world can say: "Well done, good and faithful servant." Guard well these words of your affectionate father.9

What about Sidney? The only Washburn never elected to

public office was yet the most beloved by all his siblings. The first of the brothers to die, the impatient financier was most remembered for his laughter and his generosity, and for his household, which they loved to visit. Tragically widowed at an early age, he produced the most successful offspring of all of his generation (see Appendix A). Sid collected no headlines, yet within the family he was regarded as a giant of love and laughter. Always there to support them, his more serious siblings loved him for his lighthearted style.

Perhaps the ultimate message of the remarkable Washburns is that everyone is a giant. Even Charles, whose intellect was the equal of his siblings, and whose skill with a pen was impressive in its own right, shared the giant-like integrity of his siblings, as well as their optimism.

In every society, some think that one way to be a giant is to make more noise than anyone else. All of the quiet Washburns—Sam, Martha, Mary, and Carrie—certainly fail this test. But these four, none of whom felt that they ever did anything worthy of the world's note, were notable in another aspect of giant-ness. With their siblings, they shared a quiet but enormous courage. They looked at pain and fear and death with eyes that were unafraid. Whether it was a North Atlantic gale or a Confederate cannon or the death of a young spouse or a complicated childbirth far from competent medical help, they faced every challenge without flinching or feeling sorry for themselves. They passed through life-threatening perils without complaint, were at all times strong and determined, and fought like tigers when threatened. Sam's laconic words to Elihu, scribbled in the heat and pain of battle from a ship that had nearly been destroyed just a few days earlier, cast Victorian form aside and speak plainly as to how every one of these quiet Washburns lived their lives: "We shelled the sons of bitches for four hours yesterday afternoon, and are all ready to give it to

William Drew and Elizabeth Muzzy Washburn in the 1890s.
This portrait of William was painted by his deaf-mute son
Cadwallader Lincoln Washburn. COURTESY MINNESOTA
HISTORICAL SOCIETY AND THE WASHBURN LIBRARY

them again today." Giants don't have to make more noise than
everybody else.

That leaves William, the enigma who did his best to appear
larger than life. He was arrogant, impetuous, and opinionated,
driven by a spirit that would never rest. He was a builder, an

innovator, a promoter, sublimely sure of himself, who rarely looked over his shoulder. A spectacular authority figure at home, he was at the same time an unbending defender of the status quo in public life. Originator of a panoply of human endeavor—a big part of the city of Minneapolis itself—he constantly reached out to the horizon, and was unconcerned about the details. He was a pillar of his church, but his real religion was activity and motion, the more and faster the better. He certainly thought he was a giant, and from his uproarious household to his multiple enterprises to his massive expeditions, everything was an adventure. As a leading conservative in a conservative age, he was still, by far, the most unpredictable person of the entire Washburn tribe. His son's painting of him, perhaps done at a time when his fortunes were highest, shows a patrician face with an enigmatic expression, offset by a brilliant red carnation in the buttonhole of his coat.

One final caveat needs to be added about William Drew Washburn. As the conditions of his growing up were different from his brothers', so, in the years after they died, he lived his life at a more exalted level than any of them ever did. No one had more gilt from the Gilded Age than did William. But all the gleam and glitter may very well have had the effect of blinding him to the moral compass by which they had all lived their lives.

The fact is that *somebody* very high up in the management of Pillsbury-Washburn bet wrong on the future of grain prices, may have pledged collateral that didn't exist in order to do it, and hid the obligation from the company's owners. Restitution was made and everyone moved on, but in the thick ledger that lists the principled deeds of the Washburn family, the last entry for William Drew Washburn may have an asterisk by it.

1. Memorial address, 33.
2. *Portland Sunday Telegram*, May 28, 1911.
3. From memo of Jack Andrews, May 10, 1943, at archives of General Mills.
4. CCW to ASW, August 12, 1859 (Duke).
5. James Gray, *Business Without Boundary* (Minneapolis: 1954), 14.
6. Edwin C. Washburn, *The 17* (Englewood, NJ: 1929), 141
7. Gaillard Hunt, "The Life of William Drew Washburn," unpublished essay written

for the family in 1922, supplied to the author by Mark Washburne, 9–10.

8. From Howell manuscript fragment (Washburn Library), 64.

9. EBW to HW, April 20, 1885, from Paul Gilbert and Charles Lee Bryson, *Chicago and Its Makers* (Chicago: 1929), 1063.

POSTSCRIPT

Five Defining Moments

IT IS SAD THAT THE WASHBURNS have not attracted more attention from scholars and historians. Although they are refreshing for the absence of propagandists and political spin-masters, they are also protagonists in a great age. For all their noble deeds and great accomplishments, we need to remember them for their humanity.

This writer has spent most of the past fifteen years in the presence of what Rosalind Wright called "the dear ghosts" of Norlands. These remarkable siblings had some memorably human moments. Let us not leave them without mentioning some of those moments. We can use our imaginations to fill in the details.

Like pictures at an exhibition or snapshots of a trip just completed, let us look at the Washburn scrapbook as if it had only five pictures—five pictures of Washburn moments to remember, even though there was no camera present.

* * *

The first page holds the picture of a moment that probably happened in Washington, D.C., in the rented rooms that the three Washburn congressmen, Israel Jr., Elihu, and Cadwallader, share. These are the lodgings to which they limp after the passage of the Kansas-Nebraska Act. It's three o'clock in the morning on a warm May night in 1854. They've been through a long, bad night on the floor of the House, the culmination of weeks of fruitless battle. The South and the doughfaces have rolled over them. Despite their battle to stop it, their colleagues in both chambers have reversed Henry Clay's compromise that has held North and South together for thirty-four years. Their own beloved Whig party has voted against them. The president opposes them. The Supreme Court is hostile to them. Timidity, apathy, and an arrogant South appear to rule the country.

Bespectacled Israel has led the hopeless fight. As he sits there amid the support and sympathy of his brothers, heartsick and exhausted, perhaps he remembers the sight back in the winter of 1839 in Orono when that ragtag line of Maine state militia went by his office on the Bangor Road. Those ordinary men had three hundred miles of snowbound and frozen wilderness in front of them, their country hardly knew they were there, and at the end of the long trek, they were going to take on the most powerful country in the world, Great Britain.

Those men thought they were right then, and he thinks he is right now. Quietly he gathers himself up. He is an unknown, homely congressman from a remote district of the remotest corner of the country, but he knows that he is right. The next day he launches a political movement that will revolutionize the country.

* * *

Page two: A civil war comes, and gives us a second scene. It is June 30, 1862. We are on the James River in Virginia, as Union and Confederate armies struggle at the battle of Malvern Hill. It is late afternoon, and uncoordinated Confederate attacks have been surging against Union lines on the hill for several hours. On the river, the federal gunboats *Mahaska* and *Galena* are cloaked in smoke and fire from the barrage of their heavy guns in support of the federals. The officers and crew of the Union gunboat *Galena* are shot up and short-handed, but they are still full of fight. As the battle reaches its crescendo, their 100-pound forward guns are sending huge projectiles more than a mile over the high ground and into the advancing lines of Stonewall Jackson's Confederates, as her 9-inch Dahlgrens fire at rebel sharpshooters in the woods along the shore.

On board the gunboat, organized chaos reigns. Amid deck timbers splintered and armor plating pock-marked from the bloody action at Drewry's Bluff two weeks earlier, the great guns are firing continuously. The patched and leaky hull shakes and shudders with every explosion. On the forward deck, deafened by the roar and blackened by the smoke and powder, for three hours a limping Acting Master Sam Washburn directs the fire of the two big Parrot guns. Consumed by the rage of battle, his eyes are narrow with the desire to destroy the rebels who came so close to destroying *him* just a few days earlier.

Behind him, in contrast, perhaps less than fifty feet away, Major General George B. McClellan, commander and architect of the Army of the Potomac, author of the grand plan to capture Richmond and end the Confederacy, sits pale and trembling. Although his army will win this day, he is a beaten man. With the sweat of fear on his brow, he has already decided to end the Peninsula Campaign and withdraw his beautiful army. His only thoughts that day are on the excuses he must manufacture to justify his retreat. That day he will earn Sam's disgust, and the anger of all his Washburn brothers, and Lincoln's search for a more resolute commander will extend the war for three more terrible years.

* * *

Page three: It is two years later, and the Civil War produces another Washburn moment for us to remember. This one is in Memphis, now entering its third year of occupation by the Union Army. It is December 1864, and the commanding general of the occupying army is alone in his quarters. He is scribbling a letter to his fourteen-year-old daughter at a boarding school in Massachusetts.

C. C. Washburn has been successful at almost everything he has done, and huge new successes are ahead for him when the war is over. Here in Tennessee, after a struggle that stretched all the way to Congress, he has just succeeded in cutting off all trade with the enemy. No more food, clothing, or other supplies will cross the lines, no matter how much cotton is offered, no matter how desperate the need. Like Grant and Sherman, after four years of war Washburn grimly realizes that the only way to defeat the South is to starve it to death. He has been implacable in pursuing this goal.

Now he is facing the one job that has always perplexed him—the job of being a parent. His daughter Jeanette has been invited to join friends in Connecticut for Christmas, and she has just asked her father's permission to go, as well as to let her buy a new outfit for the parties that will be held while she is there. The general, who is slow to realize that his little girl is becoming an adult, turns her down. He commands her to protect herself against "extravagance and folly" and not to imitate other girls who are "foolish and giddy."

Then, looking out his window, he sees another reason. He turns the sheet and writes, "You must make your old clothes last as long as possible, for these are very hard times, and if you could see the suffering that these poor southern people undergo, you would not wish to be clad in purple and fine linen. Ladies that were so rich from years ago that they never assumed for wants, but had fine houses, splendid wardrobes, and everything that heart could wish, I have seen begging bread often and again, with hardly clothing enough to cover them."[1] The ruthless conqueror is not as pitiless as he seems.

It is no surprise then, that when the war was finally over, the general was feted by citizens on both sides. And when he died, his greatest bequest was to the city of Minneapolis for a magnificent institution for the care and upbringing of orphan children—perhaps children like his own.

* * *

Next page: A fourth moment comes four months later, immediately after Lee's surrender at Appomattox. A mob of exhausted men, victors and vanquished alike, makes its way slowly across the muddy and starved Virginia backcountry, heading back from the surrender ceremony to the railhead at Petersburg. Most are marching, but two are riding. One of these two is in Confederate gray and wears a general's stars. The other, equally weary and traveled-stained, is in a rumpled suit of civilian clothes. Neither man has eaten or slept much for the past ten days. The Southerner is General John B. Gordon of Georgia, who has just surrendered the last ten thousand men of Robert E. Lee's army. The civilian is Congressman Elihu B. Washburne of Illinois, who has raced a thousand miles in abominable conditions to be here. The two men, former colleagues in the House of Representatives, are in earnest conversation. As each hour passes, and they approach the former Confederate capital, Gordon looks more and more relieved.

Washburne, who is close enough to Lincoln to know, has spent the entire two-day journey persuading the Southerner that his fears of a vengeful Northern dictatorship are groundless. Lincoln's intentions are moderate, and his skills and fame are enough to bring the entire North with him. The South will be dealt with fairly. The nation will bind up its wounds. Gordon has nothing to fear. The two men part amicably at Petersburg in the morning of April 14, 1865.

What neither man can know, but what both men will learn that night, is that a madman's bullet at Ford's Theater has changed everything.

* * *

Last page: The final image of the Washburns, the one to leave
with, is from forty-five years later—1912. The Civil War is
long over, and the excesses of the Gilded Age are about to produce the world's first global war. The great ship *Titanic* is taking
shape on the ways in Belfast, Ireland, to provide another symbol of the frailty of man's works.

Here in Minneapolis is another poignant scene of the end
of an age. The setting is the huge Washburn castle at Fair Oaks.
Its construction was an act of self-glorification by one of the
greatest speculators in the city. It is the home of Senator and
Mrs. William Drew Washburn. The image we need to note is
not so much of the man there. Rather, let us look at his wife of
more than fifty years, Elizabeth Muzzy Washburn.

For more than five decades this beautiful woman has followed every fortune and misfortune of her mercurial husband.
From a happy youth of privilege and gaiety in Bangor, to a tiny
house on the dusty frontier whose previous tenants were a flock
of chickens, and now to this eighty-room stone pile, she has
stuck by her man through every trial. She has borne him nine
children and seen six of them survive to successful adulthood.
In an often uproarious household, she has calmed a thousand
tumults, healed a thousand hurts. Through all of their growing
up, through every tempest within their walls and without, she
has maintained a calm and loving environment for them all.
Now the children are all well educated and settled into distant
places with lives of their own—most with families of their own.

She has provided her husband with every kind of support.
From Washington, D.C., to Peking to Moscow to Livermore,
Maine, she has played the role of gracious hostess flawlessly.
Right here at Fair Oaks she has entertained presidents and all
the national leaders of the Republican party.

She has managed every aspect of her enormous household

with aplomb and humor—from the stables to the gardens to the kitchen to the labyrinth of bedrooms large and small. She has managed vast traveling entourages to the far ends of the earth. She has dealt with setbacks as varied as the drowning of her oldest son and the loss of a Senate seat that her husband should have been able to retain. She has endured political calumnies directed at her husband and she has shared in his business defeats—ranging in scale from disappointing to disastrous. She has seen him get fired twice—once by his very own brother. She has seen him go bankrupt once already.

But now is the worst time of all. Now, at a time when they should be enjoying the quiet of their final years, an army of creditors is at their door, and the taint of disgrace hangs heavy in the air. The great house is almost empty. Outside, the winter winds howl around the battlements, and the chill is constant. Inside, most of the rooms are empty, and the halls echo with her footsteps and her memories of great events held here. The children and most of the servants are gone, as are the days of the great entertainments. There are few callers now.

It is all over. The place doesn't even belong to them anymore. In lieu of unpaid taxes, they live in it at the pleasure of the Minneapolis city fathers. For five years, a relentless phalanx of lawyers from New York has been stripping away every asset—every certificate of stock, every gilt-edged bond, every property, every forest acre. One piece at a time, they have removed almost every trace of her husband's fifty years of spectacular enterprise.

What is left is the shell of her once-proud husband—the last of the seven Washburn sons of Livermore, Maine. He is far from the glittering prince he once was, but she will stay by his side. She even goes with him for one last trip to Europe, and she is with him on his race home to die at Fair Oaks. As he has been flashing and glittering and in constant motion for all of his eighty years, so she has been steady and constant and true to him and to the family they have created together. Even now, next to the bloated but still impeccable husk that is all that is left of the prince who swept her away from Bangor fifty-four years earlier, she stands erect and looks you squarely in the eye.

There could be no better example of a nineteenth-century woman. Elizabeth Muzzy Washburn is quietly magnificent.

* * *

Looked at over the five or more generations that have passed since their time, the Washburns and their ladies may not all be godlike, but they are certainly impressive. In what they did, and in where they did it, and in how they did it, they are impressive for their dreams, for their energy, for their self-assurance, for their integrity, and for their courage.

Above all, they are impressive for their origin. They are one generation of one farm family, raised as brothers and sisters amid poverty and few advantages, in a remote area of the country's most remote state, at a time of great crisis. It was a time which most of them turned into a time of great opportunity.

We are not likely to see their like again.

1. Letter from CCW to JWK, December 5, 1864 (Washburn Library).

APPENDIX A

The Next Generation

WILLIAM'S DRAMATIC FINISH overshadowed the last years of his two remaining siblings, as well as the impressive records of his children.

His older sister Martha, following the death of her husband Charles L. Stephenson in St. Paul in 1880, lived in that city with her widowed and childless daughter, also named Martha. Both women went west to live with her youngest son, Benjamin, in Mandan, North Dakota, in 1898, not far north of William's coal mines in Wilton. The very next year her remaining daughter, Elizabeth, who had founded the first kindergarten in Minneapolis, and later went east to teach in Massachusetts, died there, in Brookline. The end came for both the Marthas in Mandan ten years later: They died just ten days apart in April 1909. Both are buried next to Captain Stephenson at Oakland Cemetery in St. Paul. Martha's remaining son, Frederick (the one who had tangled with the Christian brothers over the management of Cad's mills back in 1878), after years in Chicago and Massachusetts, and two marriages, died back in Minneapolis in 1913.

There is a faint trace of dysfunction about Martha's family. From little Nettie Washburn's memories of Martha's harshness to Captain Charles Stephenson's long absences, one gets a hint that hers was not a happy home. Of her four surviving children, all left Galena and only two were ever married. One step-grandchild, Frederick's adopted son Walter, is recorded. Although Walter had a daughter, the death of Martha's bachelor son Benjamin in California in 1925 brought a quiet end to her bloodline of the family.

$$* * *$$

Quietest of all the Washburns was Caroline, the youngest sister. She remained in her little house in Minneapolis, and continued to serve on the board of the Washburn Memorial Orphans Asylum after William's death. When she died in 1920, it was her wish to be returned to Foxcroft, Maine, and buried next to Freeland Holmes, her husband from fifty years earlier. Neither of her children, Fanny and Frank, perhaps the unsuspecting victims of too much of their mother's love, ever married. Sadly, both of them died within two years of their mother. All three, perhaps, were indirect casualties of the Civil War.

$$* * *$$

The quiet finales of both Martha's and Carrie's branches of the family contrasts vividly with the families of most of their brothers and sisters. Despite the differences, a few general observations can be made about the group.

None of Patty Benjamin's children approached her in either fertility or generation-building. None matched her success in having children, in seeing their children survive, or in seeing their children multiply. Patty had eleven children; ten survived. All of the survivors found spouses, and all of them produced children. Reduced to percentages, that's 91 percent, 100 percent, and 100 percent respectively.

The next generation consisted of forty-seven children, of whom only thirty-four survived to adulthood. That's 72 percent. Although many of these did in fact distinguish themselves, only twenty-five of the thirty-four got married. That's 73 percent. Of these twenty-five, only sixteen had children. That's 64 percent. The fall-off in fertility is notable. Only Elihu and William came anywhere close to imitating the size of the family they had grown up in. Looking across the rest of the children of the Livermore Washburns, there seem to be too many bachelors, too many spinsters, and too many childless couples.

The group of thirty-four Washburn children who survived to adulthood ranged from famous to invisible. All of them had to deal with the effects of the fame and fortunes of their parents. Many had to deal with the extensive absences of their fathers. Many had to deal with intense exposure to public notice, as well as the constant pressure—real or imagined—to keep up with their parents. Physical comforts varied widely among the families, as did parental expectations. Many of the children received excellent educations. A significant number took up writing, and one did it well enough to earn a living at it. Several were successful in business, and several others tried politics, but had less success than their forebears. All seemed to be well liked, but not all were happy. Of the quietest, hardly anything is known.

Here, in the order of age of their parents, are thumbnail sketches of what we know, beyond Martha and Caroline, about the children of the other eight Washburns of Livermore.

* * *

Israel Washburn, Jr., had four children. His oldest was Israel Henry—the one he named after his Whig idol, Henry Clay. Henry saw action with the Union Army at both Fredericksburg and Chancellorsville while serving as an aide to Maine general Hiram Berry. When Berry was killed at Chancellorsville, Henry was a first lieutenant in the 16th Maine Regiment. He resigned because of ill health in 1863, but thanks to his father's intervention with Secretary of the Navy Gideon Welles, Henry was commissioned in the U.S. Marine Corps in 1864. Based on his army record, he asked to be made a major, but second lieutenant was what he got. In addition, he got a notation in his record about "strong political connections."[1] Henry loved the

Marines and served for thirty years, mostly at various navy yards. He retired as a captain in 1886 and settled in Portsmouth, New Hampshire, near the Navy Yard in Kittery. He was happily married and saw three children survive to adulthood.

Henry's younger brother, Charles Fox Washburn, whom his father described as both unhealthy and unlucky, died just a year after his father. Charles Fox lived in Minneapolis and despite a long history of poor health, served in both houses of the state legislature there. He never married.

Israel Jr.'s two daughters, named Ada and Maud, enjoyed the social life of Washington and Augusta, and were a great comfort and help to their father during his years in Portland—especially after the death of their mother. They participated in many trips—saw the world—but neither ever met a husband. So, although successful in finding mates for two of his three sisters, and probably for two of his brothers as well, plus a second wife for himself, Israel Jr. never found a partner for either of his daughters.

* * *

Algernon Sidney Washburn had four sons, but only the second and third, named John and Robert respectively, survived to adulthood. Both boys, known affectionately as "the mackerel brigade" during their various stays at Livermore, attended Bowdoin College, but neither graduated. When their father died in 1879, John left the college and went west. He was twenty-one. His younger brother Rob, just eighteen, entered Bowdoin that year and attended for three years, but in 1882, perhaps with the help of his Uncle Israel, transferred to Tufts. Upon his graduation there in 1883, he, too, left Maine and its sad memories and moved west.

The oldest son, John, turned out to be the most successful of his entire generation. After leaving Bowdoin, he determined to learn the flour business in Minneapolis. He rapidly turned himself into an expert in the most critically important area of that business—grain buying. Urged on by his Uncle William, he joined Washburn Crosby just as the ownership and reorganization of the company was being resolved in the wake of his uncle Cad's death in 1882 and John Crosby's death in 1887. Probably to carry on the names of the deceased principals, since William Drew was about to be eased out, both John Washburn and John Crosby, Jr., were named to the board of the new corporation. Washburn was only thirty, and John Crosby was still in college. However, John Washburn served the company for the next thirty-two years. He helped guide Washburn Crosby through the First World War, and he gained fame for the company through its contributions to the famine relief programs that followed the war—the same relief programs that helped Herbert Hoover win the presidency. John Washburn helped build the foundation for what was to become General Mills a few years later. When he died suddenly in 1919, he had just been named board chairman. He was married and had three daughters.

John's younger brother Robert, after graduating from Tufts College in 1883, moved even further west—to the state of Oregon. There, in 1887, he married Mary Louise Savier, daughter of a successful Portland businessman and flour miller named Thomas Savier. Rob and Mary Louise bought a ranch in the southern part of the state, near Medford, Oregon, and went into raising apples. He later served in both the lower and upper houses of the state legislature, while combining careers as an editor, writer, and co-owner of the *Seattle Post Intellegencer*, as well as continuing as an apple grower. He died in 1929 in Portland, Oregon, without children.

* * *

Elihu and Adele Washburne had a total of eight children, six of whom survived to adulthood. Of the six, the oldest was

Gratiot, the son who distinguished himself with his father during the siege of Paris. When they returned to America, his father got Gratiot a job in the New York Customs House, where he worked for several years. At the age of only thirty-seven, Gratiot died suddenly in a hotel in Louisville, Kentucky, where he had gone on business to promote a trade exposition to be held in New York. He never married.

His younger brother Hempstead was the political star of the family. Schooled in Europe and the University of Wisconsin Law School, Hempstead went to work for a law firm in Chicago headed by his father's old political ally, Lyman Trumbull. Leaning toward public service, Hempstead ran for and was elected city attorney for Chicago in 1885. He was in this position during the difficult period when his older brother, his mother, and his father all died—the latter at his home. He served as city attorney for four years, and followed this up by being elected mayor of Chicago in 1891. His most memorable accomplishment—from conception to reality—was the World's Columbian Exposition in that city—the biggest, most elaborate trade show America had ever seen. His "reform" administration was also memorable for its resistance to the political machines that dominated the city at the time. Hempstead married and had four children who survived to adulthood.

Elihu's next son was William Pitt Washburne, known as Pitt. After receiving medical training in France, he returned to America when his father's term in Paris expired. He married twice, lived in the "Oxford" house at Livermore, which his father willed to him in 1887, and later in Galveston, Texas, where he died without children in 1898.

The youngest son was named Elihu Benjamin Washburne, Jr. He was still in prep school when his parents died, and little is known about him, other than he was a sickly child and that he died in New York in 1908 without issue. These two sons, Pitt and Elihu Jr., appear to have been the black sheep of the family, and their father directed that the bulk of his estate, $500,000, be held in trust specifically for their benefit.

Elihu and Adele also had two daughters. Susan Adele, who was born during a visit of her mother to the Washburn relatives in Raynham, Massachusetts, married William D. Bishop, a Yale graduate, in Chicago two years after her famous coming-out party there. The couple settled in his hometown of Bridgeport, Connecticut, where they had two children, and where she died in 1923. Her younger sister was Marie Lisa, named after her mother's fur-trading uncle in St. Louis, Manuel Lisa. Marie became quite attached to the estate at Norlands and chose to be married there in 1885 to Amos Fowler of Denver. She had three children in Colorado, including a daughter named Sally Reyburn who was a great supporter of Norlands. In 1927, assisted by a Yale professor named John Allison, Marie wrote a delightful little book about her mother called *Reminiscences: My Mother and I*. Marie died in 1937 and is buried with her sister in Bridgeport.

* * *

Cadwallader Colden Washburn, in the short three years that his wife was healthy, sired two children, his daughters Jeanette and Fanny. Raised as virtual orphans, both girls fiercely embraced married life at an early date. Jeanette was first. Following a courtship that involved his boyhood friend, the painter Winslow Homer, and that stretched from Belmont, Massachusetts, to Paris, France, Jeanette married Albert Warren Kelsey of Boston in 1869 at La Crosse. (A Homer painting now at the Wadsworth Atheneum in Hartford titled *The Red Feather*, is supposed to be of her.) Warren gave her all the love and attention she had never gotten from her father, and they were happily married for over fifty years—most of it lived in a mansion Cad provided for them in Chestnut Hill, outside Philadelphia. She presented Warren with nine children over fourteen years—two sons and seven daughters—eight of whom survived to adulthood. Both the sons made names for themselves, one as an architect and the other as a manufacturer and inventor.

Cad's other daughter, Fanny, married a translator at the State Department named Charles Payson, whom she had met while with her father in Washington. The wedding was an extravaganza at the governor's mansion back in Madison in 1872. When Fanny wished to follow her husband back to Washington, Cad built a house for them there. Of her children, two daughters survived to adulthood. Both the girls married foreign husbands in Washington during 1895 and 1896, following their father's tour as consul in Denmark. Fanny and Charles moved to France and then permanently settled in Switzerland. They are buried together in Vevey, a popular expatriate haven on Lake Geneva.

Except for Jeanette's brief visit back to Edgewood College in Madison in 1919, there is no record that either of Cad's daughters ever returned to Wisconsin.

* * *

Charles A. Washburn and his wife Sallie had three children. Both of their daughters were writers. Hester, who was born in Paraguay, transcribed her father's memoirs and left a lively personal journal that was not complimentary to her mother. Her sister Lilian, born in Livermore, wrote the first book about her famous uncles and grandparents, which she titled *My Seven Sons*. Their brother Thurlow, after knocking about for some years in the West, put himself through MIT, became a mining engineer in New Mexico and Colorado, and rose to be assistant superintendent of the Bonnie Bell Gold Mine near Telluride. At the age of only thirty, Thurlow Washburn was tragically killed in a snowslide there in 1899.

Hester Washburn married Willis Howell, moved to New Jersey, and had four children. Her sister Lilian married Frank Vilenius, but had no children, and spent her last years devoted to preserving the Norlands property.

* * *

Information is as scarce about brother Samuel's family as it is about him. The only surviving child by his first wife Lorette, named Samuel Benjamin Washburn, Jr., but always called Bennie, was brought up and educated through high school in Maine. He went west to work in the Washburn mill at Minneapolis and married a Fanny (also known as Lena) Henderson there in 1895. They were childless. Like his father had in Owatonna, Bennie joined a Masonic lodge in Minneapolis, and served as its leader for five years.

Of his two stepsisters, only Katherine survived to adulthood. She and her mother stayed in Avon, New York, after her father's death, and she married John Kellogg there in 1898. They had four children.

* * *

Mary Benjamin Washburn Buffum, whose brave effort to find a husband took eight years, and whose effort to increase her family cost her life, would be proud today of the family tree that she started. Although her twins died with her at Lyons, Iowa, two other sons and a daughter, named Frank, Charles, and Ada, survived to live long and fruitful lives.

Her two sons, Frank Washburn Buffum and Charles Gustavus Buffum, worked side by side with their father at the lumberyard in Lyons. When the yard's operations were consolidated at Louisiana, Missouri, in 1873, the whole family moved there. Father and sons continued their efficient and even-handed management of the company after Cad's death in 1882. When Cad's estate was settled in 1888, father and sons purchased the Louisiana yard as equal partners. Interestingly, their purchase included the name La Crosse Lumber Company, but not Cad's great mill at La Crosse. In this they were prescient, for the mill in La Crosse was shut down in 1900 and torn down in 1903. Perhaps this was because, at last, the great Wisconsin forests, which had fed all the mills for so long, were gone.

The La Crosse operation in Missouri grew and prospered as a sales organization, however. In 1901, partly to fill the need for rapid communication with their several branch yards across central Missouri and southern Illinois, Frank started up a telephone company. He also established a tool-making company that became famous for its swastika logo—long before Adolph Hitler gave that symbol a different connotation. He also helped set up a pearl button factory that still exists today. Frank married twice and had two children who survived to adulthood. One was a daughter who, with her husband, George Ruth, followed the lumber business to Longview, Washington, and established a large and respected family there. The other was Frank's son, Frank G., who stayed in Louisiana, married, and had two children.

Frank's younger brother Charles continued the management of La Crosse Lumber following his father Gustavus's death in 1899. He became president in 1914. By the time of his death in 1934, he was also president of the leading bank in town, had spearheaded the construction of a highway bridge across the Mississippi, and was chairman of the local hospital. Charles married and had a daughter and a son. The latter was educated at Princeton and in 1934 succeeded his father as the third Buffum to be president of La Crosse Lumber. His son, Charles III, presently serves on the board of the company, which is still headquartered in Louisiana, although it now has seventeen locations across Missouri and Illinois.

Mary's only daughter, Ada Mary, also grew up in Louisiana.

There is a record of her visiting The Norlands in 1881, when she was not yet twenty years old. She married twice and had a daughter, still another Mary, by her second husband, James Ovid Stark. Ada Mary Buffum Stark lived to be a hundred years old, dying in 1962. Her daughter, Mary Stark, also stayed in Louisiana, in turn married Henry Burns, and had five children. Two of her five children are presently directors of the La Crosse Lumber Company.

It was almost 150 years ago that Mary Washburn married Gustavus Buffum in the parlor at Livermore, and her brother Cadwallader, in turn, hired the young man to help him with his lumber business in Wisconsin. The La Crosse Lumber Company stands today, together with a long succession of competent Buffums who have administered it, as a fitting memorial to the good judgment of its founders and early managers.

* * *

Of all the Livermore Washburns, it was William who had the most well-known children. Somehow, amidst the almost royal surroundings of their mother and father—the servants, the private schools, the trips to Europe, the private railroad cars—the six children of William and Elizabeth Washburn who survived to adulthood managed to live normal and productive lives. As strong-willed as their father, no less than five of them achieved national notice.

The oldest surviving son, William Drew, Jr., after graduating from Yale, returned to the Midwest. Although prone to bouts of depression, he started out as a journalist in Chicago, then returned to Minneapolis to run a business in farmlands. He inherited the family interest in public affairs and served sixteen years in the state legislature representing his city. He even ran unsuccessfully for Congress in 1918. He married Florence Savier from Oregon, sister of Mary Louise Savier, who had married his cousin Rob (Sid's youngest son) a year earlier. They had four children, one of whom, Thomas Savier Washburn, with his wife Katherine, were described by Billie Gammon as "the best friends that Norlands ever had."

The second son, rendered deaf and mute by an early attack of meningitis, was named Cadwallader Lincoln Washburn. Young Cad never acknowledged his handicap, graduated from Gallaudet College, and got a graduate degree in architecture at MIT, where he won a First Award in Design. He then defied his father and went off to study art in Europe. He taught himself the intricate art of etching. Eventually he came home to join his brother Stanley at the *Chicago Daily News*, and together they went to the Far East and enjoyed great success in reporting the Russo-Japanese War, a success which Cadwallader duplicated later in Mexico, covering the revolution of 1910 as head correspondent for the *News*. Despite his deafness and lack of speech, with his ever-present writing pad he became fluent in several languages, including Spanish. After Mexico, he returned to his etchings, completing a phenomenal 970 of them by 1937 and building a worldwide reputation. His subjects ranged from peasants in Japan to cannibals in the Marquesas Islands of the Pacific. He was called by some "the world's greatest living drypoint etcher."[2] He was also a world traveler, and lived in Europe, Africa, Mexico, and Asia. His work is hung in several of the great museums of the world today, including the Louvre in Paris and the San Francisco Museum of Fine Arts, which has a substantial collection. Of special note is the painting he did of his father before William Drew died.

Cadwallader Lincoln Washburn was a man of wide interests. He even became an expert in insects in his later years. He eventually returned with his wife Margaret Cowles Ohrt to a house on the family property in Livermore, where he died without issue in 1965 at the age of ninety-nine. Four years later Gallaudet College named its new $2.5 million art center after him.

A third son, Edwin, also attended Yale, and worked in railroading all his life. Edwin wrote several books, including *The 17*, which was based on his experiences with his father building the Minneapolis and Sault Ste. Marie line across northern Michigan. He was associated with his father in an enterprise called the Washburn Steel Casting and Coupler Company, became well known in the steel foundry business, and invented a coupling and other equipment that was widely used by the nation's railroads. He rose to be special assistant to the president of the Baltimore and Ohio Railroad. Edwin married Ethel Fraser and moved to Englewood, New Jersey. They had two children. After William Drew died, it was to Edwin that his mother Lizzie moved for the last years of her life. She died there in 1916 and Edwin in 1937.

William and Lizzie's first daughter was Mary Caroline Washburn. Educated at the prestigious Ogontz School, which had just moved to Jay Cooke's lavish estate outside of Philadelphia, Mary married Williams graduate Elbert Francis Baldwin in 1892. He became editor and writer for the popular *Outlook* magazine. They lived in Lakewood, New Jersey, where she founded the Arden School for Girls, and summered in France. She instituted summer study groups in Geneva, Switzerland, for college girls interested in promoting international relations. She had two sons and three daughters, all of whom had extensive exposure to international affairs. She, too, enjoyed writing, had poems published, and wrote a charming forty-nine-page memoir about her mother's early years.

Another daughter, named Elizabeth like her mother, was educated in private schools in the U.S. and in Europe, and at Radcliffe College. She married Dr. Hamilton Wright, who was an early crusader against the opium trade. She was with him in

Kuala Lumpur for the births of the first two of their five children, and wrote a book titled *The Colour of the East* about her travels there. Upon her husband's death in 1917, Elizabeth continued the fight against drugs, ultimately becoming the first American woman ever to be given plenipotentiary diplomatic powers as a delegate to the Second Geneva Opium Conference in 1924. She was influential in bringing about the establishment of the Federal Bureau of Narcotics in 1930, and in the passage of the Boggs Act that introduced mandatory sentencing for drug violations. The Wrights lived in Washington and, during the summers, at a house her father provided for them at Livermore. She died in Washington in 1952 and was buried at the Waters Hill Cemetery behind the house where she had summered.

William's youngest son, Stanley, was a dashing figure whose early life reminds one of Jack London. He graduated from Williams College in 1901, then had a year at Harvard Law School. Back in Minneapolis, he was a police beat reporter for his father's paper, the *Minneapolis Journal*, then went to the competition as a market reporter for the *Minneapolis Times*. In 1904 he was made a foreign correspondent of the *Chicago Daily News*, and sent to cover the Russo-Japanese War. There he showed a talent for gaining the trust of both the Japanese and their Russian opponents. Operating out of a dispatch boat, he got a scoop with the fall of Port Arthur. Later he covered the Russian Revolution of 1905, and he wrote several books from this experience.

Stanley came home to lead two pack trips exploring the interior of British Columbia in 1909 and 1910. In World War I he was a correspondent for *Collier's Weekly*, and then in Russia for the *Times* of London, where for twenty-six months he was said to have been the only American with access to the Russian front. In 1916 he was with the French at Verdun and, later, with the Rumanians. Back in the U.S. he made a speaking tour through thirty-five states on behalf of the Russians, and then became a military advisor to Secretary of State Robert Lansing. Commissioned a major of cavalry, he was a military aide in the 1917 Russian railroad mission, and to the Elihu Root diplomatic mission in Vladivostok. After this, he served in military intelligence for the 26th Division in France in 1918. He was invalided home and promoted to lieutenant colonel of military intelligence. He was part of the American delegation to the disarmament conference of 1921, and was a military aide to Queen Marie of Rumania during her visit to the U.S. in 1926.

Stanley wrote a total of nine books about his experiences. Many of them are in the Washburn Library collection (see Appendix C). He also ran the Washburn Lignite Coal Company during its labor turmoil in the 1920s, until it was sold in 1929. He then left the Midwest, married the wealthy Alice Langhorne of Philadelphia, and had three children. (Alice and her two Langhorne cousins were renowned for their beauty; Nancy became Lady Astor and Irene was the original Gibson Girl.) Stanley moved to Lakewood, New Jersey, and like his older brother William, ran unsuccessfully for Congress—from New Jersey's Third District in 1932. Stanley died in Lakewood in 1950, and became the only Washburn buried at Arlington National Cemetery. He left a trail that, though completely different, was every bit as spectacular as his father's before him.

1. Note to author from Charles R. Smith, Senior Historian, USMC, March 19, 2004.
2. From *A Man Called Cad* by Stan Griffin, Deaf Friends International (Washburn Library).

APPENDIX B

Famous Cousins

SO FAR, THIS BOOK HAS CONCENTRATED on the family of Israel and Patty Washburn of Livermore, Maine. Although there have been a few references to visits they made to the grandparents in Raynham, Massachusetts, there has been no mention of their well-known Washburn cousins. Given the fact that all the Maine and Massachusetts Washburns descended from the same John Washburn, who came to Duxbury in 1631, we can generalize that the ten Livermore siblings had some pretty remarkable cousins. Six of the best known were their direct contemporaries. For readers who may be curious—especially those who may be, like the writer, Washburn descendants themselves—these six should be remembered, even if they were only faintly related to the Livermore group.

Three distant cousins who achieved much were from central Massachusetts. From Leicester, there was the brilliant lawyer named Emery Washburn, who was nominated as a Whig candidate for governor of Massachusetts, who got the most votes over two opponents but not a majority, and who was chosen by the state senate while he was in Europe and without his knowledge. He served a single term, but was swept away in the Know-Nothing tidal wave in 1854. He subsequently was a much-respected professor at Harvard Law School, where both Israel Jr. and Elihu knew him.

Also from Leicester, and a classmate of Emery at Leicester Academy, was Ichabod Washburn. He never entered politics, but went from blacksmith's apprentice to founder of the world's largest wire mill, the Washburn and Moen Manufacturing Company. Before he died in 1866 he made a lot of money from the Civil War. He made bequests, together with his cousin Emery, to found both the Worcester Polytechnic Institute and Washburn College in Topeka, Kansas. The latter was probably the result of his prewar abolitionist concerns about the future of the Kansas Territory.

Then there was the brilliant young officer of the Massachusetts Fourth Cavalry Regiment, Colonel Francis Washburn. Within a few days of the end of the Civil War, he led his eighty men in a suicidal charge against a thousand Confederates at the Battle of High Bridge, Virginia, near Farmville and not far from Appomattox Court House. This was a desperate attempt to delay Lee's army in its retreat from Richmond. Lee surrendered to Grant at Appomattox just two days later. Young Colonel Washburn was fatally wounded in the action at High Bridge, and Elihu visited his dying second cousin in a hospital at Point of Rocks, Virginia, just before he learned of Lincoln's assassination. Francis was posthumously awarded a brevet brigadiership for his heroism.

Born in Winchendon, Massachusetts, and a graduate of Yale College in 1844, was William Barrett Washburn. He engaged in manufacturing in Erving, was elected to the state legislature from 1850 to 1855, and moved to become a banker in Greenfield in 1858. He was elected to Congress as a Republican and served in the House from 1863 to 1871, much of that time with Cadwallader and Elihu. He was elected governor of Massachusetts in 1872, and then, upon the death of Senator Charles Sumner, was selected to finish out his term from 1874 to 1875 in the U.S. Senate. After declining renomination, he retired from politics and returned to banking in Greenfield.

There were two other well-known Washburn cousins who

grew up in Vermont. One of them, Henry Dana Washburn, grew up in Windsor, then migrated westward to Indiana—to Newport in Vermillion County. There he became a lawyer. No doubt in return for raising troops there, he entered the army in 1861 as a lieutenant colonel and later rose to major general. He was elected to Congress and served from 1866 to 1869 (along with his cousins Elihu, Cadwallader, and William B.). He subsequently was named surveyor general of Montana. In the course of leading an expedition to find the headwaters of the Yellowstone River, he discovered what is now Yellowstone National Park. Mount Washburn, the tallest peak in the park, is named after him.

The other Vermont cousin, Peter Thatcher Washburn, graduated from Dartmouth College, studied the law, and was admitted to the bar in Windsor County. He first practiced in Ludlow, then Woodstock. He was a member of the Vermont delegation that nominated Abraham Lincoln at the 1860 Republican convention in Chicago. He too joined the Union Army as a lieutenant colonel of his Vermont regiment, served three months near Fortress Monroe, and saw action at the Battle of Big Bethel, then finished the war as adjutant general in Vermont. His performance gained him nomination as governor, and he was elected to that office in 1869. Unfortunately, he died in office the following year, at the age of only fifty-five.[1]

1. Refer to Mark Washburn, vol. II, pp. 207, 416; vol. III, pp. 12, 428, plus Wikipedia.

Appendix C

Washburn Books
at Norlands

By Israel Washburn, Jr.:
Notes, Historical, Descriptive, and Personal, of Livermore, Maine
(Portland, 1874).

By Elihu B. Washburne:
Recollections of A Minister to France 1869–1877, 2 vols. (New
York, 1887).

By Charles A. Washburn:
Gomery of Montgomery, 2 vols. (New York, 1865).
Philip Thaxter (New York, 1861).
Political Evolution (Philadelphia, 1885).
*History of Paraguay, with Notes of Personal Observations and
Reminiscences of Diplomacy Under Difficulties*, 2 vols. (New
York, 1871).

By Elizabeth Washburn:
The Colour of the East (New York, 1913).

By Stanley Washburn:
Nogi (New York, 1913).
Victory in Defeat (London, 1916).
The Russian Offensive (London, 1917).
The Russian Advance (New York, 1917).

The Cable Game (New York, 1912).
Trails, Trappers, and Tenderfeet in Northern Canada (New York, 1912).

BY STANLEY WASHBURN, JR.:
Facts, Fables, and Frenzy on Land, Sea, and Air (Raleigh, North Carolina, 2001)

BY EDWIN C. WASHBURN:
Caleb Cutter (Englewood, New Jersey, 1929).
John Read, American, (New York, 1928).
The 17 (Englewood, New Jersey, 1929).
Men or Cogs (privately printed).

BY JEANETTE GARR WASHBURN KELSEY:
A Diverted Inheritance (Philadelphia, privately printed, 1904).
Weathering the Storm (Patience Warren), privately printed, 1920.

BY LILIAN WASHBURN VILENIUS:
My Seven Sons (Portland, Maine, 1940)

Bibliography

Books

Allen, Howard W. and Lacey, Vincent A., eds. *Illinois Elections, 1818–1990: Candidates and County Returns for President, Governor, Senate and House of Representatives* (Carbondale, IL: Southern Illinois University Press, 1992).

Angle, Paul M., ed. *The Lincoln Reader* (New Brunswick, NJ: Rutgers University Press, 1947).

Benedict, Michael Les, *A Compromise of Principle: Congressional Republicans and Reconstruction, 1863-1869* (New York, 1974).

_____. *The Impeachment Trial of Andrew Johnson* (New York: W. W. Norton, Inc., 1973).

Bicha, Karel. C. C. *Washburn and the Upper Mississippi Valley* (New York: Garland Publishing Co., 1995).

Bless, Robert C. *The History of Washburn Observatory* (Madison, WI: University of Wisconsin Publication 2000-7M8A141-78, 1978).

Boston Ship Register, 1841–1850.

Box, Pelham Horton. *The Origins of the Paraguayan War, Vol. 1* (Urbana, IL: University of Illinois Press, 1929).

Bryan, Charles F., Jr., and Nelson d. Lankford, eds. *Eye of the Storm, Written and Illustrated by Private Robert Knox Sneden,* (New York: Free Press, 2000).

_____. *Images from the Storm, Private Robert Knox Sneden,* (New York: Free Press, 2001).

Caldwell, Bill. *Rivers of Fortune: Where Maine Tides and Money Flowed* (Camden, ME: Down East Books, 1983).

Carroll, Howard. *Twelve Americans, Their Lives and Times* (New York: Harper & Brothers, 1883).

Catton, Bruce. *Grant Moves South* (Boston: Little, Brown & Company, 1950).

Chadbourne, Walter W. *A History of Banking in Maine* (Orono, ME: Gazette Publishing Co., 1936).

Chetlain, Augustus L. *Recollections of Seventy Years* (Galena, IL: State historical Society, 1899).

Current, Richard N. *The History of Wisconsin, Vol. II* (Madison, WI: Wisconsin Historical Society, 1976).

DeForest, John William. *A Volunteer's Adventures* (New Haven, CT: Yale University Press, 1996).

Dougherty, Sister Patricia. *American Diplomats and the Franco Prussian War* (Washington, D.C.: Institute for the Study of Diplomacy, Georgetown University, 1980).

Edgar, William C. *The Medal of Gold* (Minneapolis, MN: The Ballman Company, 1925).

Faust, Patricia A., ed. *Historical Times Illustrated Encyclopedia of the Civil War* (New York: Harper & Row, 1986).

Frame, Robert M. III, ed. *Railroads in the Nineteenth Century*, volume from *Encyclopedia of American Business History and Biography*, biography of William Drew Washburn. (New York: 1988), 425–28.

Fuller, Joseph V. Sketch of Elihu B. Washburne from *The American Secretaries of State and Their Diplomacy*, Vol. VII, Samuel Flagg Bemis (ed.). (New York: Pageant Book company, 1928).

Gara, Larry. *Westernized Yankee, The Story of Cyrus Woodman* (Madison, WI: State Historical Society, 1956).

Gilbert, Paul and Charles L. Bryson. *Chicago and Its Makers* (Chicago: F. Mendelsohn, 1929).

Goodwin, Doris Kearns. *Team of Rivals, The Political Genius of Abraham Lincoln* (New York: Simon & Schuster, 2005).

Gjevre, John A. *The Saga of the Soo*, 3 vols. (Moorehead, MN: privately published by the author, 1973, 1995, and 2006).

Gray, James. *Business Without Boundary: The Story of General Mills* (Minneapolis, MN: University of Minnesota Press, 1954).

Hepner, Adolph, ed. *America's Aid to Germany in 1870–71* (St. Louis, MO: 1905).

Hess, Stephen. *America's Political Dynasties: From Adams to Kennedy* (New York: Doubleday, 1966).

Hoffman, Wickham. *Camp, Court, and Siege* (New York: Harper's, 1877).

Horne, Alistair. *The Fall of Paris, The Siege and the Commune 1870–71* (New York: Penguin Books, 1965).

Howard, Robert P. *Illinois: A History of the Prairie State* (Grand Rapids, MI: W. B. Eardman's Publishing Co., 1972).

Hunt, Gaillard. *Israel, Elihu, and Cadwallader Washburn* (New York: Macmillan, 1925).

Johnson, Allen, ed. *Dictionary of American Biography* (New York: 1928).

Jordan, William B., Jr. *Maine in the Civil War: A Bibliographical Guide* (Portland, ME: Maine Historical Society, 1976).

Josephy, Alvin M. *The Civil War in the American West* (New York: Knopf, 1992).

Judd, Richard W., Edwin A. Churchill, and Joel W. Eastman, eds. *Maine: The Pine Tree State from Prehistory to the Present* (Orono, ME: University of Maine Press, 1995).

Kane, Lucile M. *The Falls of St. Anthony* (St. Paul, MN: Minnesota Historical Society Press, 1987).

Katz, Philip M. *From Appomattox to Montmartre: The Americans and the Paris Commune* (Cambridge, MA: Harvard University Press, 1998).

Kelsey, Jeanette Garr Washburn. *A Diverted Inheritance.* Privately published in 1904 (Washburn Library).

Kelsey, Kerck, *Israel Washburn, Jr.: Maine's Little-Known Giant of the Civil War* (Rockport, ME: Picton Press, 2004).

Kingsbury, Henry, ed. *An Illustrated History of Kennebec County* (New York: 1892).

Kolinski, Charles J. *Independence or Death! The Story of the Paraguayan War*, (Gainesville, FL: University of Florida, 1965).

Lash, Jeffrey. *A Politician Turned General: The Civil War Career of Stephen Augustus Hurlbut* (Kent, OH: Kent State University Press, 2003).

Lewis, Lloyd. *Captain Sam Grant* (Boston: Little, Brown & Co., 1950).

Liebert, A. *Les Ruines de Paris* (Paris: 1871), Washburn Library.

Long, E. B., with Barbara Long. *The Civil War Day by Day: An Almanac*, (Garden City, NY: DaCapo Press, 1971).

Love, William DeLoss. *Wisconsin in the War of the Rebellion: A History of All Regiments and Batteries* (Chicago: 1866).

Magdol, Edward. *Owen Lovejoy: Abolitionist in Congress* (New Brunswick, NJ: Rutgers University Press, 1967).

Malone, Dumas, ed. *Dictionary of American Biography, Vol. XIX* (New York: 1936).

Mahoney, Timothy R. *Provincial Lives: Middle Class Experience in the Antebellum Midwest* (New York: Cambridge University Press, 1999).

Marquis, Albert Nelson, ed. *The Book of Minnesotans* (Chicago: 1907).

McPherson, James M. *Battle Cry of Freedom* (New York: Oxford University Press, 1988).

_____. *Ordeal by Fire* (New York: Knopf, 1982).

Merk, Frederick. *The Fruits of Propaganda in the Tyler Administration* (Cambridge, MA: Harvard University Press, 1971).

Merrick, George Byron. *Old Times On The Upper Mississippi* (Minneapolis, MN: University of Minnesota Press, 2001).

Monroe, Ira Thompson. *History of the Town of Livermore and Its*

Pioneers (Lewiston, 1928).

Moore, Wm. F. and Jane Ann, eds. *His Brother's Blood* (Urbana, IL: University of Illinois Press, 2004).

Morgan, H. Wayne. *William McKinley and His America* (Syracuse, NY: Syracuse University Press, 1963).

Nesbit, Robert C. *The History of Wisconsin, Vol. III* (Madison, WI: Wisonsin Historical Society, 1985).

Nichols, Theodore E. *A Victorian Honeymoon* (Cloverdale, CA: privately printed).

Official Records of the Union and Confederate Navies in the War of the Rebellion, entries from Series I, vol. 7, covering March–Septtember 1862, and vol. 21, covering March–December 1864.

Peskin, Allan. *Garfield* (Kent, OH: Kent State University Press, 1978).

Phelps, Gilbert. *The Tragedy of Paraguay* (London: C. Knight, 1975).

Porter, David D. *A Naval History of the Civil War* (New York: C. P. Hatch, 1886).

Powell, William J. *Pillsbury's Best: A Company History From 1869* (Minneapolis, MN: 1985).

Ramsdell, Charles W. *Behind the Lines in the Southern Confederacy* (Baton Rouge, LA: Louisiana State University, 1944).

Ridge, Martin. *Ignatius Donnelly: The Portrait of a Politician* (Chicago: University of Chicago Press, 1962).

Sears, Stephen W. *Controversies and Commanders* (Boston: Houghton Mifflin Company, 1999).

Shutes, Milton H. *Lincoln and California* (Palo Alto, CA: Stanford University Press, 1943).

Simon, John Y., ed. *The Personal Memoirs of Julia Dent Grant* (New York: Putnam Press, 1975).

Simpson, Brooks D. *Ulysses S. Grant: Triumph Over Adversity,*

1822–1865 (Boston: Houghton Mifflin, 2000).

Storck, John and Walter Dorwin Teague. *Flour For Man's Bread* (Minneapolis, MN: University of Minnesota Press, 1952).

Taylor, Richard. *Destruction and Reconstruction*, Richard Harwell, ed. (New York: Longmans, Green & Co., 1955).

Thompson, George. *The War in Paraguay* (London: 1869).

Trefousse, Hans L. *Andrew Jackson: A Biography* (New York: W. W. Norton & Co., 1989).

Warner, Ezra J. *Generals in Blue, Lives of Union Commanders* (Baton Rouge, LA: Louisiana State University Press, 1964).

Warren, Harris Gaylord. *Paraguay: An Informal History* (Norman, OK: University of Oklahoma Press, 1949).

Washburn, Charles A. *History of Paraguay, With Notes of Personal Observations and Reminiscences of Diplomacy Under Difficulties*, 2 vols. (New York: 1871).

Washburn, Lilian. *My Seven Sons* (Portland, ME: Falmouth Publishing House, 1940).

Washburn, Stanley, Jr. *Facts, Fables, and Frency on Land, Sea, and Air* (Raleigh, NC: Pentland Press), 2001.

Washburne, Elihu B. *Recollections of a Minister to France, 1869–1877*, 2 vols. (New York: Scribner's Sons, 1887).

Washburne, Mark. *A Biography of Elihu Benjamin Washburn, Vols. 1-4* (New York: self-published, 1999–2005).

Webb, Theodore A. *Impassioned Brothers, Ministers Resident to France and Paraguay* (Lanham, 2002).

_____. *Seven Sons, Millionaires and Vagabonds* (Victoria, B.C.: self-published, 1999).

Welles, Gideon. *Diary* (Boston: Houghton Mifflin, 1911), 3 vols.

West, Emmet C. *History and Reminiscences of the Second Wisconsin Cavalry Regiment* (Wisconsin State Register Print, 1904).

Wescott, Richard R. *New Men, New Issues: The Formation of*

the Republican Party In Maine (Portland, ME: Maine Historical Society, 1986.

Whigham, Thomas L. and Kendrik Kraay, ed. *I Die With My Country* (Lincoln, NE: University of Nebraska Press, 2004).

_____. *The Paraguayan War, Vol 1* (Lincoln, NE: University of Nebraska Press, 2002).

Willey, Rev. Austin. *The History of The Antislavery Cause in State and Nation* (Portland, ME; Brown Thurston, 1895).

Williams, John Hoyt. *The Rise and Fall of the Paraguayan Republic* (Austin, TX: University of Texas Press, 1979).

Wills, Brian Steele. *Nathan Bedford Forest: The Confederacy's Greatest Cavalryman* (Lawrence, KS: University of Kansas Press, 1992).

Wilson, Henry. *History of the Rise and Fall of the Slave Power in America* (Boston: J. R. Osbood, 1874).

Wilson, James Grant, ed. *General Grant's Letters to a Friend 1861–1880* (New York: T. Y. Crowell & Co., 1897), reprinted 1973.

OTHER SOURCES

Article titled "The President Elect" by "JQT" (*New York Times*, November 17, 1868).

Adams, Elmer E. "The Washburn–Nelson Senatorial Campaign of 1894–1895," reprint of article in *Fergus Falls Journal* for January 1924, from Minnesota Historical Society.

Balcom, Thomas W. *Washburn's Century of Helping Children, from Orphanage to Child Guidance Center* (Minneapolis, MN: 1983).

Baldwin, Mary Washburn. *Early Memories of Elizabeth Muzzy Washburn* (Washburn Library).

Bennett, Dean B. "E. S. Coe and the Allagash Wildlands," *Maine History Magazine* 41:2, summer 2002.

Bowe, Frank G., Jr. "The Incredible Story of Cadwallader Washburn," *Deaf American* magazine, vol. 23, no. 3, November 1970.

Correspondence between Maj. Gen. C. C. Washburn and Maj. Gen. Nathan B. Forrest, June–September, 1864 (Washburn Library).

Dougherty, Sister Patricia, O.P. *American Diplomats and the Franco-Prussian War, Perceptions from Paris and Berlin* (Washington, D.C.: University Institute for the Study of Diplomacy, 1980).

Executor and probate reports for C. C. Washburn, William D. Washburn, and Elizabeth Muzzy Washburn.

Fowler, Marie Washburn. *Reminiscences—My Mother and I.* Privately published in 1927 (Washburn Library).

Frame, Robert M. "William Drew Washburn," biography from "Railroads in the Nineteenth Century," *Encyclopedia of American Business History and Biography* (New York: 1988).

Frye, Roland M. "The Relationship Between Elihu B. Washburne and Ulysses S. Grant," unpublished thesis for Princeton University, 1972.

Gammon, Ethel W. "The Three Daughters of Israel and Patty Washburn." Unpublished paper dated August 10, 1973 (Washburn Library).

———. Complete transcriptions of Washburn family journals, on file at Washburn Library; also miscellaneous pamphlets on the Norlands School and the Washburn family.

Howell, Hester. Manuscript fragment (Washburn Library).

Hunt, Gaillard. "The Life of William Drew Washburn." Unpublished paper written circa 1922 (Mark Washburne).

Kane, Lucille. Transcript of 1955 interview with John Crosby, Jr., from Minnesota Historical Society.

Kelsey, Jeanette Washburn. Uncatalogued journals, letters, and reminiscences (Washburn Library).

Kelsey, Kerck. "C. C. Washburn: The Evolution of a Flour Baron," *Wisconsin Magazine of History*, vol. 88, no. 4, summer 2005.

Kelsey, Kerck. "Maine's War Governor: Israel Washburn, Jr., and the Race To Save the Union," *Maine History*, vol. 42, no. 4, July 2006.

La Crosse *Republican Leader* (La Crosse County, WI, Historical Society).

Lewiston Evening Journal for December 6, 1888 regarding CCW estate.

Maine State Bank Commisioner's Annual Report, (Augusta, ME: 1853).

Mack, Edgar J. "The Mack Brothers—Real Trouble Makers?" Unpublished paper prepared for the family, February 2005, and kindly loaned to the author.

Marquette, Clare L. "The Business Activities of C.C Washburn." PhD thesis, University of Wisconsin, Madison, 1940.

Martin, Dolores Moyano. "A Sanguinary Obsession," *Military History Quarterly*, vol. 4, no. 4, summer 1992.

McMahon, Martin T. letter to *New York Evening Post*, January 17, 1871.

_____. "The War In Paraguay," *Harper's New Monthly Magazine*, vol 40, issue 239, April 1870.

Memorial Addresses on the Life and Character of C. C. Washburn delivered before the Wisconsin Historical Society, July 25, 1882, and printed by the society, 1883.

Miscellaneous correspondence relating to final disposition of Washburn Crosby Company (Washburn Library).

Miscellaneous military pay records of C. C. Washburn (Washburn Library).

Nelson, Russell K. "The Early Life and Congressional Career of Elihu B. Washburne." PhD dissertation for University of North Dakota, August 1953.

Northwestern Miller Magazine, biographical sketch of William Drew Washburn (no author listed), September 30, 1892.

Nichols, Theodore E. *A Victorian Honeymoon* (Cloverdale, CA: privately printed).

O'Meara, James. "Early Editors of California," *Overland Monthly*, vol. xv, no. 83, November 1889.

Owatonna *Journal*, misc. articles on S. B. Washburn, April 1867 through April 1868.

Paynter, Mary, O.P. *Phoenix from the Fire* (Madison, WI: privately printed history of Edgewood College).

Simon, John Y. "From Galena to Appomattox: Grant and Washburne," *Journal of Illinois State Historical Society*, LVIII, summer 1965.

St. Paul Daily Globe, special edition of May 3, 1878.

Tarshis, Rebeccah. "Col. Edward D. Baker, Lincoln's Constant Ally," *Oregon Historical Quarterly*, 1960.

Taunt, Robert B., comp. *A Brief History of the Steamboat War Eagle* (La Crosse, WI: privately printed, 2000).

Washburn, Algernon Sidney. *Correspondence 1832-1884*, collection at Duke University Library, Durham, NC.

Washburn, Charles A. Miscellaneous articles in the *Hesperian Magazine*, June–September 1859, and the *Pioneer Magazine* 1854 and 1855.

Washburn, Israel, Jr. *Dedication of the Soldiers Monument at Cherryfield Maine* (Portland, ME: privately printed, 1874), Maine Historical Society.

_____. *The Northeastern Boundar* (Portland, ME: Maine Historical Society, vol. VIII, 1881).

_____. *Remarks at Orono Centennial Celebration, March 3, 1874*, privately printed.

_____. *The Telos Canal: Evidence Before the Committee on Interior Waters*, privately transcribed, 1928 (Portland Public Library).

Washburn, Julia Chase. *Genealogical Notes of the Washburn Family*, privately printed, 1898 (Washburn Library).

Washburn, Sallie. *Diary* (Washburn Library).

Washburn, Samuel B. Miscellaneous correspondence relating to application for disability pension, 1881, Washburn Library.

Washburn, Stanley, Sr. Manuscript of autobiography (Washburn Library).

Washburne, Elihu B., *Dedicatory Excercises of the Washburn Memorial Library*, (Chicago, privately printed, 1885).

Washburne, Elihu B. "Early Recollections." Private paper written by Elihu in Archason, France, in March of 1873, edited by Wayne Dimond, and kindly copied for the author by Thomas D. Washburne, Elihu's great grandson.

Washburne, Elihu B. *The Papers of Elihu B. Washburn 1829–1882*, 102 vols., Library of Congress.

Webb, Theodore A. "Men of Mark." Address to Unitarian Universalist Historical Society, Columbus, Ohio, June 1984.

_____. "Washburn: A Pivotal Figure." Unpublished paper given to author.

Wigham, Thomas and Juan Manuel Casal. Draft of introduction to "Gauchoism" essay, on Charles Ames Washburn, never included (Washburn Library).

Wold, Frances. "The Washburn Lignite Coal Company: A History of Mining at Wilton, North Dakota," *North Dakota History Magazine*, vol. 43, no. 4.

Woodman, Cyrus. *To the Legatees and Divisees*. Pamphlet written in January 1884, regarding C. C. Washburn's will (Portland Public Library).

Acknowledgments

This book is the story of the most famous family in America that nobody ever heard of. The manuscript comes from lectures and papers that I have been asked to prepare over a period of some fifteen years—ever since my Harvard advisor, the late William E. Gienapp, alerted me to the oldest son of this remarkable group.

Putting ten different biographies into a single volume presents challenges. For one thing, there is vastly more material on some of the siblings than on others. There is virtually nothing available about the three Washburn sisters, for example, but eighty-five boxes of Elihu's papers are available in the Library of Congress alone. There are huge gaps in documentation about Sam's eventful life, and it appears that a significant portion of William's story has been expunged deliberately. A second problem in telling the story of ten brothers and sisters is the challenge of avoiding duplication. All ten stories have the same beginning, and the siblings' various paths crossed repeatedly. Telling their stories separately is easy. Interweaving all their stories and avoiding duplication is harder.

I have tried to keep a chronological order to the stories, but also to group them around similar adventures. Hence, there are chapters about the lawyers in the 1830s and 1840s, and of the politicians in the 1850s and 1860s. The women are covered in one chapter. There is a chapter on the brothers' military contributions during the Civil War, the diplomats during the 1860s and 1870s, and one on the businessmen from the 1850s through the Panic of 1873. There's a long chapter on how they all ended up after 1873. An early introduction provides an overview, and a final chapter provides some evaluation and perspective on the group. I have added a special postscript section of great moments to help remind us that these people were simple human beings, and I have added material on their children and cousins who achieved fame elsewhere. If the reader gets lost in the chronology, the fault is entirely mine.

In a way, I was lucky. I am a Washburn descendant, and I was welcome to browse through the collections of papers now held at the Washburn Library in Livermore. I am a member of the Fraternity Club of Portland, which gave me many opportunities to tell Washburn stories and confirm that they were worthy of putting into print. After a while, I got to know Billie Gammon at The Norlands, by far the most important figure in the modern-day revival of the place. Through her I was invited to do enough programs about the Washburns to confirm a high degree of public interest in the family.

Many, many people have helped me with the current project. From the academic world, besides Professor Gienapp, also from Harvard there was John Stauffer, who gave me a lecture spot on the *Delta Queen* and liked what I had to say about Major General C. C. Washburn. Thomas L. Whigham of the University of Georgia, whose knowledge of Paraguay and the Paraguayan War is without equal in this country, was indispensable in tracing the adventures of Charles and Sallie Washburn there. I am grateful to Dean Bennett at the University of Maine at Farmington for background on the Telos Canal, and to Robb Lively at the same school for constant encouragement in the various lectures he invited me to give at the Washburn humanities conferences over the years. Also in Maine, at the University of Maine in Orono, Dick Judd helped me get an article on Israel Washburn, Jr., into *Maine History*, which he edits, and at the University of Southern Maine, Professor Emeritus H. Draper Hunt was a source of encouragement and also information on his favorite subject, Hannibal Hamlin. Doug Hodgkin, now retired from Bates College, was a great resource about the mills of Lewiston and the use of water power in the nineteenth century. I cannot forget the awesome fount of Civil War knowledge represented by James McPherson at Princeton, or his personal attention during a fabulous tour he gave a group of us at Gettysburg.

Not much formal scholarship has been devoted to the Washburns, but I have been privileged to speak or correspond with three people who made key contributions. The first was Karel Bicha of Marquette University, whose 1995 book on C. C. Washburn's business activities was an essential resource to me. The second was Roland Frye, whose unpublished 1972 senior thesis at Princeton on Elihu Washburn and Ulysses S. Grant has not been equaled for its insights into these two men. The third person, from the College of Morris in New Jersey, was my always-helpful cousin, Mark Washburne, whose massive work on his ancestor, Elihu B. Washburne, is an unparalleled source of information and references. He also led me to John Y. Simon at Southern Illinois University for help about Ulysses Grant.

Ed Bearss, the Civil War guru of the National Park Service, was extraordinary in the encouragement he gave me, and the spectacular job he did in proofreading my first book on Israel Washburn, Jr. For a man as busy as he is, his keen eye and fast turnaround were truly impressive. So was Earle G. Shettleworth, Jr., Maine State Historian, director of the Maine Historic Preservation Commission, and the faithful custodian of a remarkable collection of photographs of Maine in the nineteenth century.

My friend Charles Haas, guide and host during a fabulous five-day speaking tour of La Crosse, and faithful bird dog of La Crosse photo and newspaper files for anything I needed, was a huge help there, as were his LCHS colleagues Carl Miller, Bob Taunt (all-time expert on Mississippi steamboats), and Mariel Carlisle, hostess extraordinaire. Also in Wisconsin, of great help were the archivists at Edgewood College, Sister Jean Richter and her successor Sister Sarah Naughton. Their quiet dedication to, and realism about, Cadwallader Washburn and his family is unequaled.

As in La Crosse, I have benefited much from the assistance of archivists at historical societies in many places. Prominent among these were Bill Barry and Nick Noyes in Portland and Sherman Hasbrouck in Orono, researchers Amy Markwyn in Madison and Mark Speltz in Mineral Point, and Dan Tindell, Carter Newton, and Steve Repp in Galena. I had help from Beverly Hermes in St. Paul, Minnesota, and genealogist Marilyn Arnold in Virginia. My tireless right arm in Minneapolis was Stan Seed, who never failed to dig up useful information there, and whose dogged search for Washburn gravesites from San Diego to Switzerland has provided a huge resource for the family.

Also in Minneapolis, I had great help from experts in both the General Mills and Pillsbury corporate families. Specifically, I owe thanks to David Nasby, Kate Houst, and Sue Lappi for showing me around the archives of General Mills, and to George Pillsbury for procuring for me a copy of the 1985 *Pillsbury's Best*, which served as my guide in analyzing the final adventure of William Drew Washburn.

I owe a lot to Megan Sheils of the U.S. State Department Library in Washington for her help in tracking down information from old Washington, D.C., newspapers about Fannie and Charles Payson there. Two archivists at the Lincoln Library in Springfield, Mary Michals and Gweneth Podeschi, filled in a couple of important holes for me about the early political career of Elihu Washburne. Other archivists from institutions as disparate as the Musée de l'Armée in Paris, the New York Public Library, the Museo Etnographico Andres Barbero in Paraguay, the Museo de Artes Visuales in Montevideo, and the University of Texas were also most helpful.

Here in Maine, I much appreciate the help from all the reference folks at the Bowdoin College Library who helped me blunder through their ProQuest newspaper files, as well as other important collections. Their collections are only surpassed by the Widener Library at Harvard. In addition, I am grateful for the cheerful assistance I received from the Rare Books Room at Bowdoin, and from the Archives Office of the college.

Some of my best support has come from the amateurs, driven by their own curiosity and enthusiasm, who were tireless in their pursuit of obscure information—often through sources that proved fruitless, for information that proved false, or colorful theories that could not be proved. Billie Gammon and Dennis Stires of Livermore are at the top of this list, which also includes Billie's son Michael, the Reverend Ted Webb out in Sacramento, and my old friend Dick Purdy of Marion, Massachusetts, who happily rooted around many a yellowed manuscript for me at the New Bedford Whaling Museum. My colleagues at the Norlands Living History Center are also high on this list: Ron Kley, Mitch Thomas, Mary Castonguay, and a whole string of receptionists and tour guides. Also at Norlands, I want to acknowledge the enormous labors in transcribing spidery, ink-blotted handwriting that have been accomplished by the indefatigable Billie Gammon, and by two magic interns we had one summer, Sarah Kozma and Katherine Hancock. My colleagues of the Fraternity Club in Portland have been wonderful cheerleaders. They not only suffered through at least six different papers I've delivered to them about the Washburns, but they even voted to upset a 135-year-old tradition and allowed me to have as my guest one evening TV producer/director Barbara Pulling, who responded with a superb program on Maine Public Television about the Washburns as part of her *Maine Experience* series.

In my travels, I ran into two individuals who own property that played a part in the Washburn story. They may not know about everything that happened there, but their interest in preserving the sites impressed me much. I refer to Dick and Judy Schlosser, whose beautiful farm includes the site of Cadwallader Washburn's Waubeek lumbercamp; and Richard Rudisill, whose property on Turkey Creek lies right next to Hexalls Landing, where Sam Washburn's guns crashed during the battle of Malvern Hill.

Even though memories are faint, and the line between mythology and fact is blurred, I owe many thanks to descendants of the Washburns all over the country. Attorney Tom Washburne in Maryland is high on this list, and so are Mark Washburne and Washburn Wright in New Jersey. Langhorne Washburn and Mark Peters in Virginia, Margaret Bergh in Minneapolis, Charlie Buffum in Kansas City, Susan Ruth in San Diego, Brent Washburne in Colorado, and Lois Herndon here in Maine all helped me get the genealogy straight. Their memories, though dimming, of things I'm sure they thought not very important, have been precious to me. I thank them for their patience with me, and I appreciate their honesty in admitting to the things they didn't know. They could easily have invented or embellished tales, and I would have been none the wiser.

I will never be able to express my thanks to people who have helped me on the technical side. Close at hand for innumerable small emergencies were my friend Mitch Thomas and my son Peter. Then came the terrible moment when I was victim to the dreaded blue flash, and with what I thought was a single keystroke, I lost the entire fourth draft of the manuscript. There was not a trace to be found until I brought my machine to John Burkhart of the B. C. Group in Westbrook, Maine. Miraculously, a few layers down on my hard drive, he found the entire two hundred missing pages. Rarely in my life have I been so grateful for anything, John.

I want to thank my neighbors here in Maine, Henry Thomas and Nick Witte and Dick Kurtz, who have suffered through more than their share of Washburn papers at the Fraternity Club without falling asleep, and have never ceased in their encouragement to me to get this book written.

And last, but assuredly not least, I thank my wife Susan, who still encourages me, despite the thousands of hours she has spent alone as a result. This book is hers, above all.

South Freeport, Maine
January, 2007

Index